X.I.

THE ROYAL NAVY'S MYSTERY SUBMARINE

X.I.

THE ROYAL NAVY'S MYSTERY SUBMARINE

Roger Branfill-Cook

Seaforth
PUBLISHING

Copyright © Roger Branfill-Cook

First published in Great Britain in 2012 by
Seaforth Publishing
An imprint of Pen & Sword Books Ltd
47 Church Street, Barnsley
S Yorkshire S70 2AS

www.seaforthpublishing.com
Email info@seaforthpublishing.com

British Library Cataloguing in Publication Data
A CIP data record for this book is available from the British Library

ISBN 978 1 84832 161 8

Typeset and designed by Ian Hughes, Mousemat Design Ltd

Printed in China through Printworks International Ltd

Contents

Rear Admiral Mark Anderson

The concept for His Majesty's Submarine *X.1* was born from the bitter experience of the First World War, where the lone combatant, holding wide areas of ocean at risk, once again took centre stage. *X.1* was designed to inflict devastating effects on naval and mercantile shipping, on the morale of those operating them and on the nations dependent on those supplies. Against the economic and political backdrop of the post-Great War era, naval architects sought to make a reality a submerged raider that was equally at home below and above the waves; carrying a potent armament and capable of conducting deadly ambush, she was conceived to bring fear to shipping, and to dominate a maritime area of operations whilst remaining largely unseen and untouchable.

In the modern context, *X.1* became the capability demonstrator for submerged sea power; a precursor of what was to come decades later, she was the modern nuclear attack submarine of her generation. As with any innovative submarine build programme, concept and reality only came together with skill and effort, sweat and tears. *X.1* suffered from severe first-of-class teething problems in much the same way that we do today, yet despite the additional weaponry, proved to have very sound underwater handling characteristics.

Unfortunately, her design concept did not match the context of the interwar years in which she operated; she paid the price of being ahead of her time and her potential in the conflict to come lay unappreciated. Her detractors, with their various agendas, ensured that she would be dismissed as a waste of taxpayers' money. Her lasting legacy to us was to prove that large submarines could dive and surface safely and that such a potent underwater capability can provide both fighting power and a powerful deterrent to an opposing maritime power. Even the threat of such a submarine being present would come to make an enemy think carefully about the risk to his capability and ambitions. A role most ably demonstrated during the Falklands Conflict.

Roger Branfill-Cook's superbly researched book succeeds in shining light on the truth surrounding the capability of *X.1* and the military and political conditions that acted as a backdrop to her short career in the Royal Navy.

Rear Admiral Mark Anderson
Commander Operations &
Rear Admiral Submarines, Royal Navy
January 2009 to March 2011

Introduction

Submarine cruisers have a great capacity to stir the imagination. The notion that a powerfully-armed vessel can rise to the surface in a deadly ambush, despatch an enemy vessel in a hail of shells, then simply slide away back into the depths has fascinated the submarine designers of Tsarist Russia, Imperial Germany, Great Britain, the USA, France and the Third Reich.

Traditionally, the cruiser type of vessel, successor to the classic sailing frigate, is both the protector and the predator of distant mercantile routes worldwide. A lone frigate or corsair, far from base and support, was always vulnerable to falling in with a faster or more powerful opponent. The Great War gives us the examples of *Königsberg* and *Emden*, and the Second World War was to produce many others – including the fatal first and last cruise of the *Bismarck*. Therefore the cruiser submarine, with her ability to hide from a hunter by simply submerging, seemed to many to be the ideal type of ocean raider. It was no surprise that La Royale should christen their own giant cruiser submarine after the great French corsair captain, Robert Surcouf.

The Royal Navy's sole example of a cruiser submarine, the *X.1*, has long been dismissed as a failure, and a colossal white elephant. She was the only major British warship designed after the First World War which was withdrawn from service before the outbreak of the Second. Her heavy gun armament was her most obvious feature, and this was perhaps her most contentious aspect. It is undeniable she had great potential if correctly used in a surface action role. Paradoxically her very success doomed her to a half-life existence, neither fish nor fowl, spurned both by the exponents of the surface cruiser force, and by the submariners who favoured the more stealthy underwater attack. From the chequered history of her advanced propulsion machinery, it is clear she fell far short of her designers' ambitions. However, alternative engines *did* later become available, which could have been fitted in *X.1* to cure her chronic mechanical problems.

Every writer who mentions *X.1*, however, completely misses the most important aspect of this monster vessel. The resounding success of her design was her docile underwater handling. Designed to prove once and for all that a huge submarine vessel could be dived with safety, *X.1* bridges the gap between the clumsy and deadly monster British submarines of the Great War – which tended to kill their own crews more readily than those of enemy ships – and all the large Royal Navy submarines which followed her, right up to present-day nuclear boats. In retrospect, her greatest failing was that her concept failed to address the political context of the age into which she was launched.

The 'X' in her pennant number stands for 'experimental', but it also brings an air of 'mystery', and the story of *X.1* is no stranger to mystery and subterfuge. This volume aims to lay to rest once and for all the deliberate, and innocent, misinformation spread about *X.1*, and tell the true story of the Royal Navy's extraordinary secret weapon and her crew.

Acknowledgments

The inspiration for this book, and much of the information contained therein, came from the Royal Navy Submarine Museum in Gosport. This excellent heritage site has four submarines to view, and a collection ranging from Art to Weapons systems. Full details can be found on their website: www.submarine-museum.co.uk.

My thanks and appreciation for their help and patience go out to the following individuals and organisations. Even when some research may have drawn a blank, they have always provided me with alternative sources to investigate.

Debbie Corner of the Photographic Section, Margaret Bidmead and George Malcolmson of the Archive Section, Alan Ferris, Volunteer Librarian, RN Submarine Museum, Gosport.

Mary Edwards, Bob Todd and Gabrielle Fabri of the National Maritime Museum, the Brass Foundry, Woolwich.

Chris Henry of 'Explosion!', Priddy's Hard, Gosport.

David Thorburn of Thales Optronics Limited.

Lesley Richmond of the Hunterian Museum, Glasgow.

Sharon Hinde of The Dock Museum, Barrow-in-Furness.

The Staff of the British Newspaper Library, Colindale.

The Staff of the Public Record Office, Kew.

Elizabeth Rees of Tyne & Wear Archive Services.

Dr Anne Thick of Hampshire Records Office, Winchester.

Andrew Brown and David Capus of the Metropolitan Police.

Ingus Vizulis of the Latvian Embassy, London.

Jason von Zerneck, Angelray Books, New York.

Trevor Parker of the Ordnance Society.

James Rankin of Birmingham, England.

David Vanner of Penarth, South Wales.

Peter Howcroft and David Mendez of HMS *Belfast*.

Martin Garnett of the Imperial War Museum.

Claire Freeman of the New Zealand Navy Museum, Torpedo Bay.

John Lambert of Bedford, England.

Gaëlle Dumont of Heller-Joustra SA.

David Bowen of Humbrol Ltd.

John Date of the Royal Institution of Naval Architects.

John Snyder of White Ensign Models, for his expertise on colour schemes.

The Photographs

For what was supposed to be a top-secret weapon system, a comparatively large number of photographs of *X.1* were taken – no doubt because she was at the time the world's largest submarine, but also because,

Left: Sir Arthur W Johns, KCB, CBE (1873–1937). Sixth Director of Naval Construction, responsible for the majority of Royal Navy submarine classes in the Great War, and the designer of the *X.1*. Born in 1873 at Torpoint, Cornwall, Arthur William Johns entered Devonport Dockyard as a Shipwright Apprentice at the age of 14. After heading the list of all apprentices in his examination year, he moved to Greenwich Royal Naval College as a probationary Assistant Constructor. In 1895 he qualified with the coveted First Class Professional Certificate. After several minor assignments, he worked on the design of Captain Scott's Antarctic research vessel, the *Discovery*, as well as the *King Edward VII* class pre-dreadnoughts and the Royal Yacht *Alexandra*. Promoted to the rank of Constructor in 1911, in the following year he began his long association with Royal Navy submarine design, becoming responsible for the later 'E' class vessels, and the succeeding 'F', 'G', 'H', 'J', 'K', 'L', 'M' and 'R' classes. In 1916 he was set to investigating rigid airship construction, and designed the successful *R.33* and *R.34*, the latter airship being the first machine to make a two-way air crossing of the Atlantic (in July 1919). In November 1920 A W Johns was confirmed as Assistant Director of Naval Construction, and it was in this capacity that he was responsible for the design of *X.1*. Made a CBE (Commander of the British Empire) in 1920 as a reward for his War service, he was made a CB (Companion of the Bath) in 1929, and in 1933 he was created a KCB (Knight Commander of the Bath). A lifelong scholar, Sir Arthur became a member of the Institute of Naval Architects in 1904, presenting many thought-provoking papers to that august body, and was elected a Vice President of the Institute in 1931. Promoted to Director of Naval Construction in January 1930, the last major vessel for which Sir Arthur was responsible was the new aircraft carrier HMS *Ark Royal*. Her first captain was full of praise for her aircraft-handling arrangements, stating that in the first 400 hours' flying, not one single airman had been injured taking off and landing. In the same period, he sagely concluded, if the same young men had been ashore driving their motorcars and riding their motorbikes, quite a few of them would have ended up in hospital. Sadly, early in 1936 illness forced Sir Arthur to retire, and he died on 13 January 1937.

with her unique outline, she was a shapely vessel, and very photogenic. However, in contrast only two on-board photographs seem to have survived – if indeed any others were ever taken – and there are no internal shots in existence. The two pictures of her upper control room are, in fact, photographs of the wooden mock-up built at Chatham Dockyard and used to plan out the layout of the multiple controls and fittings which had to be shoe-horned inside.

Some photographs of worse-than-average quality are included, on the grounds that they illustrate interesting features or events. Most were taken with a Kodak 'Box Brownie' or similar 'pocket' camera, and are typical of the snapshots of the era.

In recreating the odyssey of *X.1*'s peacetime service in the Mediterranean, I have unashamedly used photographs taken by the crew members of 'L' class submarines, notably *L.27*. Some of these are typical shots of submariners at play, but others illustrate the actual cruises in which *X.1* participated.

Photographic and Line Drawing Credits

Page 8 the photo of Sir Arthur W Johns appears by kind permission of the Royal Institution of Naval Architects.

Plans of the 'K' class and 'M' class boats by kind permission of Mr John Lambert; the cutaway photograph of *M.1* is by the Author.

U 155 on page 14 is a US Navy photograph which appeared in <<L'ALBVM DE LA GVERRE 1914-1918>> published by *L'Illustration*.

The line drawings of *K.26* and *U 139* appear in *Submarines of World War Two* and are reproduced by permission of Erminio Bagnasco.

The cartoon of the Battleship Bombing Experiment: *The Chicago Herald*.

Vickers gun turret and mechanism drawings, Admiralty Fire Control Clock and Fire Control Table drawings, details of the Asdic fitted to *X.1*, photos used by the *Daily Herald*, the photo of Commander Colin Mayers and the cutaway drawing of a 5.25in Mk II turret: Public Record Office, Kew.

The photographs of the Admiralty Fire Control Clock and Straddle Indicator were taken by the Author with the co-operation of the staff of HMS *Belfast*; the photographs of the sub-calibre 2pdr barrel and case were taken by the Author with the help of Mr Chris Henry of 'Explosion!'.

Sub-calibre cutaway on page 49: Hampshire Record Office, Item Ref 109M91/GL127.

The basis for the periscope view of *Akikaze* is derived from the box art for PIT-ROAD destroyer kit W13, *Minekaze*, and is reproduced by kind permission of the artist, Mr Y Takani.

The illustration of a Mark IV torpedo is reproduced from *Britain's Wonderful Fighting Forces* by Captain Ellison Hawks.

The frontispiece, the photos of *U 126* on page 25, of *X.1* on pages 61 (upper), 65, 78 (upper and lower), the upper control room photos on page 66, the rangefinder blueprint, and the Ship's Plans: the National Maritime Museum, Greenwich.

The excellent drawings of the interior of *X.1* are reproduced by kind permission of David Hill, being selected from an extensive range of internal views of *X.1*.

Captain Gilbert H Roberts on page 90 and Admiral Beatty on page 98: the Imperial War Museum.

The map of the Mediterranean in 1929 is taken from the *Atlante Internazionale del Touring Club Italiano*, in the David Rumsey Map Collection, by permission of Cartography Associates, at www.davidrumsey.com.

The Salmon postcard of *X.1* is reproduced by permission of J. Salmon Ltd.

Illustrated London News cutaway on page 105 and photos of *Narwhal* on pages 105 and 110: the Newspaper Library, Colindale;

Narwhal, *Nautilus* and *Argonaut* on pages 109, 110, 111 and 112: Naval History and Heritage Command, Washington Naval Yard.

The Heller box art for *Surcouf* is used with the kind permission of Humbrol Ltd and of Heller-Joustra SA.

The photograph of the wreck of the Japanese submarine *I-1* off Guadalcanal is reproduced by permission of the New Zealand Defence Force, Torpedo Bay Museum.

The illustrations of the Besson MB-41.1, Watanabe E9W1, Yokosuka E14Y1, Aichi *Seiran* and the Arado Ar 231 appear in *Warplanes of the Second World War Volume Six – Floatplanes*, by William Green and Dennis I Punnett.

The line drawing of the Type XI U-Boat is reproduced from *U BOAT* by Eberhard Rössler;

The photograph of the rear of a 5.25in turret: The Vickers Photographic Archive, Barrow Museum Service, Cat No. 4909.

All other photographs and illustrations are reproduced with the kind permission of the RN Submarine Museum, Gosport.

CHAPTER 1

Giant Submarines

Russian Plans

In warships, the old adage that 'Size Does Matter' seems to be true. It was the Imperial Russian Navy which had built the first armoured cruiser, and they aimed to be in the forefront of development of the latest naval weapon, the submarine. Buying in experience from several foreign inventors, the Russians were the first customers for German U-boats, purchasing the electric prototype *Forelle* and ordering the *Karp*, *Karas* and *Kambala* from Germaniawerft in 1904. In 1906 they went on to build the second submarine in the world with a diesel engine, the *Minoga*, and laid down the first submarine minelayer, the *Krab*. A Russian submarine commander was the first to try out his own design for a snorkel device. And it was to be the Russian Navy which first conceived the idea of a 'cruiser submarine'.

As early as 1911 a Russian designer named Zhuravlev proposed a submersible cruiser of 4,500 tons, powered by eight diesel engines for a surface speed of 26 knots, and armed with no less than five 4.7in guns, plus torpedoes and mines. For surface action she would be protected by up to 3in of armour plate. Needless to say, the industrial capacity of Tsarist Russia was quite incapable of building such a vessel, although under the impetus of wartime a reduced design was actually drawn up in December 1916, for a 20-knot cruiser submarine displacing 3,000 tons submerged and mounting four 4in guns. This project paralleled a similar German design of the time. the chaotic industrial conditions which stymied Russia's war production, and the political turmoil of the following year, doomed these cruiser submarines to remain on the drawing board.

A later project for three 'fleet submarines', armed with two twin 130mm gun turrets and endowed with a surface speed of 24 knots was drawn up by the Soviet Navy in 1930. Once again, however, technical difficulties led the struggling Soviets to downgrade the boats' armament to just two single 100mm guns, when they were completed as the *Pravda* class.

Royal Navy Monster Boats

Mr A W Johns served on the Submarine Development Committee of 1915, when the question of building submarine cruisers for '*guerre de course*' was discussed, but dismissed, since the German merchant fleet had been swept from the seas by then. However, during the Great War the British Admiralty went on to build large numbers of giant submarines, with disappointing results.

They had been alarmed by rumours of high speed German U-boats – one was credited with the phenomenal surface speed of 22 knots. Survivors from the old battleship *Formidable* reported – mistakenly – that the U-boat which sank them had kept pace with their old pre-dreadnought in the teeth of a gale. Admiral Fisher himself was convinced that at least two German U-boats could achieve 19 knots. So it was decided to build high speed 'Fleet Submarines' to accompany the dreadnoughts on sweeps of the North Sea. In the spring of 1915, Commodore Sydney Hall had told Lt Cdr Godfrey Herbert (who eighteen months later would take command of the ill-fated *K.13*) that the Admiralty were considering a new class of 'submersible steam-driven destroyers'.

HMS *Dreadnought* had not only ushered in a new class of all-big-gun ships – giving her name to the type – but her turbine engines had also significantly raised the maximum speeds of this new class of battleship. If a foreshortened range was accepted, the turbine-engined ships could also maintain their higher maximum speed for much longer periods compared with the old reciprocating-engined vessels. If a submarine were to keep pace with the dreadnought squadrons on offensive sweeps then she would need to be able to maintain at least 21 knots – the speed of the main battlefleet – or even exceed this speed to be able to take up an ambush position and lie in wait for retreating or damaged enemy battleships. Diesels could not yet give speeds matching that of a dreadnought, so the Admiralty had turned, fatally, to steam power for its new class of fleet submarines. The result was the dreaded 'K' class (or 'K for Killer', as some crews named them).

Their steam turbines certainly gave these monsters a high surface speed, but at a terrible price. The enormously long and narrow (and flimsy) hulls were pierced by a multitude of openings, for retractable funnels, ventilators and the like, which all had to be closed by remote control before they dived. The

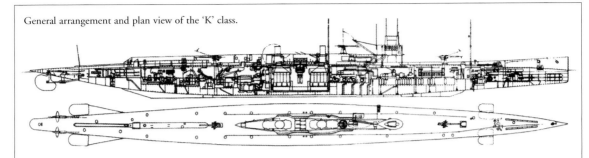

General arrangement and plan view of the 'K' class.

'K' Class Specifications

Displacement: 1,883 tons surfaced/2,565 tons submerged

Length: 338ft; **Beam:** 26.66ft

Twin screws: Geared steam turbines 10,500shp plus auxiliary diesel 800bhp = 24/25 knots surfaced/electric motors 1,400hp = 9 knots submerged

Up to 2 x 4in guns plus 1 x 3in AA; *K.17* had 5.5in; 8 x 18in torpedo tubes (4 bow, 4 beam)

Crew: 60 officers and men

slender hull – copied from cruiser designs – brought severe hydrodynamic problems. When a 'K' boat dived, the water pressure on the long flat plane of her deck would tend to force her into a much steeper dive than planned. Conversely, when she was rising to the surface, the hull suffered from an unwanted lift force about one-third of the distance back from the bows, leading to a steeper than planned rise.

The extreme size brought other problems to a crew desperately attempting to compensate for this perverse hydrodynamic behaviour. The distances between the commander and the crew members operating the hydroplanes and ballast controls throughout the enormous length of a 'K' boat made co-ordinated effort extremely difficult, and delays in

relaying commands could be fatal.

And when a 'K' boat dived, all hell usually broke loose. Most of the tragi-comic unintentional crash dives by 'K' boats usually ended in an embarrassing thump into the sea bed nose-first. Commander Ernest Leir's *K.3* even dived out of control when carrying the young Duke of York, the future King George VI. But it was no laughing matter when the unfortunately-numbered *K.13* dived in the Gareloch. More than half her crew and the members of the dockyard staff on board for the trial drowned when her engine room vents were accidentally left open and she was unable to surface.

A 'K' boat was 338ft long, and at periscope depth it took only a slight miscalculation in trim, or a dive

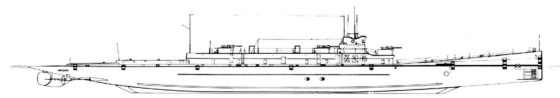

K.26, last of the breed and the only example of the so-called 'Improved K' class. Completed and commissioned exactly two months before *X.1* was launched, *K.26* served alongside *X.1* in the 1st Submarine Flotilla at Malta, and survived until 1931.

***K.26* Specifications**

Displacement: 2,140 tons surfaced/2,770 tons submerged

Length: 351½ft; **Beam:** 28ft

Twin screws: Geared steam turbines 10,000shp plus auxiliary diesel 800bhp = 23.5 knots surfaced/electric motors 1,400hp = 9 knots submerged

3 x 4in guns; 10 x 21in torpedo tubes

Crew: 65 officers and men

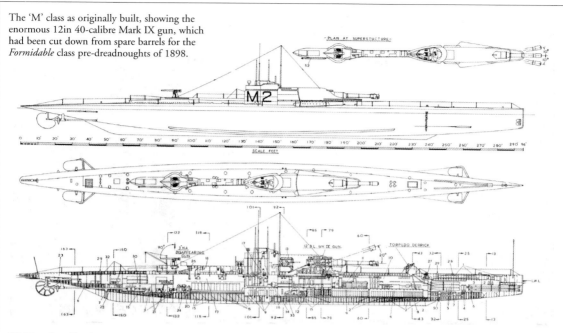

The 'M' class as originally built, showing the enormous 12in 40-calibre Mark IX gun, which had been cut down from spare barrels for the *Formidable* class pre-dreadnoughts of 1898.

'M' Class Specifications

Displacement: 1,600 tons surfaced/1,950 tons submerged

Length: 296ft (*M.1*)/305ft (*M.2* & *M.3*); **Beam:** 24½ft

Twin screws: Diesels 2,400bhp = 15.5 knots surfaced/electric motors 1,600hp = 9.5 knots submerged

1 x 12in/40 gun; 1 x 3in AA gun; 2 x .303in Lewis machine guns;

4 x 18in (*M.1*)/4 x 21in (*M.2* & *M.3*) torpedo tubes (all forward)

Crew: 60–70 officers and men

A cutaway model of *M.1* in the Science Museum, London, showing the armament arrangements.

accidentally steepening, to send the bow plunging to a depth where the pressure of water might easily crush the hull, and this was probably the cause of the loss of *K.5*, which tragically disappeared off the Atlantic shelf during Fleet Exercises in January 1921.

The three huge 'Mutton Boats' of the 'M' or 'Monitor' class which followed were almost as clumsy, weighed down by an enormous 12in gun of the type mounted on pre-dreadnought battleships. It is difficult at this distance to appreciate why the 'M' class were built in the first place. With adequate aerial spotting they could be useful for bombardment of a lightly-defended coastline, but the effect of their slow-loading single 12in gun could only ever be considered as having a nuisance value and of no real military significance, and the gun had to be aimed by pointing the whole submarine at the target. As coast bombardment types they were completely outclassed by the surface monitors, in the design of which the Royal Navy excelled. And lacking the huge side bulges of these surface monitors with their 12in, 14in, 15in and even 18in guns, the submarines were highly vulnerable to attack by mine, torpedo and remote control explosive motor boats – as used by the Germans to defend their seaward flank in Belgium.

The contemporary notion that an 'M' boat could

compensate for the comparative lack of success of submarines using torpedoes, by taking a single pot-shot at a passing German capital ship with their 12in gun, must rate as high fantasy or even worse. The gun itself, after the initial shot, could only be reloaded on the surface. Hit or miss with the first round, exposing their position in their classic 'dip-chick' manoeuvre would bring down a hornets' nest of destroyers, and the large and cumbersome 'M' boat's chances of survival would be minimal.

The wreck of *M.1* was discovered off Portland in 1999, and reconstruction of the circumstances of her loss showed just how difficult these monsters were to control under water. The daughter of one of the crewmen, Able Seaman H G Jewell who was lost with *M.1* in 1925, recalled her father's unease about the handling of the top-heavy boat, and his premonition on his last leave ashore that he might not survive the planned exercise. When *M.2* was also lost with her whole crew in 1932, old sailors recalled that the keels of the 'M' class had originally been laid down as units of the 'K' or 'Killer' class.

The U-Cruisers

It was to be Imperial Germany which built the first practical cruiser submarines. They were to serve as the inspiration for many prototype vessels between the wars. Many distinguished naval authors feel that the German construction of U-Cruisers was a failure. A large boat absorbed a disproportionate amount of scarce dockyard labour and equally scarce materials, while being able to accomplish nothing that the medium-sized boats could not do equally well. Mr A W Johns, designer of *X.1*, closely studied surrendered German U-boats and presented his findings to the Institute of Naval Architects in 1920. His audience agreed with him that, in every respect besides the horsepower of their diesel engines, Royal Naval submarines of the Great War compared favourably with the German boats. In particular he noted that the larger U-boats took twice as long to build as the standard units.

German U-boat commanders also preferred the smaller boats. German design in any case tended to isolate the commander in the conning tower above the control room. The widely-separated crew operating a long boat presented severe problems of co-ordination, and split-second co-ordination between all members of the diving team was precisely what safely submerging an early submarine required. The big U-Cruisers were difficult to control, according to Commander Fechter, a former U-boat captain writing in *Marine Rundschau*. He felt a small boat gave one centralised control.

One of the ex-mercantile U-Cruisers (probably the *U 155*) inspects the Spanish liner *Infanta-Isabel-de Borbon* off Cadiz on 18 March 1918. Note that the U-Boat is 'rigged' for surface running, with washing hung out to dry! Her crew obviously think they have little to fear, armed as she is with two huge 15cm guns.

U 155 **Specifications**

Displacement: 1,512 tons surfaced/1,875 tons submerged

Length: 65m; Beam: 8.9m; Draught: 5.3m

Twin screws: Diesels 760bhp = 9.5 knots surfaced/electric motors 800hp = 7.5 knots submerged

Using diesels + electric motors on the surface = 12.4 knots

2 x 15cm/45 guns; 2 x 8.8cm AA guns; 2 x 50cm torpedo tubes (bow), 18 torpedoes

Crew: 56-76 officers and men

Why then did the Kaiser's Navy persevere with these large U-Cruisers? The answer is partly logistical, and partly psychological. All the German cruisers stationed overseas in 1914 had been quickly run to ground and destroyed. Apart from raiders disguised as merchant ships, no cruiser replacements were sent out, as they could hardly be expected to survive the Royal Navy's surface blockade of Germany. Submarine cruisers, on the other hand, could evade the naval blockade and continue to show the flag in distant waters. And very large submarines could carry much more fuel, ammunition and supplies for extended cruises.

German designers had gained valuable experience with the handling of large, long-range submersibles with the four mercantile 'Deutschland' class unarmed cargo vessels, designed to circumvent the British naval blockade of the North Atlantic. As early as September 1916 the German Navy had decided to convert a second batch of four mercantile submarines under construction into long-range corsair cruisers, to carry the numbers U 151 to U 154.[1] When the entry of the USA into the war rendered the mercantile submarine redundant, the surviving trio from the first batch were also converted to combat use as U 155 to U 157 (the Bremen having been lost in the meantime). In order to raise the low speed of the three ex-mercantile boats, they were fitted with new propellers which allowed the use of both diesel engines and battery power driving their electric motors, for boosting surface speed in an emergency. The Royal Navy was able to study this engine arrangement in detail when the U 155, ex-Deutschland, was handed over to the UK in 1918.

At the same time the Imperial German Navy threw itself into a major construction programme of extremely large U-Cruisers of a new design. Their plans included the heavily-armed cruisers of Projects 46 and 46a and the armoured cruisers of Project 47.

Because of the time delay in designing 4,000bhp diesel engines, the latter vessels were dropped in favour of the ultimate U-Cruiser of the Great War, Project 50, or Kreuzer 44. This huge vessel, also known as UD 1, with a surface displacement of 3,800 tons, was to be powered by steam turbines for high surface speed. The Germans accepted the larger-than-normal number of openings in the pressure hull which steam power required, but looked to solve the major problem of retained boiler heat when dived, by adopting the special 'diving boiler' patented by Schäfer and Wölke – which was contained in a tank free to flood with seawater when the vessel submerged, thus dissipating the heat.[2]

Due to the deteriorating war situation, the lack of raw materials, and a severe manpower shortage – especially of trained construction workers – only four of the planned fourteen U-Cruisers laid down were actually completed prior to the Armistice, and the armoured steam turbine boats of Project 50 never left the drawing board.

Nevertheless, the first of these large vessels (Project 46) were commissioned, with names as befitting their large size and cruiser status:

U 139, named Kapitänleutnant Schweiger in German service, was taken over by the French Navy, rechristened Halbronn, and served until July 1928, not being broken up until eight years later. The French Navy was very impressed with her armament arrangements: U 139's two 15cm (5.9in) guns each fired up to fourteen rounds a minute, fed by an armoured and powered ammunition hoist from refrigerated magazines. When submerged the gun barrels were sealed watertight by a tompion at the muzzle and by a special short cartridge case in the breech. After surfacing, the 3m base stereoscopic rangefinder could be raised by compressed air to a height of 7.5m (more than 24 feet) above the waterline, giving an excellent spotting facility out to a useful effective range. Her conning tower was armoured to a maximum of 90mm, and the above-water portions of her hull to 35mm thickness.

This heavy armament and armour meant that U 139 was very clumsy underwater, but on the surface she was very stable and provided a good gun platform.

U 140 was named Kapitänleutnant Otto Weddigen. She was ceded to the USA in 1919, and two years later was sunk as a target to fulfil the terms of the Versailles Treaty. In the interim no doubt the US Navy took full advantage to test and copy the design, features of which were to appear some years later in the Americans' own submarine cruiser designs.

U 141 came to the UK in 1918, and was not scrapped until 1923, after use as a target for firing trials. Key aspects of the class design, such as the thick pressure hull, the horizontal rangefinder for her 5.9in guns, and a separate diesel generator for battery charging, were to reappear in X.1. Her name, if she was allocated one, did not accompany her into British hands.

A fourth cruiser, the U 142, was the only vessel to be completed under Project 46a, with slightly larger displacement (2,158 tons surfaced/2,785 tons submerged). With a nominal range of 20,000 miles,

Internal arrangements of the
U 139 class boats.

U 139 at sea during the war.

U 139 Class Specifications
Displacement: 1,930 tons surfaced/2,483 tons submerged
Length: 94.7m; **Beam:** 9m
Twin screws; Diesels 3,500bhp = 16 knots surfaced/ electric motors 1,780hp = 8 knots submerged
2 x 15cm guns; 2 x 8.8cm AA guns; 6 x 50cm torpedo tubes (4 bow, 2 stern);
Crew: Between 62 and 80 officers and men

and carrying two 15cm guns, two lighter guns and
twenty torpedoes, the British Admiralty considered
her to be a most formidable antagonist. The
Armistice found her not quite ready for sea. She was
broken up in Germany in 1919, as were her
uncompleted sisters still on the stocks.

Thus it can be seen that the Imperial German
Navy not only continued with the design of U-
Cruisers, but persevered in their construction – even
when the deteriorating war situation should have
required the concentration of all available manpower
and materials on the rapid construction of much
smaller boats. This penchant for 'blue water U-boats'
was to return to feature prominently in Admiral
Raeder's ill-fated 'Z-Plan' twenty years later.

In the meantime, the ceded U-Cruisers, and the
plans of *U 117* and *U 142* which Germaniawerft and
Vulkan were permitted to sell to the Japanese in
1920, made a great impression on the Allied Navies,
and their descendants were to take to the water in
some numbers in the inter-war period.[3] And the first
of these, incorporating many of the lessons of the U-
Cruisers, would be *X.1*.

A painting by the famous German marine artist Willy Stöwer:
'U-Boot-Kreuzer im Gefecht (1 Oktober 1918)', depicting a
supposed attack on an escorted convoy of armed merchant ships.
An escort and several of the merchant ships are replying to the
fire of the unnamed U-Cruiser. The number of shell splashes
around the escort at left may indicate that a pair of U-Cruisers
has concentrated to overwhelm a convoy. The low height of the
15cm guns above the waterline, in comparison to the turrets on
X.1, means that they can only be served efficiently in relatively
calm conditions. The painting also reveals the rangetaker perched
on the rear of the conning tower, at the short-based rangefinder
which could only be used on the surface. Obviously, fire control
relies on the officers on the relatively low conning tower spotting
the fall of shot with binoculars. Moreover, they are dangerously
exposed to blast from the aft 15cm gun.

CHAPTER 2

Design Criteria

A Ship of Extremes

Given the moves by the British after the First World War to outlaw the submarine as a weapon of war, a contemporary observer would have been at a loss to explain why the Admiralty conceived, and then continued with the construction of the vessel which was to become *X.1*. She could be described as the latest, and possibly the very last example of the 'Fisher Doctrine', emphasising speed and gunpower over all other qualities – and even to excess – which had led to the spectacular failures of the 'K' class submarines during the Great War and later the 'M' boats. And of course, the Silent Service was no stranger to the contradictions built into her conception and possible future employment, given the ambivalent attitude of the Admiralty towards the earliest submarines. After all, it was no less a personage than Rear Admiral Wilson VC, Third Sea Lord and Controller of the Navy, who in 1900 had dubbed the submarine as a 'damned un-English weapon'. Wilson, who had won his VC on land during the Sudan campaign, went further when he declared that we should 'treat all submarines as pirates in wartime and . . . hang all the crews'. And this when the first five out of hundreds of these 'un-English weapons' had already been ordered from Vickers in Barrow for the Royal Navy.

The secrecy which was to surround *X.1* all through her chequered career began with a total news blackout, leading to the most fantastic rumours which persisted for years. She was to have an incredible speed of *33 knots*, to keep up with the *Hood* and other fast warships . . . She would carry guns bigger than 12in, or else an armament of six 5.5in guns . . . She would be difficult to dive and control underwater, just like the old 'K' boats and the U-Cruisers. In fact her secrets were not to be displayed to the British public at large, who had paid for her, until August 1930. This was more than seven years after her launch, when she had returned home from the Mediterranean with a large question mark against her future. During Chatham's Navy Week members of the public were allowed on board her for the first time, and to coincide with this event the *Illustrated London News* of the same month published a large cutaway drawing.

X.1 was to be a ship of extremes. At the time of her launch she was the largest, the longest and the deepest-diving submarine in the world. Her designers intended her to be also the fastest diesel-powered submarine, and she was to carry the heaviest surface armament ever fitted in a submarine. Finally, she was to be the most controversial submarine design the Royal Navy ever produced, and the subject of the longest-lived policy of deliberate misinformation ever attempted by the Admiralty.[1] The success or otherwise of that policy of misinformation can be seen in Chapter 11.

Captain Nasmith's Preferences

When *X.1* was laid down in 1921 the Admiralty was seriously considering the possibility of war with Japan. It was becoming clear that the Anglo-Japanese Alliance which was due to expire in July 1921 was unlikely to be renewed a third time, in view of the frenetic naval race which was taking place between Britain, the USA and Japan. The Imperial Japanese Navy was eagerly planning new super-dreadnought classes armed with ten 16in and even eight 18in guns.

The starting point for *X.1* was the committee on designs, which after 1919 interviewed the most successful submarine officers of the First World War. The majority opinion, led by Captain Martin Nasmith of *E.11* fame, called for the development of a long-range submarine capable of raiding enemy commerce, and with a powerful gun armament to drive off escort vessels.

The committee's views were taken to heart in that the new experimental submarine planned for in the 1921/22 Estimates would carry a large gun armament. However, although it was to be *X.1*'s most obvious visual feature, her gun armament did not start out as the prime consideration for her conception. In fact it probably came a poor third.

Design Aims

She was to be experimental in three major areas:

Her designed surface speed

The fastest diesel boats during the Great War had

Martin Nasmith VC won his Victoria Cross during the Dardanelles campaign, for his exploits in disrupting Turkish supplies being sent to Gallipoli. Told to 'go and run amuck in the Marmora', he braved the nets and minefields of the Narrows in *E.11*, and began his first patrol in Turkish waters on 20 May 1915. On his triumphal return he asked for a deck gun, to greatly increase his chances of scoring damage on the enemy when far from a friendly port and carrying only a limited supply of precious torpedoes. Again, some enemy vessels were too small to rate a torpedo, and there were tempting opportunities to shell enemy troops and installations ashore. Subsequent incursions were made by boats armed with 6pdr, 12pdr and even 4in deck guns. They fought it out on the surface with armed Turkish ships, shelled railways and troop columns, and bombarded powder mills. Lt Cdr Bruce in *E.12* had even taken on and defeated a battery of Turkish field guns with his 4in gun. The damage Nasmith and his fellow commanders were able to inflict was considerable, and at one point threatened to destroy the morale of the Turkish V Army facing the ANZAC troops. During the Second World War, Martin Nasmith made an important contribution to the Battle of the Atlantic against Hitler's U-boats, by recommending the introduction of Rescue Ships in convoys, to pick up torpedoed seamen. The twenty-nine Rescue Ships would go on to save more than 4,000 men from the sea.

been the 'J' class, whose maximum surface speed of 19.5 knots was felt to be disappointing. It fell some two knots short of allowing them to operate as 'fleet submarines', accompanying the dreadnought battleships and battlecruisers on sweeps. This failure had led directly to a reversion to steam power for the succeeding 'K' class. In this area *X.1* was also to be a bitter disappointment.

Underwater control and diving trim

The disastrous experience with the preceding 'K' class had shown that it was far from easy to safely dive and control such huge submersibles. The 'K' class were so long and narrow, with large flat deck areas, and initially, a lack of buoyancy forward, that they frequently dived out of control and struck the sea bed. Their crews' difficulties were compounded by the fact that their very length made control cumbersome. The commander and diving officer were so far removed from the planesmen fore and aft that their orders had to be relayed by remote control – voice tubes or telephone. This control problem had been noted by U-boat commanders who preferred the smaller classes to the large U-Cruisers for that very reason. Most of the inadvertent dives to the bottom by 'K' class subs ended merely in embarrassment. However, on Thursday 20 January 1921 during Fleet exercises off the Atlantic Shelf, it is likely *K.5* went out of control when diving, exceeded her safe diving depth of 150ft and was lost with six officers and fifty-one men.

The quick-blow tanks built into the last of the 'K' class, the *K.26*, were intended as a safety device, in case the sub took on a steep diving angle by the bow. Cdr Raikes' proposals to fit quick-blow and quick-flood tanks at both ends of *X.1* were the key to her complete success in underwater handling, as demonstrated by her flawless diving, underwater control and surfacing performance.

For a corsair submarine, especially one with no scout aircraft embarked (as would be carried by *M.2*, the French *Surcouf* and many later Japanese boats) the necessity to dive rapidly under control was essential. The ability to surface rapidly in good control was equally crucial to her role as a surface gun platform to take her opponents by surprise. Her secondary role of underwater ambusher with a heavy bow torpedo outfit also required handiness when submerged. In all these respects *X.1* met or exceeded the hopes of her designers.

Surface gunpower

'What can submarines do? They can be built to do anything that a surface ship can do and can "get there" unseen to do it, but when there they cannot do it as well.' So wrote the Technical History Section of the Admiralty in 1921.

The *X.1* was built to test theories on how to successfully operate a corsair submarine, designed to range far from base on extended patrols to disrupt and destroy enemy convoys and communications, in an oceanic context. Examination of captured U-

Cruisers had revealed the potential of a large long-range raider carrying a heavy surface armament. However, the Armistice had intervened before many U-Cruisers could show their form in actual combat situations, and the U-boat war had hinged on the efforts of smaller boats – which could operate as far away as the US coast but relied on stealth and torpedoes rather than gunpower. Drawing on successful Allied developments of the latter part of the

Great War, it was to be expected that enemy convoys would be escorted by sloops or frigates, but also by first-rate destroyers. Recent experiences told submariners how difficult it was to sink or disable one of these fast, highly manoeuvrable, shallow-draft opponents.[2] Imperial Germany's High Seas Fleet had launched and commissioned 235 destroyers. The number lost to all causes, principally mining, was sixty-eight ships – of which only four were torpedoed

X.1 seen from her bulbous bow, showing her forward turret.

by British submarines.[3] Out of 170 German torpedo boats in service, forty were lost during the Great War, but none to submarine torpedo. On the British side, of the 523 destroyers built and in service before 1919, plus the 100 older torpedo boats still in commission, sixty-four destroyers and nine torpedo boats were lost to all causes. These ranged from collision – an ever-present risk to flotillas manoeuvring at high speed in close formation – to the deadly mine, but only nine destroyers and two torpedo boats fell victim to U-boat torpedoes.[4] But to succeed, a corsair submarine would have to face up to and sink escorting destroyers.

Traditional submariners harboured serious doubts about the feasibility of successful surface gun actions against a well-armed, aggressively-handled destroyer. Despite her low profile and minimum of hull exposed to fire, a submarine like the *U 141* had the odds stacked against her in a stand-up gunfight with a destroyer. Her opponent would have a director control tower (DCT), high-set rangefinder and a higher rate of fire from smaller guns than the clumsy hand-operated 15cm carried by the U-Cruiser. With only two main guns, mounted one before and one aft of the conning tower, the U-Cruiser would have to expose her beam to the onrushing destroyer, bearing in at full speed and eager to ram . . . And the destroyer captain, staring down the muzzles of a pair of 15cm guns, would be certain to throw his ship into a series of high-speed zigzags to throw off the German gunners.

The submariner's traditional *modus operandi*, dating all the way back to Bushnell's *Turtle* and Fulton's *Nautilus*, was to strike unseen from a submerged position. When self-propelled torpedoes gave them the opportunity to stand off and attack, they perfected the underwater ambush to sink more powerful prey. *X.1*'s design aimed to utilise the 'ambush' advantages of a submerged attack but using surface guns. Torpedoes were expensive and bulky. Raiding far from home, expenditure of the last torpedo could bring a premature end to a cruise. As well as her twelve torpedoes, *X.1* was to carry more than 100 rounds of 5.2in 70lb shells for each of her four guns – which gave her a huge logistical advantage over the submarine relying mainly on torpedoes. Her unique Barr & Stroud periscopic rangefinder could give accurate range to a target destroyer while still submerged. Her watertight DCT allowed her gunnery officer and his spotting crew to sit calmly in their seats having pre-selected the elevation and bearing of the target, with the gun target dials ready laid even before surfacing.

No frantic rush up ladders and onto the gun deck for the gunners – this was the role of the loading numbers, tugging the cartridge cases and shells from the power hoists between the twin guns and placing them into the tray for power ramming into the semi-automatic breeches. Engaging a rapidly-manoeuvring target destroyer, the DCT and transmitting station on *X.1* held an incomparable advantage over *U 141*. The odds were tilted back firmly in favour of the corsair sub.

Proposals to arm the future '*X.2*' with three twin – or even two triple – turrets were supported by enthusiastic gunnery officers' claims that this would enable her to surprise and overwhelm light cruisers.[5] Far-fetched as this might seem in hindsight, it was only the logical extension of the successful gunnery trials run by *X.1*. Such unproven optimism was likely to have played into the hands of *X.1*'s major opponents, the torpedo specialists. However, even in his fatal report which condemned *X.1* for her costly and protracted development, Captain (S) George P Thompson could not refrain from closing with the telling comment 'The tactics of engaging surface targets is unsound in principle, although her armament and the small part of the pressure hull exposed above the surface should occasionally enable her to achieve useful results'. Praise indeed from the opposition.

The Alternative Capital Ship

Finally, one needs to consider whether there was a 'hidden agenda' behind the design and construction of *X.1*. A clue to this is the opinion voiced by the new First Sea Lord, Sir David Beatty, that the decisive future warship would be a submersible battlecruiser.

Although the super-dreadnought battleships and battlecruisers planned for the post-Great War period greatly exceeded the original *Dreadnought* of 1906 in size and power, their cost had also escalated, to the point where even the strongest Powers could only afford to build a comparative handful of the latest monster vessels. This factor in turn would have rendered them so valuable in the event of a conflict that fleet commanders or their political overlords might have been reluctant to expose them in the line of battle, or indeed anywhere outside heavily protected anchorages as a 'fleet in being'.[6] This upward spiral in size and cost threatened to become self-defeating. It also severely limited a navy's ability to wield influence on a world-wide scale, if one's few capital vessels were never to be risked outside home bases.

There were some wiser heads in the British

Admiralty who decided to explore other avenues of exerting sea power. They experimented with aircraft carriers, small torpedo craft and of course submarines. These prophets, as in the US Navy, had to fight fiercely to defend their corner against the traditionalists, who continued to favour the heavily armed and armoured dreadnought as the ultimate arbiter of naval conflict. However, the tide of post-war opinion was beginning to turn against the dreadnought. The vast costs involved and the fear of another Armageddon had at last brought some kind of sanity to international relations, and the bold US proposals to restrict and scrap battleships resulted in the Washington Conference and the Naval Treaties.

Meanwhile, that notorious iconoclast, Colonel Billy Mitchell, had demonstrated that dreadnoughts could be fatally vulnerable to attack by aircraft. On 21 July 1921 he had arranged for an extravagant public demonstration, in which the surrendered German dreadnought *Ostfriesland* was attacked off Cape Henry by Martin bombers carrying the largest bombs then extant, each weighing 1,000kg. Six of these weapons sufficed to sink the stationary and defenceless *Ostfriesland* in just ten minutes. Two years later it was the turn of the old USN battleships *Virginia* and *New Jersey* to fall victims to Mitchell's bombing trials, both vessels going down off Cape Hatteras on 5 September

1923. Battleship exponents could argue that the vessels were not under way when attacked, they did not manoeuvre out of harm's way and they were not shooting back. However, the very fact that aircraft had developed out of all recognition in less than twenty years, to the point where they already posed a very serious threat to surface ships meant that, for the armoured behemoths, the writing was well and truly on the wall. If dreadnoughts were becoming too expensive, and yet remained so vulnerable, what form should the capital ships of the future take?

As the first major exponents of air power at sea, the Admiralty pushed ahead with the conversion and construction of a substantial fleet of aircraft carriers, and at the same time planned a series of innovative experiments with submarines, which ultimately created the aircraft carrier *M.2*, the minelayer *M.3*, and of course, the cruiser *X.1*. If dreadnoughts were to be driven from the seas by political whim, or by air power – whether based ashore or afloat – then the way ahead could lie with the type of vessel which could avoid air attack by simply submerging out of harm's way. First a submersible cruiser prototype, and then a more powerfully armed sister-ship, and finally a whole submersible fleet with battleships, cruisers, aircraft carriers, monitors, minelayers and support vessels. In this ambitious programme the Royal Navy was some forty years ahead of events, when the nuclear boats and in particular the ICBM missile 'boomers' became a major factor in international affairs. It has been said of *X.1* that she was conceived years ahead of the technology which would have made her a success. In this her detractors were thinking of her experimental machinery, but the same holds true for the operational doctrines which would make her successors the *de facto* capital ships of their era.

A cartoon of the Mitchell 1921 bombing trials which appeared in the *Chicago Tribune*. The 'German Battleship' was the *Ostfriesland*, one of the first-generation German dreadnoughts and hardly comparable with the contemporary monsters of three times her displacement. However, she bore the title of 'battleship' and her sinking must have been a salutary lesson for big-gun advocates worldwide.

CHAPTER 3

Propulsion Machinery

Main Engines

However powerful she may have appeared on paper, *X.1* had her Achilles heel: the fragility of her main diesel engines. Initially it was proposed to use four ex-German U-boat engines to keep down the cost. The stated aim of saving cost would rear its head in other areas, notably the torpedo tubes, the air bottles, and the ballast tanks. Understandably, wherever standard items could be fitted into the design there would be cost savings, but the use of patently second-hand equipment would lead to major problems. However, it must be said that Vickers-designed submarine diesels during the Great War had a poor reputation, based on the perception that German engines produced far more horsepower per cylinder. Arthur W Johns acknowledged this difference in his overall analysis of German submarines. However, in retrospect it must be noted that the total power output of the larger (and therefore less efficient) Vickers diesel engines did in fact match that of the later German U-boats, producing the same nominal 1,200hp per engine. From the experiences of *X.1* it must be questioned whether the U-boat diesels were more reliable in service than the Vickers designs.

The Germans had planned to fit diesel engines of up to 4,000bhp in their armoured U-Cruiser designs, and the *Kaiser* class dreadnought *Prinzregent Luitpold* was designed for a huge Germania six-cylinder two-stroke diesel engine driving the central shaft. In the event none of these engines was actually built: the Project 47 U-Cruisers were dropped, and the *Prinzregent Luitpold* had to make do with the turbines fitted to her two outer shafts, which restricted her top speed to only 20 knots. In designing *X.1* the Admiralty would attempt in one leap to go from 1,200hp diesels to diesels producing 3,000hp, and it soon became clear that in 1921 they were reaching beyond the technology of the day. Just ten years later, diesel engines of the power and reliability needed for *X.1* would go to sea in HM Submarine *Thames*.

On 2 November 1920 the Engineer in Chief estimated that *X.1* could attain a total output of 8,000hp using Electric Motors and main engines working together, at a shaft speed of 390rpm. Two days later he produced the following power to speed

chart. It can be seen that to increase speed by just 50 per cent required a quadrupling of the power output.

BHP	2,000	4,000	6,000	8,000
Surface Speed	14 knots	17.5 knots	20 knots	21.75 knots

Arthur W Johns responded the next day with an unduly optimistic power prognosis, calculated from the trials using the scale model in the tank at Haslar, carried out on 30 September previously.

EHP	4,005	4,490	5,070
Surface Speed	20 knots	21 knots	22 knots

The scale of the engines can also be gauged from the fact that the air storage reservoirs for starting them on compressed air were estimated to weigh a total of 6 tons.

Bench testing of these massive main engines appears to have proceeded satisfactorily. There were minor annoyances due to broken valve springs and burnt exhaust valves, but these were commonplace faults given the technology and metallurgy of the day. The built-up construction was an advantage in that such faults could readily be rectified *in situ*. When mounted in the long, flexible hull of the submarine, however, and coupled rigidly to an 80ft long propeller shaft, the main engines began to behave in an unsettling manner. Apart from piston problems, it appeared that whenever maximum revolutions were called for, one or other of the camshaft drives ran hot and the engine was shut down just prior to a complete, and probably catastrophic, failure.

The Admiralty designers had gone for sheer size, scaling up existing design technology to obtain the power output necessary to drive *X.1* at high speed. Unfortunately they adhered to a Straight-Eight engine layout – with an overhead camshaft it is true. The Straight-Eight is structurally one of the weakest of all the traditional reciprocating engine layouts, requiring an extremely rigid bed plate, with the Vee-Eight conversely being one of the strongest. Marc Birkigt had pointed the way during the Great War with his compact and strong Hispano Suiza V-8 aircraft engine, and both the Rolls-Royce, Liberty and

A series of photographs showing the port main engine under construction.

Note the massive engine bed and substantial crankshaft.

Here the crankcase is being constructed around the individual cylinders, using a vertical framework.

Here the individual camshaft bearings and valve boxes are being bolted in place.

Views of the completed engine ready for bench testing, complete with exhaust manifold and temporary piping.

One of the main engines completed. Note the scale rule (graduated in feet) showing the enormous size of these engines.

Main engine control gear. A view of one end showing the regulator gear – which was later to fly to pieces in use.

Main engine bench testing.

Curtis aero engines used the equally efficient V-12 layout.[1] However, the stresses involved in the compressed-ignition engine would have produced shear forces on the bearing journals of opposite cylinders which would have been beyond the capacities of the lubricating oils of the day. High-speed V-form marine diesels would not appear for many years after *X.1*'s launch. Although *X.1*'s engines were intended to run at relatively low speeds compared with smaller aero engines, the Straight-Eight was notorious for producing torsional oscillations and cyclical vibrations, due to the long, whippy crankshaft. *X.1*'s main engines never appear to have suffered from crankshaft breakages or main bearing problems, so the design of the bottom end seems to have been adequate, even massive. However, static and dynamic balancing of such a long crankshaft was difficult, and the torsional out-of-balance forces would tend to be greatest at the ends of the shaft. For this reason the camshaft drive was taken off the crank in the centre of the engine by gearing. Using chain drive for the overhead camshaft, as suggested by Engineer Officer Lt Bigwood, might have helped, with chain tensioners to maintain accurate valve timing. Even eccentric rod drive to the overhead camshaft, as in W O Bentley's aero and car engine designs, may have helped. But vertical shaft drive, with huge bevelled gear wheels in such a non-rigid unit, were doomed to failure whenever high power outputs were demanded. Finally, it would appear that the torsional vibration problems may have been accentuated needlessly by rigidly connecting the engines to the propeller shafts. Lt Bigwood records that he himself was able to examine the flexible couplings used by German designers for the auxiliary engines taken from *U 126*. It is possible that flexible couplings were considered for the main engines and rejected because of the much higher power output to be transmitted. This analysis may appear to be with the advantage of hindsight, but it must be said that all the problems, and a range of solutions, were extant and well-understood at the time *X.1*'s main engines were on the drawing board.

In 1920 it was recognised that using full power would cause problems due to high piston speed. This

A drawing by David Hill showing the main engine room, looking aft. The compartment was more than 50ft long.

problem had arisen before the Great War in the last of the pre-turbine engined torpedo boat destroyers, with their vertical triple-expansion engines. Since then, British naval designers had a wealth of experience designing and operating large, high speed reciprocating steam engines. To withstand the stresses and reduce the reciprocating weight, the pistons of X.1's main engines were to be made of light alloy, at the time the largest light alloy pistons yet built. They were to suffer two major failures, one piston breaking up during the initial full power trials in January 1924, and the second seizing in the cylinder and causing an explosion in February 1931 – but the second incident may have been due to faulty lubrication.

The traditional steam triple- and quadruple-expansion engines could be built to a massive scale, yet they always remained relatively short compared to their size. The main engines of X.1, on the other hand, were extremely long compare to their height, to include the eight in-line cylinders. Patently, the built-up construction of the crankcase, with separate cylinder heads and valve boxes, militated against overall engine rigidity. On top of all these integral engine faults, during one Mediterranean cruise it was decided to try to use shale oil in the main engines as an attempt to save money. The comments by the long-suffering engineering staff were not complimentary.

As a first brave attempt to scale up a high-powered engine from existing models, the X.1's main engines were fatally flawed, and remained too fragile for dependable use. No-one seemed willing to admit that they were, and would always remain, a costly failure. Such an admission would have required grasping the nettle of what to replace them with. In 1931 X.1's main engines were officially downrated to a total output of only 4,500bhp, and the motor-assisted drive was discontinued for surface propulsion. Sadly, it was clear that X.1 with her original main engines was not capable of running down a scattering convoy of merchant vessels, at her 'reliable' top speed of only 16.5 knots. However, admitting this would open the Pandora's Box of what she was intended for, and against whom.

At high revolutions, X.1's main engine room must have been an exciting, not to say dangerous, place to stand, with the excessive oil-throwing from the vibrating engines adding to the sense of drama. Little wonder that several of her engineering staff are reported as suffering from virtual nervous breakdowns. They were continually in the firing line, and breakdowns which they could do little to prevent would be held to be their fault.

Auxiliary Engines and Generators

A minute dated 7 May 1921 in the Ship's Cover noted it was planned to use the auxiliary generators to add 1,000hp per shaft, plus the main engines, giving a total of '10,000hp' (*sic*). The 'K' class had been supplied with a diesel generator set in addition to their steam turbines, in order to boost surface propulsion capability when shutting down or starting up the boilers during diving and surfacing. On two occasions this diesel had brought 'K' boats home in an emergency: K.3 had shipped water down her funnels, flooding the boiler room, and K.11, diving to avoid an unidentified ship, suffered a serious fire which wrecked her boiler room.

U 155 and U 141 both had dual surface drive capability. The former boat, with her stubby hull and low length to breadth ratio derived from her merchant origins, plus low-powered diesels for

U 126 in Royal Navy hands leaving Portsmouth in 1920.

mercantile operation, could use her electric motors in conjunction with her diesels for surface running, to boost the power of her main engines and give a higher top speed for emergencies. No commentator picked up the fact that this was tactically unsound – because it drained the batteries just when they could be needed to escape underwater. The later *U 141* could run her diesel generator set at the same time as her main engines, resulting in less of a drain on the battery when the electric motors were clutched in on the propeller shafts for emergency full speed. Drawing on tests with *U 141*, the auxiliary engines in *X.1* were to be similarly employed.

When engaging the auxiliary diesels on *X.1* the order traditionally given was 'Start the *Deutschland*s'. It has been suggested that this term arose by misconception, since the engines originally came from the *U 126* and not the *U 155*. However, it is probable the term

came about through the use of both main engines and the electric motors to drive the ship on the surface – as in the original *Deutschland*. That vessel had entered into public imagination through her visits to several UK ports after her surrender, on show for charity. *X.1*'s auxiliary diesel engines should have been reliable, lifted as they were out of the ocean minelayer *U 126* which had served briefly under the White Ensign. But the Admiralty had overlooked the effectiveness of their own Great War blockade on Germany. The 'Rape of Belgium' and similar predations in north-eastern France had involved German occupation forces systematically stripping out domestic pipes and fittings from houses to salvage non-ferrous metals, and even removing the lead from roofs. Motors built under wartime conditions of brass and copper shortages simply did not last long into the 1920s. Rated at 1,200hp each they were stretched to achieve 800hp.

David Hill's drawing of the auxiliary engine room, looking aft towards the gun turret trunking. The ladder on the left leads up into the main superstructure where there was a small galley and the boat stowage. Compressed-air cylinders which were used for starting the diesels can be seen on either side of the compartment. To port and starboard of the rear of the platform are toilets for the engineering staff with an engineers' storeroom further aft on the port side. Lockers for the crew are sited around the turret trunking on the starboard side. This rear area was used by the engineering staff for maintenance and contained a drill, a lathe and an emery wheel which can be seen on the right. Immediately below the platform was a large electric motor driving an air compressor and a low pressure blower used during the final stages of surfacing the submarine.

David Hill's drawing of the dynamo switchboard, looking to starboard.

The first of several problems with these auxiliary engines began on 6 June 1924, during trials on the Maplin Sands Measured Mile. On that occasion it was noted that the after pedestal bearing on the starboard ex-U-boat diesel was defective, the nature of the fault not being specified. On 14 January 1925 Commander Raikes noted in his report on X.1's diving trials off the Tongue Light Vessel: 'The Auxiliary Engines gave trouble during the trials. It is considered that the crankshaft of the Starboard Auxiliary Engine is out of line. This is to be fixed at Chatham Dockyard.' The next day the starboard auxiliary engine had to be shut down due to a worn camshaft bearing.

A major breakdown occurred at Malta on 21 May 1929, when X.1 was charging her batteries using the auxiliary engines. After running for fifty-five minutes, the crankshaft on the port auxiliary engine actually fractured. One has to wonder where a spare crankshaft was obtained for an old U-boat engine eleven years after the war had ended.

Three years earlier, Rear Admiral (S) had

commented that the old German engines were not wearing well, and he recommended at the time that running all four diesel engines on the surface should be abandoned. Since the German engines could not produce their rated horsepower, using the main motors at the same time as the main engines was bound to drain the batteries. This could leave the ship vulnerable in the event that she needed to dive urgently, for example if under air attack. This had been the main drawback of the old *Deutschland*s and the *U 139* class boats, but their entry into service at the very end of the Great War had failed to show up the problem in protracted service.

Main Motors

Rated at 1,000ehp each, X.1's two main motors were very reliable. In fact Lt Commander Ruck-Keene wrote in his analysis of X.1 that 'The electric motors were excellent.' In his period of duty on board that was undoubtedly so. Initially, the main motors did cause some problems, mainly due to the after bearing on the port main motor overheating twice during the first full power trials of January 1924. Just over a year later, the forward coupling on the starboard main motor also overheated. It is clear that the lubrication problems were solved, since on many occasions X.1 returned to harbour after one or other main engine mishaps on the reliable power of her electric main motors. These were also used exclusively for manoeuvring X.1 when in harbour, no doubt because they could be relied on absolutely, unlike her two other sources of propulsion.

Batteries

Before the days of the Dutch use of the snorkel, or closed-circuit propulsion such as the Walther system and the later nuclear reactors, a submarine relied totally on electricity stored in her batteries for propulsion underwater. Once again in proposals for the X.1, penny-pinching reared its ugly head, with the suggestion of using second-hand battery cells taken from existing submarines laid up in reserve, but the DNC commented in a note dated 25 January 1921 that on the contrary it was necessary to install larger cells than standard. These would obviously need to be specially made to suit the size and planned performance of the new experimental cruiser.

Each lead acid cell measured 17in by 21in and was 46in high, and weighed 12½ cwt (43.18cm x 53.34cm x 116.84cm; weighing 635kg). The 330 cells were arranged in three groups or batteries of 110 cells each, and weighed just over 216 tons.

Other equipment associated with the electric main motors was equally massive:

- the dynamo and battery switchboard weighed 3½ tons;
- the Port and Starboard Motor switchboards weighed 2½ tons each;
- the main cables weighed 21½ tons; and
- battery connecting strips totalled 2¼ tons.

X.1 was fitted with a closed-circuit ventilation system for her battery cells. In fact she was the second submarine to be so fitted, *H.32* being the first. After the 'O' class boats all submarines reverted to an open ventilation system for their battery cells. After June 1924 *X.1*'s system incorporated CO_2 bottles in the event of a fire in the cells. In addition, for duty in the Tropics, *X.1* was fitted with a battery cooling plant. This was arranged to pump 9,000 cubic feet of air per minute into the three batteries, entering at 65°F to keep the cell temperature within safe limits.

Despite these state-of-the-art precautions, *X.1* suffered two battery explosions. The first occurred in No 3 Battery on 2 February 1927 at Gibraltar. The report stated that hydrogen explosions occurred in No 3 battery compartment while charging, due to a ventilation valve being shut instead of open. The cause of ignition was not determined. The amount of damage caused was not recorded, but just five days later *X.1*'s Log showed that she was carrying out underwater speed trials and depth changing trials. Either the Dockyard had been very speedy in effecting repairs, or else (which is more likely) the damage was of a minor nature. The second explosion occurred in No. 1 Battery at 04.20 on the morning of 11 July 1929, when *X.1* was in Greek waters to participate in Exercise 'OG'. She returned via Navarino to Malta Dockyard where the battery was repaired.

In his analysis of the performance of *X.1* and his proposals for her successor, Lt Commander Ruck-Keene noted that in *X.1* there was enough distilled water carried on board to top up the batteries twice. For use in the Tropics he wondered if this small supply would be adequate.

David Hill's drawings of the main motor room looking forward.

CHAPTER 4

Handling

There is no such thing as a 'safe' submarine. By the very nature of her environment she is constantly exposed to potentially dangerous situations, and her safe working requires the highest standards of training and co-ordination from her crew. While learning the task of controlling such a large and complex submarine as *X.1*, it was natural there would be moments of excitement or high drama, especially if they involved unexpectedly steep dives, but on the whole her crew found *X.1* to behave in an exemplary manner underwater. It is certain they would have taken her to war with complete confidence, if ever she had been called upon to fight.

The Lessons of Experience

In June 1921, the dramatic leap in size of *X.1* and the concommittal requirement for safe underwater handling, led to thoughts of a 1/48th scale model to be built and tested in the tank at Haslar on Hornsea Island, to investigate the best hull shape and performance.

Three months later, Mr M P Payne, the Superintendent of the Admiralty Experiment Works, determined that the test model should be built to 1/20th scale. This would allow them not only to check on hydrodynamic performance, but also to estimate the horsepower of the electric motors needed for submerged running. Rather than being towed as with surface ship models, the test model of *X.1* was to be self-propelled, using an electric motor, in order to be able to determine its free underwater characteristics.

The model tests were supervised by Commander J F Hutchings DSO, and the invaluable contribution they made to *X.1*'s performance underwater were to be given fulsome praise by Commander Raikes.

Commander Robert H T Raikes DSO and Bar

Her first commanding officer, Commander Raikes can justly be called the 'Godfather' of *X.1*. He nursemaided her through construction and commissioning, and she was his 'baby'. He also had crucial input into certain design features regarding her trim control gear and fittings. Whereas earlier craft had been referred to by the apellation of 'submarine boats' (and, in the US Navy, they are still called 'boats') it is noticeable in the reports of Commander Raikes, that he refers to her as 'the ship'.

The experimental self-propelled model of *X.1* used at Haslar, with the test team.

Commander R H T Raikes, *X.1*'s first Commanding Officer, and the 'godfather' of the ship. In just one month in 1916, Commander Raikes in *E.54* had tangled with three U-boats. One, the minelayer *UC 10*, went to the bottom off Schouwen. On 1 May 1917, Raikes and his crew accounted for the *U 81*, sunk to the West of Ireland, the German CO and six crewmen surviving. He ended his RN service as Vice Admiral, Flag Officer Submarines.

Experience with the notorious 'K' boats had shown the necessity for ballast tanks of the quick-blow high-pressure air type, and in fact the surviving 'K' class had all been retrofitted with enormous swan bows containing quick-blow tanks. So successful would the system be in *X.1*, that when in February 1926 plans were advanced for converting the second of the 'monitor' submarines, *M.2*, to an aircraft carrier, it was minuted that 'Experience with quick-flood and blow tanks on *K.26* and *X.1* shows they are of great value in controlling the vessel.' In August 1921 A W Johns reported that he planned to make use of 135 submarine high-pressure air bottles stored as spares for existing boats.

In October 1921 tenders were invited for three rotary blowers for blowing the ballast tanks, each rated at 1,700 cu ft of air per minute at a pressure of 11lbs above atmospheric at 750rpm, capable of up to 15lbs above atmospheric pressure. The successful bids were received from Messrs Reavells of Ranelagh Works, Ipswich, who were contracted to provide the rotary compressors.

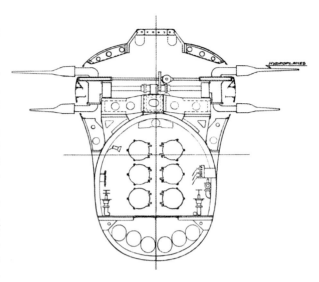

Forward hydroplanes, of the 'biplane' type, showing the substantial structure used to brace them to the pressure hull. Below the torpedo tubes are their compressed-air cylinders.

Hydroplanes

The official photograph of *X.1* shortly after launch shows her with just one set of forward hydroplanes, retracting backwards into the hull, in line with the stowed anchors. These single hydroplanes can also be seen in the photograph of *X.1* secured to a buoy at Sheerness at the time of her first gunnery trials (without tops to her gun turret shields).

It soon became evident that these small forward planes were completely ineffectual, and the main control effort was exerted by the stern planes alone. In

order to increase the 'bite' of the forward planes they were changed to the 'biplane' type which appear in all other photographs of *X.1*. These were installed above and below the old position of the forward planes, and also retracted backwards into the hull. They were the only twin forward hydroplanes ever fitted to a British submarine. Both the original and the new sets were positioned clear of the normal waterline, so as not to interfere with surface running, even when retracted.

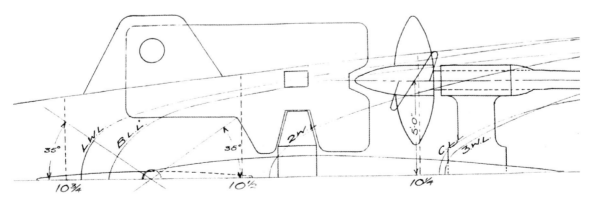

Rear hydroplanes in plan view. The fin shown upper left is the hydroplane guard, to protect them when coming alongside, as the planes projected beyond the hull sides.

The rear hydroplanes were extremely large even compared with the size of the ship. It is likely that very large hydroplanes were specified to ensure maximum controllability. In fact, the tank tests at Haslar on 4 January 1921 showed it would be possible to reduce the size of the aft hydroplanes, but it is unlikely this recommendation was acted upon. It is safer to assume that the final arrangement was the original design. Constructor Commander Stanton, following his cruise to Gibraltar and back in *X.1* in April 1926, reported on the 29th of that month that 'The rear hydroplanes were highly effective'. All three pairs of hydroplanes acted through 30 degrees of rise and 30 degrees of dive.

Diving

A W Johns was familiar with the depths reached by RN submarines during the Great War. When depth-charged in error by the US destroyers *Davis*, *Paudling* and *Trippe* in early 1918, the *L.2* had dived out of control and hit the sea bed at a depth of 300ft. Managing to blow the ballast tanks and surface, Lt-Commander Ackworth fired Very recognition signals which the Americans finally recognised, but not before one of them had put a 3in shell into *L.2*, fortunately without piercing the pressure hull. This sort of depth was way beyond the capabilities of the monster 'K' class boats and their offshoots, the clumsy 'M' class submarine 'monitors'.

X.1 was designed and built to prove if a large submersible could be successfully controlled underwater. But she was to be no dangerous 'K' boat or dip-chick *M.1*. She dived smartly, once underwater she handled like a dream, and she was the deepest diving submarine of her day, designed for a depth of 450ft, and a test depth of 500ft. It was this deep diving ability which marked *X.1* out as a 'submarine' rather than a huge 'submersible'. A W Johns was painfully aware of the dangers of diving a large submersible such as the 'K' class. With a length of 338ft, and a maximum diving depth of only some 200 to 250ft, in deep water a sharp down angle could take the bows, if not the whole boat, below crush depth before the crew could regain control. *X.1* was even longer, at 363ft, and to ensure she could dive with safety, A W Johns gave her the unprecedented maximum diving capability of 450ft (her crush depth was estimated at 500ft) – which of course brought problems of the watertight integrity of all fittings and openings, and the glands on the propeller shafts and periscopes – but especially the two revolving turret trunks.

As her natural operational environment would be surfaced, or running just below the surface hunting and ranging on her prey, this deep diving ability was built in purely as a safety margin. It would also, of course, help her evade A/S attacks from a flotilla of large destroyers which would be too numerous to engage in a surface action.

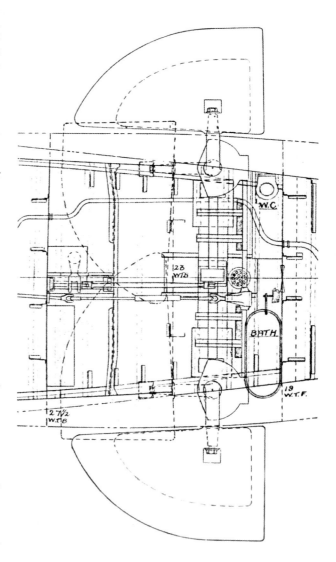

Plan view of the forward hydroplanes, showing their extended and retracted positions. Note that when retracted the upper set overlapped slightly. Also shown are the bathtub and WC ('heads') used when on the surface.

Trimming

Maintaining the trim of a submarine was a crucial element of control. To dive rapidly a bow-down angle was desired, and the opposite effect was needed when surfacing rapidly. At all other times underwater, it was preferable to keep the vessel on as even a keel as possible, and vary the depth by means of flooding and blowing the various ballast tanks built into much of the length of the hull. With an extremely large, and particularly an extremely long, submarine, co-ordination of the ballast tank filling and emptying was made much more difficult, to say nothing of the delays built in through the need to pass orders throughout the length of the ship.

X.1 was to be used in an experimental role to perfect the use of fore and aft quick-blowing and flooding tanks to aid trim. These were incorporated initially to help overcome the hydroplaning effect noticed in the hull of the 'K' class which exerted an upward lift at around a quarter of the length from the bow when the hull was inclined upward. The firm of Drysdales were required to design a blower pump capable of operating at a depth of 400ft, and this unit would need to be cross-connected to be able to pump any tank.

Following his experiences with *X.1*'s control arrangements, on 10 July 1924 Commander Raikes minuted the following recommended performance figures for quick-blow and quick-flood tanks, to be arranged near the planes in succeeding classes of submarine:

Floods 1 ton in 5½ seconds, blows 1 ton in 4 seconds (as in 'X.1')

There must be a blowing and flooding tank at each end of the submarine in order to:

- *have the ability to blow and flood at the same rate at all times;*
- *prevent wastage of stored air by continual blowing and venting;*
- *prevent, if an inboard vent is used, continually venting into the ship.*

One tank fitted with HP blow is merely an emergency or safety device, not a system for trimming or control.

Trim and control are talked of rather as being separate functions but are of course really the same thing up to a point.

Trim is either corrected by Thrust exerted by the Planes or Thrust exerted by Weight.

And Control is roughly the rate at which you can exert this Thrust in tons per second.

Control apart from Trim is affected only by excessive angles of Inclination and Swing in the Vertical Plane.

The effect of these is difficult to estimate but they have to be eventually dealt with by Thrust exerted by the Planes or by Weight.

Three months later he noted that a Martin tank depth indicator had been fitted on 1 October 1924. When switched on it continually recorded the water level in each tank. Commander Raikes hoped to also use this device to measure the quantity of oil in the self-compensating tanks, to replace the space occupied by the large gauge glasses 'of doubtful efficiency'.

In addition to the ballast pumps, there was a need to provide an additional pump to wash the anchor cable, since the cable locker would not be open to the sea at both ends as in previous submarine designs. More importantly, Commander Raikes requested arrangements to pump out a flooded magazine caused by diving with a shot hole in the hull or with a gun hatch unlatched. These arrangements had been planned for the original design but had been omitted during construction. His eagle eye had spotted the discrepancy and steps were put in hand to fit the necessary pump connections. For a submarine vessel which intended to shoot it out on the surface these were crucial arrangements, and *X.1* would be the only submarine with this backup safety feature.

During the basin trials on Thursday 10 April 1924 unspecified damage was caused to No 14 external tank which would take a fortnight to repair. No delay was expected in overall completion, Commander Raikes noted, as the engines, equipment and guns were not ready at that time.

Commander Raikes' report on the trimming and inclining trials which were carried out in the Basin at Chatham Dockyard on 21, 22 and 23 May 1924 showed the following:

- The vessel was inclined on the surface and also submerged. She showed a greater margin of stability than had been anticipated.
- As for trim, the ship proved to be light. It was not possible to get more than the main hull fully under and the water level more than about 3ft up the superstructure. However, this was seen as an error on the right side. He noted it was a very satisfactory result on the whole.
- 96 tons of ballast were calculated as being necessary. This ballast would go to the bottom of the ship and would compensate for weights still

to go on higher up. Eleven months earlier an Engineering report had recommended that, if extra ballast were ever required, then consideration should be given to fitting an additional nine compressed-air bottles, which were described as 'always an advantage'.

- The operation of the quick-blow and quick-flood tanks was most satisfactory and it was thought these would be of great use.
  Times for moving water in these tanks were:
  Blowing: 1 ton in 4 seconds average.
  Flooding: 1 ton in 5.5 seconds average.
  The quick-blow tanks held about 11 tons each; the quick-flood tanks held 15 tons in one and 19 tons in the other.
- The weights appeared to be distributed evenly throughout the ship, and the ship was quite easy to control for list when blowing and flooding, in fact there was very little tendency to list at all.
- It was thought that the time taken to get the main hull under, at 36 seconds, was very satisfactory indeed.

The after tanks flooded more slowly than planned, giving the ship an angle by the stern of two degrees, and steps were put in hand to rectify this. These measures in fact accentuated a bow-up angle instead, and led to re-ballasting.

Six months later he added a footnote on dynamic, as opposed to static, trim: 'Varying trim angles and depths for surface running will have an effect on the speeds and range attained. On trials at deep draught (18 inches deeper than planned) 18.5 knots was achieved.'

Commands for diving and trim were passed to the various hull stations by telephone. Lieutenant Rucke-Keen commented in 1928 that, despite a specially-trained communications party, the telephone was much slower than the loudspeaker for diving.

Diving Trials

These took place on Wednesday 14 January 1925 in the vicinity of the Tongue Light Vessel. *X.1* was shepherded by the destroyer HMS *Shamrock*.

Results were satisfactory except that the stern planes seemed to exert much more control than the bow planes. It was recommended that the bow planes be redesigned for more control. Going from power to hand operation on the planes was satisfactory. The trials were curtailed when a control cable on the port side plane balance weight parted, and Portsmouth Dockyard effected repairs.

On 27 January 1925 *X.1* dived south of the Isle of Wight, again accompanied by *Shamrock*. The ship took an angle down by the bow during the first minute (about 40 to 50 seconds after flooding the main ballast tanks). After diving for about an hour the aft planes jammed at 7 degrees of rise. The ship was proceeding at 2 knots submerged. The fore planes were quite incapable of counteracting the effect of this. Dismantling in harbour found no visible fault. After reassembly the gear worked easier than before and it was thought something found its way into the screw gear but afterwards worked clear.

The maximum depth reached was 125 feet. There were some slight leaks:

- Port side of Rangefinder Compartment;
- Stern Glands;
- Engine Room hatch;
- Aft gun trunk;
- Starboard Auxiliary Engine Circulating System;
- Forrard gun trunk;
- Both Muffler Valves (Aft Main).

The quick-blow and quick-flood tanks worked very satisfactorily. Practically no other tanks were used to obtain correct trim. Commander Raikes confirmed that the trials of the model had been most valuable in estimating what the ship was likely to do under various conditions. Control at very slow speeds was remarkably good. Battens were fitted to observe the movements of the gun trunks. The aft trunk showed no movement. The forward trunk moved $1/64$in into the ship and out again! On 13 March 1925 Commander Raikes made proposals to counter what he took to be an unsatisfactory angle down by the bows, which would cause problems if diving quickly.

Submerged turning trials were undertaken when *X.1* was *en route* to Gibraltar on 17 April 1926. The best times for turning were obtained with full speed on the outside propeller, slow speed on the inside propeller, 25 degrees of helm, series parallel grouping. The actual recorded results were: 90 degrees in 5 minutes 7 seconds; 180 degrees in 9 minutes 4 seconds. During the same trials, when she was officially taken down to a maximum of 190ft, changing depth on an even keel from 35ft down to 70ft without altering trim, took 1 minute 23 seconds.

'Ain't Misbehavin'

Lieutenant Gilbert Roberts took part in *X.1*'s fourth set of gunnery trials. In a letter written fifty years later he described an alarming incident during a mock attack on a target vessel posing as an enemy 'carrier'. *X.1* fired all six bow torpedoes while submerged. She then surfaced on a circular course, opening A-arcs before diving at speed on the turn. It turned out to be a difficult dive, with a steep down angle by the bow. Lieutenant Roberts suggested this was possibly due to the rear ballast tank being positioned higher than the forward one, meaning it flooded later. The manoeuvre led to concerns over acid spillage from the battery cells, and *X.1* surfaced heeled over at an angle.

Obviously her size and length required precise control during such a violent manoeuvre . . . No doubt the torpedo and gunnery departments had gained experience quicker than the diving team! What was notable was that, however she misbehaved on occasions, she always remained under control and was able to surface and dive freely, at will.

Diving Time

X.1's average diving time was officially recorded as '2 minutes 20 seconds'. The Ship's Cover preserved at Woolwich shows:

Main hull under in 36 seconds
Periscope depth in 2 mins 27 secs

It must be borne in mind that these were the figures for a normal dive under controlled conditions. If leaked, they could serve to dissuade potential enemies, and especially Japan, from copying such unwieldy large submarines. Crew members knew from experience that *X.1* could 'crash dive' in an emergency – going full ahead on engines and motors and flooding her quick-flood bow tank – in less than a minute.

Surface Handiness

During her preliminary engine trials off the Maplin Sands between 17 and 20 December 1923, without gun mounts fitted but with no ammunition on board either, it was noted that *X.1* rolled 4 to 8 degrees each way with a period of about 7 to 8 seconds in a slight swell. An accompanying destroyer (not named) rolled slightly less but with a shorter period. This made her a very stable gun platform and simplified the work of the director control party.

No surviving record notes her surface turning circles. That she turned and handled in an exemplary manner can be deduced from the total lack of critical reports to the contrary. However, at first her enormous length did cause a couple of minor mishaps. On 20 December 1923 she fouled the mooring of a flying boat off Sheerness, and a month later she collided with the barge *Suez*, again off Sheerness. It was clear that her helmsmen then became used to the size and handiness of their charge. She certainly managed to avoid collision with an onrushing German merchant vessel, the *Stettin*, in the early morning of 29 July 1927, when outbound from Salonika *en route* to Skiathos.

The only other navigational error occurred when she was under tow at Malta in August 1929, when the inexperience of the dockyard hands allowed her to go aground off Conspicua Slips.

Engines full ahead to full astern took 30 seconds. Full astern to full ahead in 25 seconds.

Due to her great length, when alongside *X.1* was normally assisted by tugs. When manoeuvring inside a harbour she would use her main motors, for ease of going astern, as well as the additional reliability of her electric drive, which never failed her. When leaving harbour she would then clutch in her main engines. All too often she would limp back home on her main motors . .

CHAPTER 5

Armament

The length, tonnage and price of a light cruiser, *X.1* was given an impressive cruiser-type armament, with the specific aim of destroying convoy escort vessels. This was her *raison d'être*, the justification for all the cost and effort put into building and operating the ship. She was designed to surface at high speed, with gun trainers and layers already at their pointers down below, and blow any unsuspecting opposition out of the water. Her 1in-thick upper hull would resist anything enemy destroyers could throw at her. And anything too big to gun, she would simply torpedo . . .

5.2in Turrets

She carried two twin 5.2in guns in fully-powered cruiser-type turrets. These were fed by power hoists, which ran down into the magazines through 4ft 6in wide revolving trunks which actually pierced the pressure hull. One can imagine the care which had to be taken to ensure these remained watertight at a depth of 450ft. Vickers built a special gun pit to assemble and test *X.1*'s turrets and their trunks. Their quote dated 19 July 1922 for the two gun mountings, including pit trials, plus DCT firing gear, came to £54,094. Each mounting on its own would cost £16,580. The quote diplomatically stated that 'Repeat orders would lower the price'.

The official turret handbook stated almost apologetically that 'the design of the mounting had been handicapped by the severe limitations which were imposed regarding weight and space, which restrictions arose from the problem of mounting a turret in a submarine. These limitations must be borne in mind when considering the total output of the turret'.[1] The range achieved by the mounting was adequate for its intended use, as was the rate of fire of twelve rounds per turret per minute,[2] dictated in part by the use of semi-fixed (i.e. two-piece) ammunition. Of course, the narrowness of the watertight gland through the pressure hull restricted the type and number of ammunition hoists. In place of the separate endless chain hoists for shell and cartridge case used in the twin and triple 6in cruiser turrets, in *X.1* only one hoist per gun handled both cartridge case and shell, and the hoists themselves were of the 'pusher' type. Compared with the experimental twin 6in turret installed in 'A' position in the light cruiser HMS *Enterprise*, the *X.1* mountings were smaller and thereby more cramped, but not more so than the later twin 5.25in dual-purpose (DP) turret. There was, of course, no provision for a store of ready-use ammunition on the mounting, since this was not intended to be watertight.

A key element in rate of fire was the power available to operate the hoists and mountings. In this respect the twin gun turrets on *X.1* had to compete with many other systems which would be operated at the same time as the guns were being brought into action, for example the periscopes, rangefinder, DCT roof rams, ballast tank vents, blower pumps, hydroplane and rudder controls, etc. The limited on-board power generation was to be rectified in the succeeding *X.2*.

What was missing of course was any form of armour or splinter protection, the gun housing being merely a wind and spray shield. This was a deliberate choice dictated by the need to limit topweight. It seems to have succeeded, as *X.1* was not plagued by a tendency to roll to extreme angles (with the risk of spilling battery acid) in the same way as did the later *Surcouf* with her enormous twin 8in turret. Also, the revolving structure which penetrated into the pressure hull and the loading facilities in the 'handling room' helped balance out the weight of the guns at the top of the turret structure. In comparison, *Surcouf*'s turret structure was completely top-heavy, the trunk actually narrowing towards its base.

There was no attempt to give the Mark I mounting any form of anti-aircraft capability, which would have required a second high-angle (HA) director and much higher gun pivots. It is probable a conscious decision was taken that *X.1* would be expected to submerge out of harm's way in the event of the approach of a hostile aircraft, rather than attempting to shoot it out on the surface.[3] Given the poor performance of RN heavy AA gunfire prior to the introduction of the proximity shell, it is likely this was the correct approach. Even the heavily-armed 'Aircraft Trap' U-boats sent to sea by Dönitz in 1943 had to admit defeat in the face of determined aircraft attack.

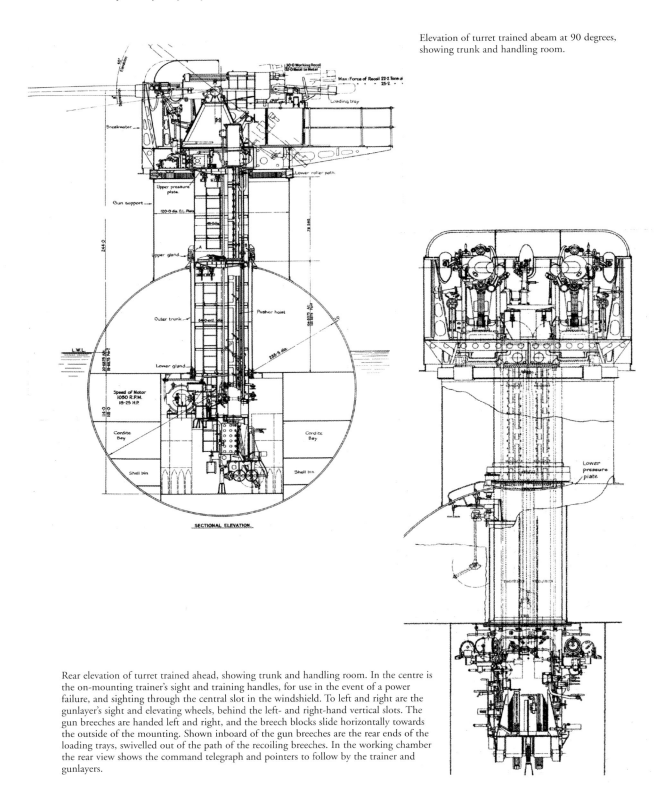

Elevation of turret trained abeam at 90 degrees, showing trunk and handling room.

Rear elevation of turret trained ahead, showing trunk and handling room. In the centre is the on-mounting trainer's sight and training handles, for use in the event of a power failure, and sighting through the central slot in the windshield. To left and right are the gunlayer's sight and elevating wheels, behind the left- and right-hand vertical slots. The gun breeches are handed left and right, and the breech blocks slide horizontally towards the outside of the mounting. Shown inboard of the gun breeches are the rear ends of the loading trays, swivelled out of the path of the recoiling breeches. In the working chamber the rear view shows the command telegraph and pointers to follow by the trainer and gunlayers.

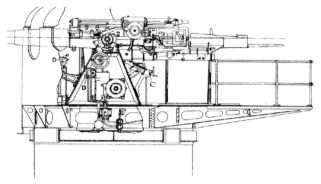

Side elevation of the left-hand gun.

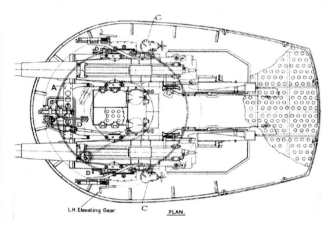

L.H. Elevating Gear.   PLAN.

Plan of the turret platform.

The turret was of the 'long trunk' type, where the gun platform formed a turntable, from which was hung a trunk 48in in diameter and carrying the ammunition hoists, electrical cables, voice pipes and rod gearing, together with the means of access from the interior of the submarine. This inner trunk revolved with the mounting. Total revolving weight of the unarmoured twin mounting, complete with trunk and guns, was 27 tons 3 cwt. The weight of the mounting was taken on a roller path, below which level the mounting was watertight. The upper pressure plate was part of the revolving structure and comprised watertight fittings through which passed the ammunition hoists, electric cables, voicepipes, rod gearing and the gun crew access manhole. The roller path was supported by vertical plating riveted to the outer hull, which formed the gun support. Below the gun mounting this vertical plating of the

superstructure was 120in wide. The outer trunk plating provided extra protection in the event of damage to the upper part of the hull or superstructure. On 18 April 1921, R Backhouse, the Director of Naval Ordnance, had specified that the trunk should be made of 15lb steel plating. Where the trunk pierced the pressure hull proper there was a second pressure plate, similar to the upper one. These two pressure plates provided the means of making the lower portion of the trunk watertight. The hole in the pressure hull was kept watertight by the upper or main gland containing a rubberised fabric packing compressed by mechanical means. A little below the level of the load waterline there was a deck pierced by the lower end of the trunk. That hole was kept watertight by a lower, secondary gland, which was regarded as an emergency measure.

Below this deck was a compartment 9ft square and about the same height, which formed the working chamber. Outside and below this working chamber were situated the cordite bays and the shell bins. The mounting's power unit was attached to the part of the trunk which protruded into the upper part of the working chamber. This was an electrically-driven hydraulic pump, and there was one for each turret. Hydraulic pressure peaked at 850 to 900 psi, but when the turret was training to port or starboard this pressure could fall to only 300 psi. In the event of loss of the hydraulic oil the system could be filled with fresh water or, in an emergency, with sea water. Also in the working chamber and attached to the revolving part of the trunk were the seats for the gunlayers and trainer, together with the director receivers. These, with their pointers which the gunlayers and trainer had to match with their own pointers, formed the primary method of gun control and firing.

The working chamber acted as the magazine handling room and was subject to all appropriate safety precautions to prevent flash and other forms of ignition. The ammunition supply passed up the trunk via two pusher hoists, one for each gun. Each hoist delivered both cordite cartridge case and shell to its own gun. The hoists were fitted with quick-closing watertight doors on the turret platform and sluice doors at the bottom as a security precaution. The original Vickers drawings show the streamlined form of the turret shield which was finalised only after underwater trials in the Haslar tank. The mounting is open overhead and at the rear, but in service the side plating was extended further back than shown in these construction drawings, and the side railings

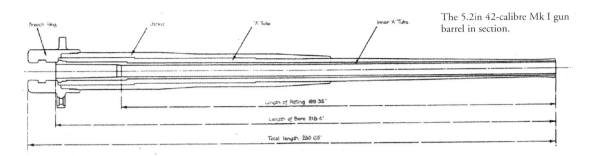

The 5.2in 42-calibre Mk I gun barrel in section.

were cut back to suit. In the handbook the shield is described as a 'breakwater and hood'. The circular watertight covers at the top of the two ammunition hoists can be seen between the guns. The watertight covers are hinged at the front and closed by a quick-release clamp at the rear. Behind each hoist can be seen the figure-of-eight foot pedal which activates the hoist mechanism. In front of the hoists are the flaps at the head of the ladder inside the trunk, through which the gun crews gain access to the turret. The shells and cartridge cases are shown in position on the loading trays which have been swung inwards to clear the recoiling breech blocks when the guns fire. Below

the loading trays are the gun wells cut in the platform floor to allow the guns their full 40 degrees elevation. The plan view shows how compact the turrets were. To achieve a high rate of fire required precise co-ordination between the loading numbers, which in turn demanded constant training and practice shoots.

The 5.2in 42-calibre QF Mark I LA (low-angle), a joint new design effort by the Royal Ordnance Factory at Woolwich & Vickers, was specially produced for *X.1*. It had a QF (quick-firing) SA (semi-automatic) breech mechanism closed by a horizontal sliding wedge, which was closed manually but opened automatically when the recoiling barrel

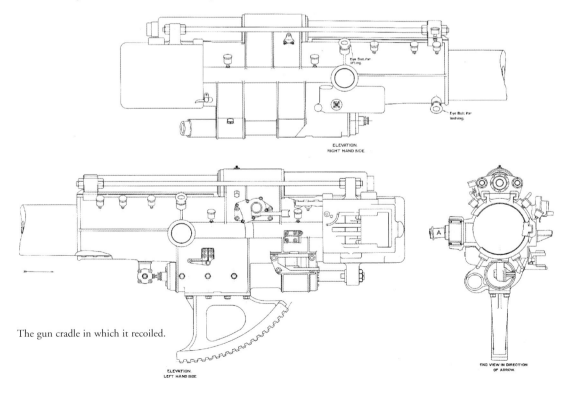

The gun cradle in which it recoiled.

tripped an actuating pawl. Weight of the gun barrel complete was 3.425 tons. The overall length was 230.65in, the bore length was 218.4in, and the rifling

breech was copied from best German U-boat practice . . . However, after some use the breech block type used on *X.1* tended to score its upper and lower

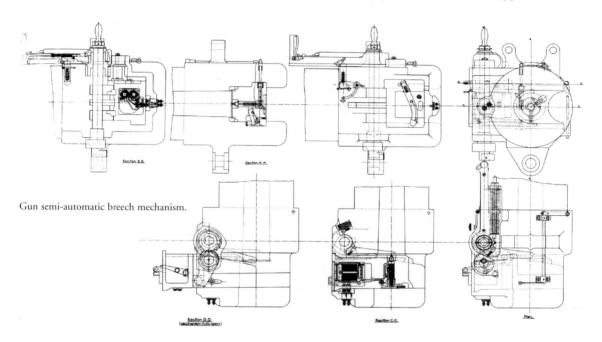

Gun semi-automatic breech mechanism.

extended for 189.35in. The chamber volume was 630 cubic inches. Only six 5.2in guns were ever built. They survived *X.1* by several years, but disappeared from history in late 1940 or soon thereafter.

The gun was an unusual choice. Close in calibre to the later 5.25in DP gun, the two breech mechanisms were similar, and both guns fired semi-fixed ammunition. When the design parameters for *X.1* were being finalised in March 1921, her role of 'fleet' or 'cruiser' submarine had not been decided. Consideration was given to arming her turrets with either twin 6in or twin 4in guns, but 4.5in – which was itself a new calibre for the Royal Navy – was also considered. For gun surface action the turrets would need to pack a punch sufficient to disable a destroyer, and they would need to be QF. It must be assumed that the existing 6in, 5.5in and 4.7in guns were rejected in favour of a brand-new design simply because they were all of the breech-loading (BL) variety, where the breech seal is effected by a De Bange obturator pad. Using these would have required a hinged tompion to seal the muzzle end, and of course the breech seal would deteriorate underwater. Also, it has to be said, the sliding wedge

sliding faces, presumably due to lubricant being washed away by immersion in sea water, and proposals for *X.2* included incorporating rollers in the breech block to avoid this problem.

Each gun was independently capable of being elevated to a maximum of 40 degrees (where the ship's structure permitted) and could in theory depress to a maximum of 8 degrees.[4] Operation was full power in both elevation and training. The rate of training was 8 degrees per second; power elevation in high was 4 to 5 degrees per second. The recoil gear mounted below the barrel was oil-filled, all but for a small air space which would expand and contract as necessary. The volume of this air space was around 6 per cent of the total internal volume of the recoil cylinder. The air space was to prevent a partial vacuum forming which tended to prevent the gun from running out again after firing – as had been experienced during the Great War. The recoil cylinder held ten quarts (or 2½ gallons) of glycerine and water. Recoil was measured between 26in and 29.9in according to the control valve settings. The air recuperator mounted above the barrel held the gun in the firing position at any elevation, and returned it to battery after firing. It

The loading tray of a right-hand gun.

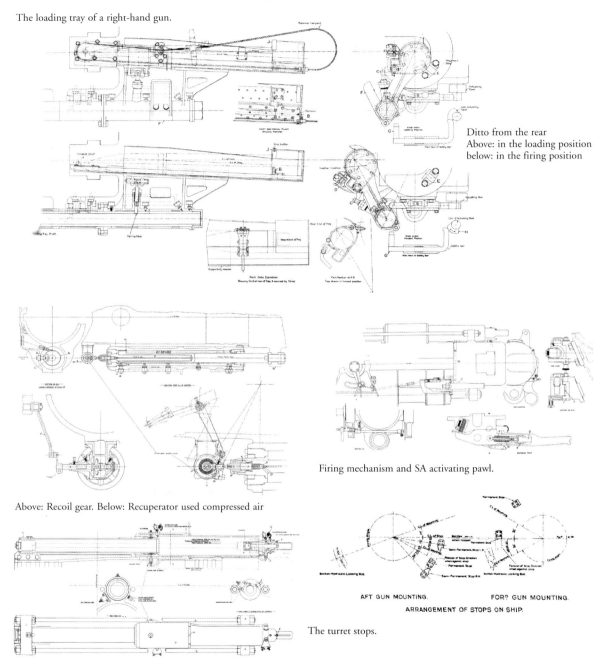

Ditto from the rear
Above: in the loading position
below: in the firing position

Above: Recoil gear. Below: Recuperator used compressed air

Firing mechanism and SA activating pawl.

The turret stops.

used compressed air from the submarine's systems at 500 psi pressure. Firing was normally by remote electrical control from the DCT, operating a solenoid to release the firing pin to strike the percussion cap in the base of the cartridge. In an emergency the gun could be fired using a manual trigger.

To load, the tray would be swivelled into alignment with its gun barrel. The cartridge case containing the cordite charge would be placed in the tray up against the rear rubber buffer and the shell would be placed in front of the cartridge case. The rammer was activated by means of a wire lanyard,

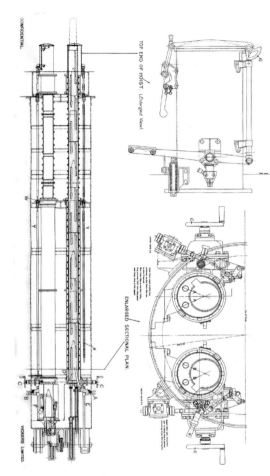

Pushing the shell . . .

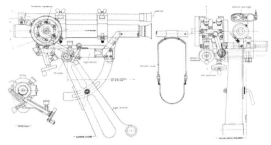

On-mounting gunsights.
Above: Training. Below: Laying.

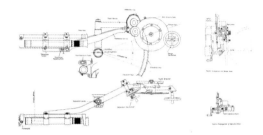

Left: gun hoists, of the pushover type
Below: Hoist loading gear.

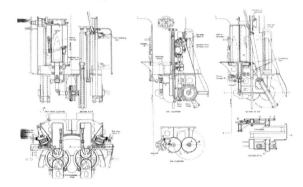

pushing the shell and cartridge case forward into the breech. When the breech block was closed by means of a lever, the loading tray was swivelled sideways to clear the recoiling breech. An interlock prevented the gun from firing until the loading tray was safely out of the way. Before the turret could be trained its hydraulic locking bolt had to be withdrawn. After firing the turret would be returned to the fore-and-aft position and the locking bolt replaced.

Each turret could train through a maximum of 150 degrees Green and 150 degrees Red, and safety stops were installed to avoid the guns firing into the ship's superstructure. Despite these, the officers of HMS *Excellent* reported on 18 February 1926 that marks on the ship's superstructure abaft the fore turret showed some part was touching the ship's structure while training. During peacetime exercises and in normal use the training arcs were further restricted by temporary stops, but in case of necessity these could be disengaged by means of a foot pedal and the full training scope restored, accepting the risk of blast damage to the superstructure. Obviously the aft turret could not fire straight ahead, but it would also not train from one side to the other facing forward, so to engage a target on the opposite beam it had first to train around past the stern.

In the event of a power failure or a hit to the DCT, each turret could fire in local control and be aimed from the mounting platform. The necessary sighting telescopes were contained in cases fixed inside the gun trunk. As the turret crews made their way up the access ladders, the gunlayers and trainer would take the gunsights from their cases and install them in the turret where they simply clipped into place using steel spring clips. The spring steel clips were prone to corrosion due to the action of seawater, and tended to lose their spring tension, so for *X.2* it was proposed to redesign these fittings using butterfly screws. Above each telescopic sight was mounted a fixed aperture or peep-hole sight, for use in the event of damage to or degradation of the telescope. HMS *Excellent*'s officers noted that hand training was feasible, but slow; also, that the guns were muzzle-heavy even with the gun or tray loaded, so the manual elevation effort required was high.

Commands were relayed from each lower control position to the turret loading crew on the mounting itself by means of a mechanical telegraph. Similar to the units used to relay orders between bridge and engine room, there was a dial at the top and bottom of each turret, the cover bearing the engraved commands Cease Firing, Close Down for Diving and Individual. The dial of each unit was engraved Lay for Loading, Ready, Individual Laying, Hand Loading and Shift Circuit. This mechanical telegraph system would come into its own in the event the turrets were firing in local control, and being manually operated it was immune to electrical power failure.

Each gun turret trunk carried two pusher hoists – one for each gun – consisting of a series of concentric tubes of sufficient diameter to allow a shell or cartridge case to pass vertically through them. In the handling room, each gun hoist ended at a revolving scuttle with two cylindrical compartments on opposite sides. Each compartment could accommodate either a cartridge case or a shell on its base. When loaded, a compartment would be rotated into line with the ascending pawls of the hoist, while the opposite empty compartment would then be open to the handling room. For ease of understanding the Turret Instruction Manual described the hoist as containing two sets of pawls, designated the 'red' series and the 'blue' series. Each series of pawls was carried on a vertical pawl rod, which reciprocated up and down at the rear end of the hoist tube. The pawls were pivoted on this rod, and were free to swivel between the 'housed' or vertical position and the 'engaged' position where they protruded out into the body of the hoist at an angle of around 40 degrees to the horizontal. Instead of being exact mirror images, the 'red' series of pawls was fixed higher up on the 'red' rod compared to the 'blue' series opposite. Both pawl rods were

connected at their bottom end to a driving crankshaft, arranged so that while the 'blue' series of pawls was descending, the 'red' series would be ascending, and vice versa. Stops on the fixed structure engaged under the tails of the 'blue' pawls at the end of the downward stroke, and fastened them into the 'engaged' position. The lowermost 'engaged' pawl would latch underneath the base of the next shell or cartridge case presented in position by the revolving scuttle, and on its upward stroke would lift the ammunition vertically. As the 'red' pawls descended, they were free to pivot upwards into the 'housed' position on meeting the ascending ammunition, before falling into the 'engaged' position at the end of the downward stroke. When the ascending 'blue' pawl rod reached the limit of its upward motion, the neighbouring 'red' pawl rod would in its turn be ready to ascend, with its pawls in the 'engaged' position. On encountering the ammunition held on the 'blue' pawl the 'red' pawl would pick it up and carry it vertically one step further. And so on, in a form of vertical rachet, until the ammunition reached the top of the hoist.

If the top watertight cover was shut, an interlock prevented the hoist from moving, as was the case if the bottom sluice door was closed. Also, if the loading number on the mounting lifted his foot off the operating pedal, the hoist would automatically stop. If motion of the ship caused ammunition to jam in the way of the sluice door, thus preventing the door from closing in the event surface action was to be broken off, the two lower pawls of each series could be manually disconnected from their respective rod to allow the offending case or shell to be removed. Obviously, in view of the loading tray arrangement, the cartridge case would be the first to be loaded into the hoist scuttle, followed by the shell, so they would arrive at the mounting in the correct order. The hoists were worked by the mounting's hydraulic pump, but if this failed the system could be worked by hand. In the event the hoists themselves became damaged, the turret crew could quickly rig up a secondary ammunition supply, using a double endless whip in the ladder way in the trunk, carrying two buckets – when one bucket was up, the other was in the lower position. As a last resort the ammunition could be sent up using a single hemp whip and ammunition bags.

On conclusion of *X.1*'s gunnery trials, on 18 February 1926 the officers of HMS *Excellent* reported that the time taken to supply six complete rounds to each gun varied from 58 to 61 seconds. They also noted that the lip of each cartridge was catching in a join of the hoist tube on the right-hand pusher hoist on the aft turret, and this was duly refitted.

Gunnery control

Normally both gun turrets were laid and fired from the DCT. This had a watertight roof which would be raised 2ft to create a vision slot. Through this slot the Gunnery Officer, the Leading Director Layer and Two Gun Layers Second Class would control and fire the guns electronically, and correct over and under shots to achieve the desired straddle of the target vessel. A W Johns had determined as early as April 1922 that all instruments and other gear were to be non-magnetic as the DCT would be within the radius of the compass. At first the hydraulic rams which raised and lowered the DCT roof were prone to leak, and this contributed to the ease with which aircraft could detect *X.1* submerged in the clear waters of the Mediterranean. Following *X.1*'s gunnery trials, HMS *Excellent*'s experts recommended on 18 February 1926 that the DCT should have a training repeater graduated around its brass cover, to comply with Admiralty Fleet Order 2486/25.

Ranges were provided by the only horizontal 9ft base periscopic rangefinder ever fitted to a submarine. The German U-Cruisers of the *U 139* class had a horizontal rangefinder mounted on the rear of the conning tower, which could be elevated by compressed air to give increased ranges for their 15cm guns. However, this arrangement could only be used once the U-Cruiser had surfaced. In *X.1*, the rangefinder was fitted atop a special periscope, which meant that ranges could be taken underwater, and the turret target indicator dials laid on their target ready to fire. Meanwhile, the whole spotting and

rangetaking crew sat comfortable and dry at their seats. Obviously, because the turret trunk glands were kept tightly sealed while *X.1* was underwater, the turrets themselves could not be trained underwater. But once the glands were freed off on surfacing, while the gun crews scrambled up the ladders into the turrets to commence loading, it was a matter of a few seconds for the gun aimers sitting at the base of the trunks to align their pointers and train and elevate the guns ready to open fire.

The specifications for this 'Submarine Periscope Rangefinder' were provided by Barr & Stroud on 11 July 1921. This special rangefinder was of the co-incidence type. Arguments have long raged about the effectiveness of this type of unit compared with the stereoscopic type of rangefinder built by Zeiss for the German navies. Barr & Stroud themselves conducted detailed surveys into the comparative merits of both types, and were proud to announce the clear superiority of their co-incidence rangefinder over the German model. Even the Germans admitted that it took a special kind of operative to produce consistent results from the stereoscopic type. The main difference was that the co-incidence unit relied on a simple visual alignment to obtain the range. The stereoscopic type required a degree of subjective analysis to determine the range. Although this might be obtained before an engagement began, the Germans found to their cost that the operatives' effectiveness declined dramatically when their own ships came under fire. A normal submarine rangefinder was arranged with two prisms in the top of the vertical periscope tube with a very short base length. It is likely that the internal arrangement of *X.1*'s horizontal 9ft rangefinder was copied from the

A close-up view of the conning tower area showing the curved roof of the DCT, which is closed (note that the rangefinder is missing, which may date this view to June 1927 at Malta).

Enlargement of the photograph of the mock gun attack on *Cyclops*, showing the DCT roof raised high above the tower on its three hydraulic rams.

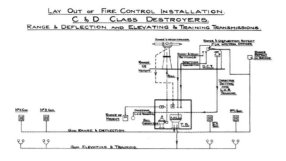

Diagram showing a typical DCT gunnery control system of the period (this example is for a 'C' or 'D' class destroyer).

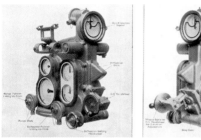

Examples of the layer's and trainer's sights fitted in a DCT of the period (these would control the fire of 6in guns).

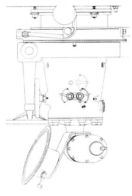

Detail from the Barr & Stroud blueprint of the lower end of the Type F.U.2 periscopic rangefinder, showing the binocular eyepieces. Research has so far failed to find any trace of the Barr & Stroud drawing for the special rangefinder head. Perhaps it may be found only by accident, since a major customer of Barr & Stroud was the Imperial Japanese Navy, whose representative had an office in the factory. At around the time *X.1*'s rangefinder was being produced, the factory was actually visited by several Japanese dignitaries, including the future Admiral Yamamoto! Doubtless the rangefinder drawing would have been labelled as some innocuous piece of equipment to avert prying eyes. The standard 9ft base FQ2 Rangefinder had a magnifying power of 28 diameters, and was accurate to within 0.5 per cent at 6,000 yards. The times taken to raise and lower the rangefinder were 27 seconds UP, and 7 seconds DOWN.

Enlargement of the photograph of *X.1* diving in Grand Harbour, showing the rangefinder in position.

The rangefinder periscope is raised high above the conning tower, possibly in salute on leaving harbour.

An Admiralty Fire Control Clock for two turrets, still *in situ* in the transmitting station of HMS *Belfast*.

standard Great War Barr & Stroud model FQ2, found on dreadnought battleships, modified of course to remain watertight at a depth of 450ft. Used with care it could appear to a distant observer as a piece of driftwood or an empty liferaft.

Data from the rangefinder, the active Asdic, the hydrophone gear, and manual observation was fed to the transmitting station, where the Admiralty Fire Control Clock[5] would provide the necessary firing solutions. In their report, HMS *Excellent*'s officers noted that the fire control Dumaresq needed to be

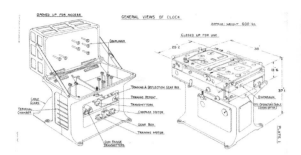

A contemporary drawing of an Admiralty Fire Control Clock showing how the unit opened up for maintenance.

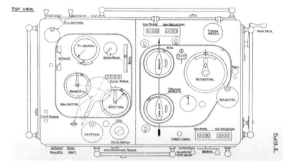

A drawing from the maintenance manual detailing the instruments and dials in the top of the Fire Control Clock.

HMS *Belfast*'s main Admiralty Fire Control Table with the top opened to show the pointer dials for the relative positions of 'Own Ship' and 'Enemy Ship'.

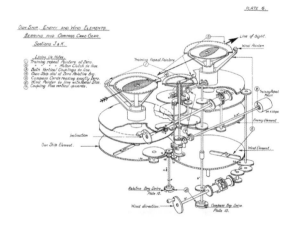

A maintenance manual drawing showing a segment of the internal gearing of a Fire Control Clock.

modified according to Admiralty Fleet Order 235/25, to enable deflections to be calculated. The Fire Control Clock itself was an extremely complicated mechanical computer. Built no doubt following the inspiration of the Victorian Polymath Charles Babbage, it obviously depended on the quality of the information which was fed into it, but when this was accurate, the machine worked extremely well. Numerous successful gun engagements by the Royal Navy stand in testament to this.[6]

The gunlayers and trainer sat on seats mounted on the revolving trunk hung from the turret turntable and turned with it. Their task was to ensure the mounting and the individual guns followed the evolutions prescribed by the gunnery officer in the DCT. To enable them to do this out of sight of the target they were merely obliged to turn their control wheels so that the pointers on two sets of dials were always matched. As the range and bearing to the proposed target vessel could be ascertained with a high degree of accuracy before surfacing, the guns were laid, ready to fire, while still under water. The only gunners who risked getting wet were the turret

The 'Fire Gong' button (with the words engraved upside down).

45

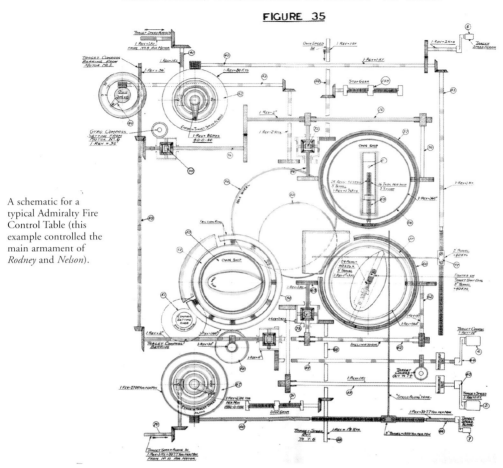

A schematic for a typical Admiralty Fire Control Table (this example controlled the main armament of *Rodney* and *Nelson*).

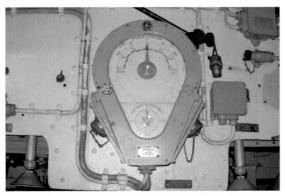

The straddle corrector dial still in place in HMS *Belfast*'s transmitting station.

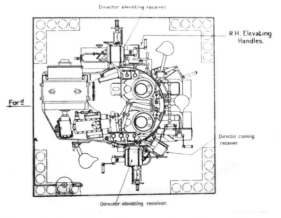

The seats for the trainer and the two gunlayers for one of the turrets.

platform crews who scrambled up the ladders into the twin mountings, took the charges and shells from the top of the hoists and placed them in the gun loading trays.

Watertight integrity

The 'K' class had been criticised for having 'too many damned holes'. *X.1* would not suffer from retracting funnels and boiler room intake vents, but she did have two much larger, and potentially worrying, openings in her pressure hull, in which revolved the trunks for her twin turrets. These were a critical element in the design, crucial to the success of *X.1*'s gun armament.

The top of the outer fixed trunk ended in a deck ring, riveted on top of the pressure hull plating. This deck ring was extended upwards in a combing, which was threaded on the outside. A large nut was screwed up and down this deck ring by a gear wheel set bearing on external teeth cut in the outer rim of the nut. The moving internal part of the gun trunk carried a horizontal flange. Between the top of the nut and the lower face of the flange was sandwiched a rubberised fabric sealing gland. Screwing the nut up the combing compressed the rubber gland and made the joint watertight. To prevent tearing of the rubber, a floating steel washer was interposed between the rubber and the flange. It was obviously critical to correctly fit and align the rubber and fabric sealing ring, and ensure its proper lubrication to preserve the

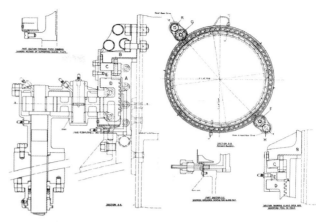

Upper gun trunk gland.

scarph joint which completed the ring. During deep diving trials *en route* to Gibraltar in April 1926, it was noted that the foremost gun trunk gland was found to be leaking worse on every occasion of diving. For comparison purposes the front gland originally had a rubber ring, compared to the aft one which had a

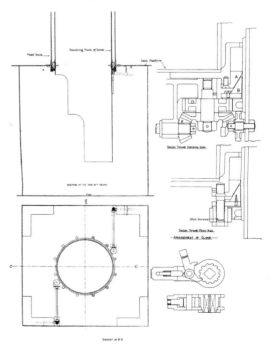

Lower gun trunk gland. This was a much simpler affair, comprising a conical section rubber ring which was forced upwards to seal. It was always intended only as an emergency backup to the main upper gland.

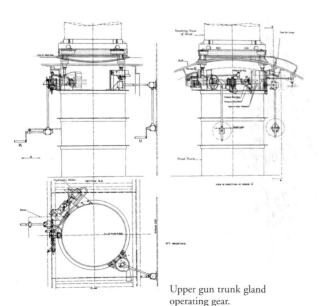

Upper gun trunk gland operating gear.

dexine ring. The aft gland gave no trouble. A dexine ring was fitted to the front gland when *X.1* returned to Chatham in May 1926.

In the event of a power failure both the upper and the emergency lower gun trunk glands could be closed and opened by hand gearing. The waterproof fittings comprised the upper and lower glands sealing the revolving trunk, the waterproof access hatch between the guns and the quick-release watertight caps fitted at the heads of the ammunition trunks. In case water found its way inside the trunk, the ammunition loading scuttle at the bottom end was fitted with a sluice door which sealed onto a rubber strip at the bottom edge of the opening. In case this sluice gate was obstructed on closing down for diving, for example by a cartridge case or shell becoming displaced and thereby preventing the sluice gate from closing, the two lower pawls of each carrier rod were clutched to the rod in such a way that they could be easily detached to allow the jammed ammunition to be freed.

The 5.2in round

X.1's main armament fired 'semi-fixed' ammunition. This meant that the shell and cartridge case containing the propellant were separate units, which only came together when placed on the loading tray. In theory this allowed for the cartridge case loading of cordite to be varied for different applications. But in practice it simply meant that the individual components were lighter and more easily carried and loaded, which was an important consideration within *X.1*'s cramped turrets and handling rooms.

The 5.2in shell was designated by the MOD Reference 2248, which covered both SAP (Semi-Armour Piercing) and Practice rounds. The shell was designed to be 21.5in long (but a later report gave its length as 23in), with a single driving band and a base fuse, and weighed 70lbs.

The separate cartridge case design was to RL Reference 30073. The breech was sealed or 'obturated' on firing by means of the brass case itself which expanded to fill the chamber. There was therefore no need for an obturator pad or sealing ring as used on the 'BL' type of gun with its separate silk bag containing a cordite charge. The brass cartridge

case contained either 10.78lbs of MC 16 propellant or else 11.36lbs of SC 109, and with the latter charge the complete case weighed 17.34lbs. Full-length clips held on a lid covering the open mouth of the case.

Its dimensions were:

Maximum overall length of case with lid	26.215in
Maximum overall length of case with lid and clips	27in
Overall diameter at base without clip	6.51in
Overall diameter at base with clip	7.00in
Diameter at mouth of case with lid in position	5.49in

The normal charge produced a muzzle velocity of 2,300 feet per second, sufficient to propel the 70lb shell to a maximum range of 17,288 yards at 40 degrees elevation.

The planned shell capacity was to be 100 rounds per gun, comprising:

240 SAP
60 SAP NT (Night Tracer)
80 HE BDF (Base Detonator Fuse)
20 HE BDF NT.

The SAP shell contained a bursting charge. Shells designated 'NT' carried a tracer compound for use in night firing. In practice *X.1* carried a total of 102 rounds for each of her four 5.2in guns, and adjacent to the magazines she had a complex system of compensating tanks, into which seawater was admitted to balance the weight of rounds fired. In this way her trim for diving and underwater manoeuvring was preserved.

The 5.2in gun may be considered as the inspiration for the much more powerful 5.25in DP HA/LA gun which served during the Second World War. In order to throw an anti-aircraft HE shell to an altitude of 49,000ft, the 5.25in had a longer barrel a larger chamber volume, and therefore a much larger propellant charge. But it also had a semi-automatic horizontal sliding wedge breech, and fired semi-fixed ammunition using a brass cartridge case and separate shell. Appendix C gives the basic characteristics of both weapons.

2pdr sub-calibre guns

Much use was made of sub-calibre firing to save both the cost of 5.2in shells and cartridges and also wear on the main armament. This particular design of sub-calibre practice barrel was used in a range of guns, the 5.2in being the largest. It was slid into the barrel and locked in place. The normal breech block sliding

The shell and separate cartridge case, as placed together in the tray.

Photographs of a preserved 2pdr sub-calibre gun at 'Explosion!', Priddy's Hard, Gosport, showing the bronze adapters at breech, muzzle and midway down the barrel. This particular barrel is fitted with adapters for the 4.7in gun.

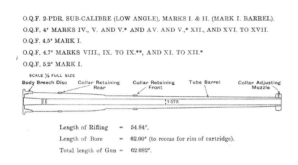

O.Q.F. 2-PDR. SUB-CALIBRE (LOW ANGLE), MARKS I. & II. (MARK I. BARREL).
O.Q.F. 4′ MARKS IV., V. AND V.* AND AV. AND V.,* XII., AND XVI. TO XVII.
O.Q.F. 4.5′ MARK I.
O.Q.F. 4.7′ MARKS VIII., IX. TO IX.**, AND XI. TO XII.*
O.Q.F. 5.2′ MARK I.

SCALE ½ FULL SIZE

Length of Rifling = 54.84″.
Length of Bore = 62.00″ (to recess for rim of cartridge).
Total length of Gun = 62.082″.

A cutaway section showing the construction of the sub-calibre 2pdr and the means of fastening it in the carrier barrel.

A case for the shortened 2pdr sub-calibre round, compared with a standard pom-pom anti-aircraft fused HE round.

wedge closed behind the brass cartridge case and the shell was fired by the firing pin in the same way as the 5.2in round. The 2pdr sub-calibre ammunition was supplied in pom-pom belts, but the brass cartridge case itself was shorter than the case used for the anti-aircraft shell in the pom-pom. Practice cases were usually cut down from standard-length cases, and their base markings were then overstamped accordingly. Two segments of the brass rim were milled like a coin edge, which aided rapid identification of the special round, especially at night. In *X.1* this precaution was unnecessary, since the ship did not mount standard 2pdr pom-poms. The practice allowance was 100 sub-calibre rounds per gun, which allowed for lengthy firing sessions at minimal cost.

Surface Gun Action

The proposed enemy for *X.1* was to be Japan. At the time she was designed, it was becoming more and more likely that Japan, locked in a costly naval race in the Pacific with her former allies Britain and the USA, would refuse to renew the Anglo-Japanese Alliance when it expired in 1921.

The plates in her pressure hull, inspired by the hull of *U 141*, were made of tough 1in high-tensile curved steel, resistant to destroyer-calibre shells. In addition much of her pressure hull would lie beneath the surface during a gun action due to her low profile. Should the pressure hull be holed by an enemy shell, her 'Godfather' Commander Raikes had ensured she had sufficient pump capacity to dive safely even with one magazine flooded, due to shell damage or a hatch being inadvertently left open in a hurry! This was also one advantage of her considerable size.[7]

It must be said that *X.1* succeeded in matching the criteria set for her in being able to engage a convoy escort consisting of the size and type of

A contemporary Imperial Japanese Navy destroyer, as she would have appeared through *X.1*'s rangefinder periscope. The exact range was obtained by bringing the two parts of the split image into coincidence in the right-hand eyepiece, reading off the range in the left-hand eyepiece. Here the forward mast is being used. Submarines normally avoided confrontation with such speedy and deadly vessels. Here *X.1* is stalking the *Akikaze*, which has become her prey.

destroyer existing at the time of her conception. Later Japanese First-Class destroyers, such as the world-beating *Fubuki*s which began to appear in 1926, would have proved a tough nut for *X.1* to tackle on the surface. However, this was less significant as the *modus operandi* of the Imperial Japanese Navy was to husband their large destroyers for actions between opposing fleets, leaving the less 'honourable' task of convoy escort to the smaller, older and weaker units. Built under the 1918, 1919 and 1920 Programmes, the *Momi* class comprised twenty-one Second-Class destroyers launched between 1919 and 1923. They were followed by eight units of the similar *Wakatake* class, launched between 1922 and 1924. These 280ft vessels displaced between 1,020 and 1,100 tons full load; they could exceed 35 knots when new, and they carried an armament of three 4.7in guns and four 21in torpedo tubes. Their main tactical drawback if attacking a large and well-armed submarine on the surface was that they presented only one gun of their main armament directly ahead. The thirty-six units of the larger *Minekaze*, *Kamikaze* and *Mutsuki* classes shared the same armament layout and the same problem.

When considering whether or not to capitalise on the design of *X.1*, by completing a more powerfully

armed sister-ship, (for which the designation '*X.2*' was long reserved), the exponents of surface gunpower may have overreached themselves. They asserted that *X.2*, armed with three twin or two triple 5.2in gun turrets, could surprise even a Japanese light cruiser 'with every expectation of being able to overwhelm her'. Such ambitions would have fallen far short of reality, given that even the weakest Japanese light cruisers were protected by a waterline belt of 2in armour plate, topped by a protective deck 1½ inches thick. Faced with such a powerful opponent, however, the 'X' class submarines, having exemplary underwater manoeuvrability and control, could use their underwater Asdic equipment and heavy bow salvo of six 21in tubes to carry out a torpedo attack, with a fair prospect of success.

On the other hand, in *defending* herself against an attack by small, manoeuvrable escort vessels with anti-submarine capability, tactically it made far more sense for *X.1* to fight on the surface. There her gunnery control systems and heavy armament weighed the scales heavily in her favour. Submerged she presented a huge sonar target, and compared with surface escort vessels, her underwater speed, turning circle and endurance were all severely limited. This problem dogged all the large submarines of the Second World War, and many boats were depth-charged to destruction or forced to the surface by much smaller ASW escort vessels.[8]

In a gun action against an escorted convoy, *X.1* would proceed as follows:

1. The approach of enemy vessels would be noted from Asdic, directional hydrophones or visual surface contact.

2. Once in position for a submerged ambush, *X.1*'s commander would raise the periscopic rangefinder, and mark off the range to the nearest escort vessel.

3. The guns would be laid on target underwater, and when all was ready the klaxon would sound for surface action.

4. Less than 90 seconds after the order to surface was given, *X.1*'s turrets would be firing accurately-controlled salvoes of 70lb shells into the unsuspecting victim.

5. With the first target escort vessel sunk or in flames, *X.1* would switch target to the next escort vessel

rushing to the aid of her compatriots. And the action would continue until all escorts were eliminated, leaving the huge corsair submarine to cruise in leisurely pursuit of her main targets, the relatively helpless merchantmen.

On the approach of a larger and tougher enemy, *X.1* would simply submerge and, using her active Asdic just like a modern hunter-killer sub to obtain the target's bearing, course and speed, she would fire her bow salvo of six 21in torpedoes. The blazing wreck could then be finished off with gunfire . . .

Practice Makes Perfect

In April 1926 *X.1* was *en route* for Gibraltar, and Commander Phillips commenced a series of full-calibre gunnery trials. On 10 April he wrote in his report:

'A' turret, forward, seen from the bridge, with the galley chimney in evidence. Obviously, this latter fitting would be removed on diving, and in a gun action.

The guns were fired at extreme training to test blast and discomfort on the bridge. This was very slight.

In a gun manning exercise: 1) Director Tower clear of the water to order 'off gun trunk glands' = 1 minute. 2) Ditto to 'Fore Turret on Target = 2 minutes 15 seconds. 3) Ditto Aft Turret = 3 minutes 5 seconds (due to the bearing of the target the aft turret had to train through 320 degrees).

The present telemotor pumps had insufficient capacity to take off both glands at the same time so a start of 15 seconds is given to the after gland. There is the question of bringing the fore turret into action first.[9]

Maintenance of the gunnery equipment will be considerable subject as it is to constant submersion.

A week later he penned the following:

Director misfires were suffered.

The foremost gun trunk gland was leaking worse on every occasion of diving. The front gland has a rubber ring compared to the aft one which has a dexine ring, which has given no trouble. Propose to fit a dexine ring to the front gland on return to Chatham.

Director misfires were diagnosed.

On 1 May 1926, following a subsequent full-calibre shoot, and a great deal of gun drill and familiarisation with the systems, Commander Phillips was pleased to report: 'Time to opening fire 1' 30". 8 salvoes fired in 2 minutes. Shoot commenced at 3,000 yards. Second shoot at 10,000 yards. Last five salvoes were straddles.'

'Y' turret trained out to port, showing the windshield segments which elevated with the guns, and the voice communication tube.

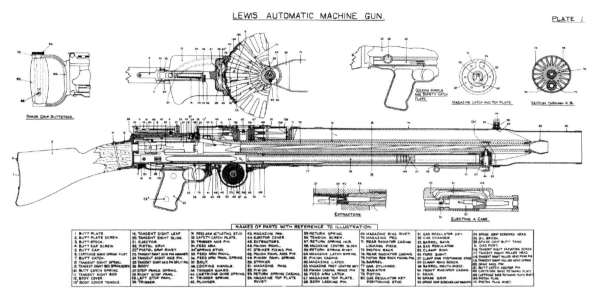

.303in calibre Lewis gun in section.

Anti-Aircraft Armament

D J Dent, Rear Admiral, Fort Blockhouse, considered the matter of anti-aircraft armament in a memo penned on 12 March 1921: 'If a 3in HA gun is fitted then it should be on a disappearing mount not to interfere with the underwater speed. This question should be deferred until development of the multiple pom-pom.' Unfortunately, it was later decided to remove the 3in HA gun as 'it was no use for K boats'. Only six days later the Rear Admiral (S) had changed his mind concerning the multiple pom-pom, and remarked prophetically: 'This gun is not even an anti-

aircraft gun'.[10] Obviously, *X.1* was intended to operate far out in the open ocean, where the threat of enemy air power was felt to be minimal. She was therefore supplied with just two single Lewis guns, with 2,000 rounds of Mk VIII ball and 500 rounds of tracer. It must be said that, during the Battle of Britain, it was the trusty old Lewis which claimed the most Luftwaffe aircraft shot down by ground fire – although virtually nothing else was available at the time. It was, however, strictly a close-range weapon. Practice anti-aircraft shoots were carried out on a kite target towed usually by another submarine, as on 6 April 1928, when *K.26* obliged. This lack of an effective anti-aircraft armament was the one serious flaw in her armament. It is clear she would be obliged to operate far from enemy shore-based aviation. This aspect is one more clear indication that *X.1* was deliberately planned as a long-range blue water corsair submarine. *X.1*, it must be said, was large enough and had enough deck space to allow her to carry a half-decent outfit of 20mm Oerlikon and even 40mm Bofors guns, had she lasted to fight in the Second World War.

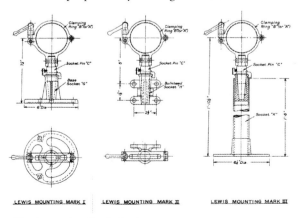

Naval mountings for the Lewis.

Torpedoes

Initially Rear Admiral Dent considered that *X.1*'s gun armament was secondary. Her torpedoes were to

A drawing by David Hill of the torpedo room, looking forward, showing four of the six 21in torpedo tubes plus their reloads. Reloads for tubes 5 and 6 were located in troughs below the walking platform. Overhead is the operating mechanism for the forward hydroplanes.

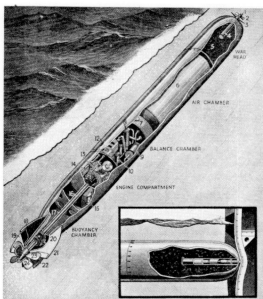

CONSTRUCTION OF THE MODERN TORPEDO

Fig. 13. *A 21-inch torpedo costs £2,000 and has 6,000 separate parts. It is probably the most lethal weapon in existence. 1, Firing pin. 2, Safety screw. 3, Whisker. 4, Detonator. 5, 500-lb. high explosive. 6, Compressed-air chamber. 7, Water chamber. 8, Hydrostatic depth control gear. 9, Steering control for horizontal rudders. 10, Paraffin bottle. 11, Trip valves and starting gear. 12, Trigger starter. 13, Four-cylinder hot-air driven radial engine of 350 h.p. 14, Servo motor. 15, Gyroscopic rudder control. 16, Propeller shaft, and 17, tunnel. 18, Upper vertical fin and rudder. 19, Port horizontal fin and rudder. 20, Gearbox driving propellers in opposite directions. 21, Starboard horizontal fin and rudder. 22, Lower vertical fin and rudder. 23, Forward propeller. 24, After propeller. Inset shows torpedo at moment of contact. The safety screw has worked off during the torpedo's passage through the water, and the firing pin which operates the detonator is driven home by the impact.*

comprise her main armament.[11] The large 'K' class boats had been severely criticised for their weak torpedo armament of only four bow tubes for 18in torpedoes. To remedy this defect, the first of the 'Improved Ks', the *K.26*, was fitted with a powerful bow armament of six 21in torpedo tubes (plus four beam tubes). The same bow armament of six tubes was planned for the *L.50* type, and cancellation of seventeen such boats made available a brand-new set of six 21in tubes for *X.1*. This economy move nearly brought disaster. The 'L' class were designed for a maximum diving depth of only 200ft, and the tube door rear clips were only safe to that depth, whereas *X.1* was designed to dive to 450ft. Just in time the error was noticed and the clips replaced with stronger fittings. In place of the 'K' class beam tubes, on 25 January 1921 the DNC noted that with angled gyros the bow tubes could be used for beam shots. On 11

Illustration of a Mark IV torpedo, from a British wartime publication unashamedly written to boost morale, but portraying the still-current Mark IV reasonably accurately.

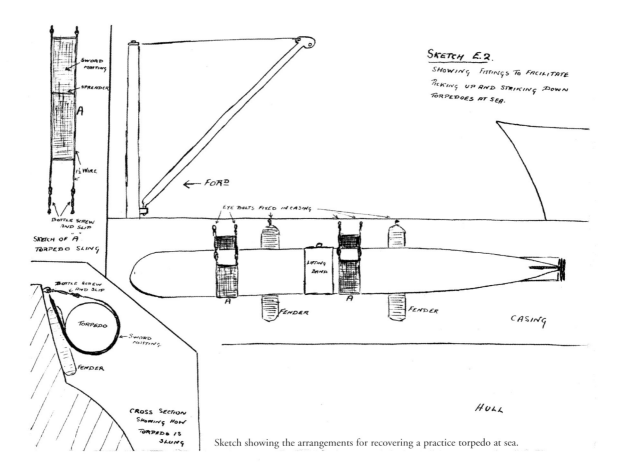

Sketch showing the arrangements for recovering a practice torpedo at sea.

November 1921 it was decided to fit *X.1* with torpedo firing reservoirs operating at the higher than normal pressure of 900lbs/sq in. The capacity of each reservoir was to be 7 cubic feet, and their internal diameter 16in.

Her slim bow had been designed to give as high a surface speed as possible. A W Johns minuted on 29 August 1921 that 'The torpedo tubes are to be fitted further forward than in previous boats. An increase in breadth of the boat behind the tubes allows greater access. This increases the water resistance but is a good trade-off. The torpedo storage compartment is to be the same as on *K26*.' On the other hand Lt Commander Ruck-Keene in his report of October 1928 noted that this did mean the tube space was somewhat cramped. This did not, however, seem to unduly impair the performance of the torpedo party. Only twelve torpedoes were carried, six in the bow tubes and six reloads. This was a small number for a corsair submarine. It is clear therefore that her main

weapon against commerce would be her 5.2in guns, leaving the torpedoes for use against major warship targets of opportunity.

Torpedo lifting gear was installed to hoist Mk IV* 21in torpedoes. The Mark IV torpedo had first entered service in 1917, and became the principal torpedo used by the Royal Navy in the Great War. Given their high cost – stated at some £2,000 apiece in 1939 – it is not surprising that a submarine would retain her initial outfit of torpedoes until they were expended in live firing or, as sometimes happened to the embarrassment of all concerned, they were fired in practice shoots and not recovered. Continuing in service throughout the Second World War, by September 1944 over 500 Mark IVs had been fired by submarines and surface vessels.

The Mark IV* was 25ft 9in (6.896m) long, weighed 3,206lbs or 1.43 tons (1,454kg), and carried a 515lb (234kg) explosive charge of amatol (a mixture of TNT and ammonium nitrate). With a

Recovering a practice torpedo in the Mediterranean. Such a procedure in cold northern waters would not be a popular duty.

all, and one was lost. Finally, the *Aberdare* class minesweeper HMS *Ross* dutifully stood in for a target, and *X.1* fired a full salvo of six torpedoes at her. Over an hour later she was still looking for two practice torpedoes which had not turned up, and they were written off as lost, making a total of three of these very expensive missiles expended. However, the official report on the trials penned on 19 October 1925 deemed her torpedo firing performance to have been 'Satisfactory'. She was to carry out many more torpedo firing exercises during her Mediterranean sojourn, including several live firings.

Proposals for a Sister-Ship

In October 1928, Lt Commander Philip Ruck-Keene wrote an appraisal of the features of *X.1*, and put forward proposals for her sister-ship, to be designated *X.2*. He made the following comments on her armament:

Gunnery: The manner in which the whole control personnel, including layers and trainers, have merely to sit quietly in their seats, and not climb rapidly through hatches, at the critical moment when breaking surface, and just before opening fire, is excellent. In fact the whole arrangement seems to have been designed almost ahead of its time.

Suggest 6 x 5.2in in 2 triple or 3 twin turrets to engage any cruiser in single combat with every chance of annihilating her. Convoys are certain to be escorted by cruisers in future wars. As X.1 has proved to be an excellent submersible, the further step of fitting three turrets instead of two is perfectly feasible. No superimposed mounts because of the blast effects in the open turrets.

Telescope carriers to have butterfly nuts in place of the special spring clips which rust and lose tension. The firing rod rusts up and is hard to strip. The trainer's sight needs a drain fitted. The sliding breech blocks are satisfactory but scoring has occurred on the upper and lower surfaces. They need rollers to support the blocks. The training rack needs better protection from floating bodies – usually debris floating in the water.

The gun trunk glands have proved satisfactory. Large volumes of telemotor pressure are required to operate. This dangerously lowers the margin for operating vents and raising periscopes etc. at the same time. Additional accumulators are suggested.

Emergency gland – the present fitting is bad and maintenance would probably be difficult under war conditions.

negative buoyancy of 445lbs (202kg), the torpedo was driven by a wet-heater four-cylinder hot-air radial engine producing 350hp. It could be pre-set for a variety of speeds and ranges, but for submarine use the Mark IV was normally set to run for 6,000 yards (5,500m) at 40 knots. Alternatively, at 30 knots it had a maximum range of 9,500 yards (8,700m). The warhead was fired by contact pistol, but had *X.1* survived to fight in the Second World War, magnetic firing pistols would have become available as an option. For practice torpedo attacks, a dummy warhead would be fitted, which allowed the torpedo to float at the end of its run and be recovered on board.

Initial torpedo trials were held off the Isle of Wight and Portsmouth between 25 September and 16 October 1925. On five days *X.1* was dived to various depths, the deepest being 100ft, and fired a total of forty practice torpedoes. Then followed a day of surface firing, when nine torpedoes were fired in

Communications: There are mechanical telltales platform to magazine.

The Gun Number Two combines the duties of breech worker and sightsetter and also is the Communications Number with the Transmitting Station by means of a voice pipe headpiece.

Suggestion to do away with the telltales. The guns <u>can</u> be loaded at any elevation.

Do away with the interceptor at the guns. The Gunlayer uses a pedal switch.

Transmitting Station to platforms – by voicepipes – are not entirely satisfactory.

In the magazines, room is too restricted. Circular magazines could overcome this.

Electrical circuits need to be completely watertight and not merely splash tight.

The pusher hoist consists of a number of sections, each one being a concentric fit upon the other. In X.1 some were not so, causing jams and damage to cartridges.

Hand training is too heavy and gearing should be fitted.

The shield supports need strengthening to cope with rough weather.

The torpedo tubes are very cramped due to design of the hull for speed.

Lt Commander Ruck-Keene's recommendations mainly concerned items which, through slight changes, could become perfected. The opening tone of his comments, though somewhat over-optimistic, is nevertheless evidence of the enthusiasm which the ship's gunnery capabilities engendered among her crew.

An aerial view dated '4th December 1928'.

CHAPTER 6

The Ship, Her Hull, Fittings and Complement

X.1's Vital Statistics

Surface Displacement was 2,425 tons Standard and 2,780 tons Normal load.

Submerged, *X.1* displaced 3,600 tons under Normal load conditions.

She was 363ft 6in (110.79m) long overall, with a maximum beam of 29ft 10in (9.09m), and a mean Normal load draft of 15ft 9in (4.80m).

When necessary, she could carry a maximum fuel load of 452 tons of fuel oil, to give a range of 16,200 miles at 10 knots surfaced; range 18
  miles at 4 knots submerged.

The Hull

The keel of *X.1*, ordered under the Estimates for 1921/22, was laid down at Chatham Dockyard on 2 November 1921. She was built under the covered Ship Shed on No. 7 Slip. Because of her length, some 60ft of the bows protruded beyond the landward doors of the Shed, and the slip had to be extended onto the roadway.

The *X.1*'s hull was more of a complete double hull than in any previous design. To once more quote the 1921 Technical History Section of the Admiralty, 'A hen's egg is strong and so is an ostrich egg, but if the shell of the ostrich egg was as thin as the shell of the hen's egg it would be very weak indeed; in the same way a "K" boat is structurally weaker to resist deep pressures than is an "E" boat'. And *X.1* was to be nearly 30ft longer than the clumsy 'K' Boats.

Rear Admiral Dent proposed on 12 March 1921 that her plating should correspond to that of the *U 139* class, and the major part of her riveted pressure hull was formed from 1in thick high tensile steel (from the Port Talbot Steel Company Limited),

annealed to make it easier to roll. This immensely thick hull allowed her to dive to the unprecedented depth of 450ft (A W Johns designed her for a maximum depth of 500ft, as per his note dated 27 February 1922, at which depth he calculated the pressure on the hull to be 225 PSI). This compared with the previous 'K' class boats and their ½in plating, which restricted them to a maximum depth of only 150ft. And the new technology brought its own risks. Her thick pressure hull was pierced by the two large-diameter revolving trunks of her turrets. Power-operated rubber glands which sealed these gun trunks were eventually made to operate perfectly. But insufficient hydraulic power to the telemotors meant that she could not free off both gun trunk glands, and open or close her vents, or raise her periscopes all at the same time. These and other minor faults – only to be expected in such a highly imaginative and experimental vessel – were planned to be corrected in the follow-up ship, the *X.2*, which was never to be built.

The pressure hull was divided up into ten watertight compartments by nine bulkheads, each

Leaving Grand Harbour, Malta, in June 1928, painted in Scheme III.

pierced by a circular watertight door 2ft 9in in diameter – the first such doors to be used in an RN submarine. The entire hull structure was fastened together by rivets – both countersunk and fan heads. In the original design estimates both types of rivet were costed at £1.00 per hundredweight (285kg). Welded construction had been used by Cammell Laird in 1921 to build the merchant ship *Fullagar*, and it may seem surprising that the technique was not introduced in *X.1*, given the highly experimental nature of so many elements of her design. However, a major drawback was that the high tensile strength D Quality steel specified for warships was not the best steel to use for welding.[1] Welding was introduced into RN submarine designs with the *Rainbow* class laid down in 1929, which had welded external fuel ballast tanks. Welding was first used for the pressure hull frames with *Talisman*, *Tetrarch* and *Torbay* of the 1938 Programme, while *Subtle* (launched on 27 January 1944) was the first RN submarine to have a fully-welded pressure hull. Even so, their ¾in thick pressure plating did not permit these later boats to exceed the design depth of *X.1*.

Keels

Two 10-ton drop keels were fitted, which could be jettisoned if her crew needed to surface in an emergency. No bilge keels were thought necessary – unlike those which had to be fitted to the *Surcouf* and the huge Japanese boats. *X.1*'s rolling characteristics were acceptable as designed.

Weight breakdown

At normal load, the weights built into *X.1*, as designed, were as follows:

	Tons
Hull	1,480
guns	50
ballast keel	170
battery	210
ammunition 300 rds	14
air bottles	6
main motors	62
gear & effects	15
auxiliary engines	90
water	24
generators	36¾
main engines	250
provisions & stores	20
torpedoes	35¾
air bottles	37

fresh water	24
trimming water	10
auxiliary ballast	20
water in compensating tanks	40
oil fuel (external)	177
oil fuel (internal)	2¾
lube oil	44
spare gear	5
	2,781 tons

Whilst her surface armament, at around 110 tons, represented only some 4 per cent of the total weights, this was much higher than in any other submarine ever built, except for *Surcouf*. Specific gunnery items were the DCT weighing 16.1 tons, the hull structure and glands underneath the guns at 19.4 tons, and hull stiffening in way of the guns, 3.4 tons. Each turret and trunk as fitted weighed 27.15 tons, and the 5.2in shells and cartridge cases added a further 15.9 tons. The weights for the four sub-calibre barrels and 400 practice rounds are not specified but would have added just under two tons.

Upper control room stiffening

An ex-crew member of *X.1*, Jimmy Lester, related an 'exciting' dive experience in his book *More Submarine Memories*.[2] As he remembered the incident, 'We heard that she was designed for an extreme depth of 750 feet which sounded unbelievable. On our way to Malta she tried it out. At 450 feet her conning tower reduced its width by 3½ inches so she blew everything a bit quick and surfaced, the Med being very deep just there. All this she told *K.26* on surfacing. We were told to keep the near-accident between us as she was secret and experimental.'

From the Ship's Cover and the papers preserved at Gosport, this may be an earlier incident which occurred during *X.1*'s first overseas cruise to Gibraltar in April 1926. Apparently, the upper control room had flat parallel sides of such area that, at 400ft there was such serious deflection, it was decided not to stay long at that depth. Commander Phillips reported on 16 April 1926 that 'Strengthening of the upper control room is "absolutely necessary", among a list of other items.'

Naval Constructor Mr A G W S Stanton accompanied *X.1* on her trip to Gibraltar, and he was able to sketch out a suitable reinforcement for this part of the hull. On his return he drew up a blueprint, which exists in the Ship's Cover at Woolwich, detailing the following measures:

1. Ribs to be doubled by inserting three new vertical. Z-section 20lbs intercostal welded into bosom of stiffeners;

2. Two horizontal 4in x 4in x 12.75lbs stiffeners to be added;

3. 20lbs flanges to be added to both upper floors.

No further comments were heard on the subject of the control room sides, so this frightening incident was not repeated.

The two bow anchors were to be carried in hawse pipes as on a light cruiser – to avoid difficulties in mooring a submarine of such large size.

Fuel and Oil Storage

X.1 carried virtually all her fuel load in external tanks. These were left open at the bottom to allow sea water to enter and replace fuel as it was used up, thus helping to preserve the overall trim. Unfortunately, allowing the fuel oil and sea water to come into contact could lead to the oil emulsifying, especially in bad weather conditions. A much more serious problem was the fact that these external fuel tanks were riveted, and tended to be far from oil-tight.

As early as 19 August 1922, Mr T Palmer, Manager of the Constructive Department at Chatham Dockyard, was defending the yard's method of sealing the oil tanks, in the following manner:

Oil tank seals use bedding material of vegetable tar and Portland cement. These are mixed to a consistency of common putty and used in association with white hemp stop waters. On testing, if slight leaks occur, a mixture of white and red lead is injected. Considerable experience has been gained at this Yard in oil tight work. In view of the above it is considered that it would be a mistake to depart from Chatham practice at this stage of the construction of s/m X.1.

The reader is left to surmise that there had already been a history of leaks from the external fuel tanks of RN submarines.

On 18 November 1924, Commander Raikes noted that the 'Rivitting [sic] in No 12 Main Ballast is not oil tight. It was suggested this might be overcome by Electric Welding all the Seams and Butts.' Obviously nothing was done, since on his return from Gibraltar in April 1926, Constructor Commander A G W S Stanton reported that 'Nos 1 and 3 Fuel Groups were leaking badly soon after

leaving England.' Again, in July 1928 X.1 reported serious leaks from external fuel tanks (the same problem as with the contemporary 'O' and 'P' classes). From Lt Commander Ruck-Keene's report of October 1928 we read: 'Oil leaks are most serious and in calm weather would undoubtedly give her away when submerged – leaks developed within 3 weeks of leaving dockyard hands. Reports from the Mediterranean Fleet show she was easily visible from the air when submerged.'[3] After the *Rainbow* class were launched with welded external fuel tanks, earlier boats such as *Oberon* (the former *O.1*) had their fuel tank seams welded up during refits. Despite Commander Raikes' proposal, and the on-going programme of refits, nothing was ever done to improve the sealing of X.1's fuel tanks, even following her disastrous drydock accident.

Colour Schemes

X.1 carried a variety of paint finishes, and her crew certainly had a great deal of free time in harbour to repaint ship. Given the total absence of specific records on the subject, the following colour schemes are indicative only, based on an analysis of the photographic record and of the Ship's Log Books. This analysis is complicated by the fact that only a small number of photographs are actually dated, and in some cases these dates appear incorrect. For example, one of the aerial views of X.1 at sea in the Mediterranean is ascribed to '4th December 1928', but her Log shows on that day her crew had gone ashore and the ship was beginning her Annual Refit. Similarly, a scene described as 'X.1 in harbour in 1931' shows her in the company of several major vessels, at a time when she seldom left the dockside. Colours actually used are difficult to deduce from black and white photography, but there are pointers elsewhere.

Scheme I

At launch, her hull above the waterline, the casing and conning tower were painted overall mid-grey. This colour was probably the standard Great War submarine grey. The Munsell neutral value was N5/0. A colour and tonal match is the USN Late WWII Neutral Ocean Gray. Below the waterline she was painted the standard anti-fouling red. Initially she had no boot topping. Her pennant number was a large sans serif 'X.1.' in white, shadowed in black to the right and below, on the side of the superstructure below the conning tower.

Scheme II

First seen in the photo at No. 1 Buoy, Sheerness (no turret windshields, single forward hydroplanes). The hull above the waterline, the superstructure, conning tower and turrets were overall grey, as were the gun barrels. This was probably the Great War submarine grey. Below the waterline the hull was anti-fouling red, with black boot topping. The depth markings can be seen on her forward hull, painted in white. In fact these numbers were raised metal characters fastened to the hull – probably in brass. She carried a smaller 'X.I.' in white, shadowed in black to the right and below, on the conning tower sides. Also in the painting by a crew member. Several bows-on photos show this scheme, as well as the shot of *X.1* 'approaching Gosport', probably during her torpedo trials.

Scheme III

By June 1928, *X.1* had been repainted overall light grey above the boot topping, including her gun barrels, presumably to suit her deployment to the Mediterranean. The appropriate Admiralty Reference for Mediterranean Grey was AP 507C. To eliminate glare from the light grey paint, the top of the DCT, a section of the conning tower roof just ahead of the surface conning position, and the tops of the windshields of both turrets were rendered in a dark colour, probably black but possibly dark grey. 'X.I.' was in black on the conning tower sides. Walkways along the centre of the hull casing and on the hull aft were a dark colour, possibly black or even covered in corticene, which was a dark red-brown colour.

Scheme IV

Later in 1928 *X.1* appeared in a striking scheme: Her hull casing above the boot topping, including the bulbous projection of the bow quick-blow tanks, was painted in a very dark colour. This area is virtually certain to be black. Were it a predecessor of the 'Mediterranean Blue' used so successfully by the famous 10th Submarine Flotilla based in Malta during the Second World War, it would more closely match the tonality of the surrounding sea.[4] Above this new colour the superstructure sides, conning tower, turrets and gun barrels remained light grey, except for the darker anti-glare panels of Scheme III. 'X.I.' was in black on the conning tower sides. This must be considered an experimental scheme, since *X.1* did not retain it for long. That the two clearest photos of this scheme were taken from an aircraft lend credence to the supposition that the experimental vessel of the Flotilla was being used as a test bed for a prototype camouflage scheme, designed to lessen the vessel's visibility from the air.

Scheme V

At some time prior to returning to the UK, *X.1* was repainted in a different two-tone scheme. In this scheme the lower part of the hull casing above the black boot topping was painted what appears to be Admiralty Dark Grey (Ref AP 507A). Her superstructure, conning tower and turrets were painted in a light grey, presumably Admiralty Light Grey (Ref AP 507C). The light grey extended some 2ft onto the curved area of her hull, and the demarcation line forward was a horizontal continuation of this level, passing between her forward hydroplane slots and just above her anchors. Her gun barrels and the rangefinder were black. Her pennant number 'X.I.' in black was retained on the conning tower sides. The depth numbers have been overpainted by the general colour scheme and are no longer picked out in white. Since the crew could readily note the raised numbers there was no need to pick them out in a contrasting colour. This distinctive scheme can be seen in the shots of *X.1 en route* to and arriving at Gibraltar.

Scheme VI

The final photographs of *X.1*, showing her keeled over in drydock on 26 June 1931, show a simpler scheme. Seen from the bow, the entire vessel above the boot topping seems to be Admiralty Light Grey (AP 507C). The light from the fading afternoon sun is deceptive, however, as the photograph taken from the stern appears to show a darker shade on those areas formerly painted in dark grey (Scheme V). It is possible, of course, that this shade differentiation results from overpainting the dark grey area in light grey. The dark stripe running from the front of the conning tower to below the waterline is actually a shadow, as it does not appear on a photo taken some time earlier the same afternoon. The boot topping was black, with anti-fouling red below this. At this time she carried her pennant number 'X I' in white, this time with no full stops, shaded in black to the right and below, on the superstructure sides below the conning tower, in the same position and of a similar size to when she was launched.

Sensors and Communications

In a memo dated 30 December 1921, designer A W Johns addressed himself to the questions of sending and receiving messages surfaced and submerged, and raised the possibility of installing the new Asdic apparatus.

Two views of *X.1* wearing Scheme V, probably at Gibraltar.

In drydock in 1931.

Asdic

Asdic[5] had been invented in the latter stages of the Great War as a replacement for the extempore hydrophone installations, which were then the only means of detecting a submerged submarine. It became widely fitted to surface ships of the Royal Navy, and it was erroneously believed to have rendered the submarine impotent.[6]

In his memo, A W Johns proposed that the question of whether or not to fit Asdic in *X.1* should wait on future trials with *H.32*. She had been built by Vickers at Barrow-on-Furness and commissioned on 27 May 1919.[7] In 1921 design work began on a submarine Asdic, based on the set first fitted to a 'P' Boat, but inverted. Designated the Type 113, it first went to sea in *H.32* the following year. The quartz transducer was fitted inside a retracting canvas-covered dome, which required a period of immersion before it became sound-transparent. This troublesome canvas dome was soon replaced by a copper one. Initial results were obviously promising, for on 12 May 1923 approval was given to fit an Asdic installation in *X.1*. She would be the first submarine to be *designed as such* to have an Asdic compartment installed. As at 26 January 1925, *H.32* and *X.1* were the only submarines so far fitted with Asdic. Four *L.50* class subs were to be fitted with Asdic while building. The special set fitted to *X.1* was designated the Type 113X, and was strengthened for deep diving. It was also provided with a hinged cover to protect the oscillator dome from gun blast. In 1930 *X.1*'s set had its electronics updated, when it was redesignated the Type 113C.

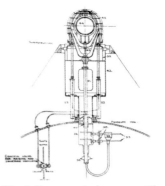

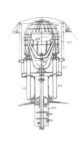

The Asdic turret raised on hydraulic rams into the operating position, Oscillator vertical, facing forward.

The Asdic turret retracted for surface action, with its hinged cover in place, Oscillator horizontal, with the original design of frame for a canvas cover.

The Asdic Type 113X turret ready to be installed in *X.1*, in a mock-up showing the control wheels and the hinged turret cover. The framework covering the oscillator was to be fitted with a canvas cover as on *H.32*, but in practice it was replaced with a thin copper dome. This item was extremely fragile and when removed for maintenance required careful handling.

Asdic brought many advantages. Since *X.1* was of a size to present a tempting target to smaller, submerged boats, her Asdic set was designed to detect other submarines as well as surface targets. The set also had an important navigational function in *X.1*, as befitted her role as a corsair submarine in the wide blue yonder. Vast areas of the sea had been surveyed by surface ships, but depths and rocks had only been investigated down to about 70ft. *X.1*'s Asdic set enabled her to detect and avoid uncharted rocks when she was proceeding submerged.[8]

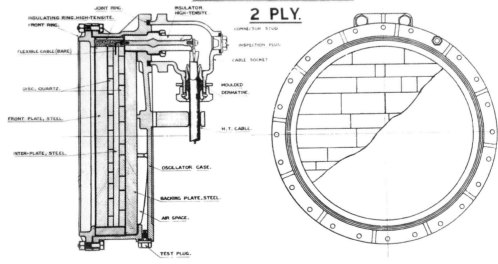

A drawing of the 2-Ply quartz oscillator of the Asdic Type 113X.

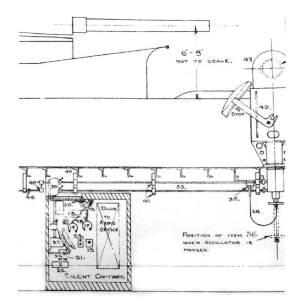

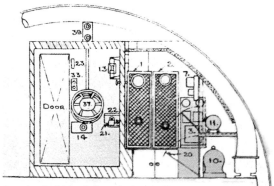

A section looking aft through the sound-insulated silent compartment on the left, where the operator sat, and the Asdic office to the right, containing the electrical equipment.

The Asdic arrangements showing the silent compartment, with its double wheel (37) for training and elevating the oscillator, the pair of headphones (17) for the operator and an officer, the Morse key (21), the operating rods for the Asdic turret (53), and the repeater rod to the control room (46). Also shown in side view is the hinged cover which protects the Asdic turret from the blast of 'A' turret's guns close overhead.

The original intentions were that Asdic was to be used for navigational and target ranging, and also for communications. It offered the possibility of co-ordinating divisional attacks by several boats at once. Trials were carried out with *H.32* between June 1925 and January 1926, and the reports were copied to Lt-Commander Phillips in *X.1* as to:

- station-keeping with another non-Asdic equipped submarine;
- attacking without periscope exposed after an initial periscope sighting had been made;
- avoiding anti-submarine attacks by surface escorts;
- transmitting of messages between surface vessels and submerged submarines;
- firing torpedo spreads on Asdic bearings.

Excellent results were achieved, and the Asdic set in *H.32* was used to complement the underwater directional hydrophone receiver.

It was found that submarine Asdic was less affected by surface disturbances. High speed, which disrupted surface Asdic, was not a problem for a submerged submarine owing to the very low speeds

David Hill's drawing of 'A' turret trunking with, on the right, the door to the Asdic silent compartment.

achieved prior to the later stages of the Second World War.[9]

Asdic pulses could be transmitted and received on a range of frequencies. This ability could be used to differentiate between attacking A/S vessels, and also to actively range on A/S vessels not transmitting if their search frequency was known, the submarine transmitting pulses on a different band to avoid the chance of the surface sets homing onto the submarine. The major problem with keeping an extended Asdic watch was the monotony of the operation, which resulted in extreme operator fatigue, and necessitated frequent reliefs. Obviously, a large submarine such as *X.1* could carry a sufficient number of operators to mitigate this factor.

Unfortunately, despite the pioneering work done by *H.32* and *X.1*, Royal Navy submariners would not use their Asdic for torpedo attacks, avoiding emitting active signals and using their Asdic set as a passive hydrophone receiver. The results achieved in all the above trials foreshadowed the much later work of the USN and RN nuclear hunter-killer submarines.

Hydrophones

In the same memo on communications, designer A W Johns ordered the installation of frame coils and revolving directional hydrophones (RDH). The retractable RDH instrument was installed as far forward as possible, in the bow just behind the Bull Ring (the steel ring on top of the bow used for mooring the ship).

Despite some notable successes during the Great War, hydrophones had proved to have limited applications for surface vessels in detecting and tracking submerged submarines in the open sea – especially when the target submarines were running near-silent or stopped on the bottom. Conversely, submerged submarines continued to make good use of hydrophones for detecting and identifying surface vessels. Experienced operators could differentiate between slow-turning mercantile screws and the faster high-pitched noise generated by a warship. They could provide accurate target bearings, an estimation of speed based on screw revolutions and the type of target, and some indication of range. Hydrophones could also warn of approaching torpedo screws, and the 'click' made by depth charge detonators as they were activated by hydrostatic pressure could prepare the crew for the resultant explosion. Hydrophones were of course the principal means of picking up submerged transmissions sent out by the Fessenden Gear, the underwater equivalent of the later 'talk between ships' (TBS) surface sets.

Fessenden Gear

Johns also instructed that Fessenden Gear would be fitted to *X.1*. In 1912 the Submarine Signal Company, which had specialised in signalling the position of lighthouses, lightships, shoals, wrecks and other hazards by means of underwater bells and the associated on-board reception devices, decided to go into competition with Marconi's aerial wireless transmission system. They hired electrical engineer Professor R A Fessenden to develop an underwater Morse Code transmitter. During the Great War the Fessenden Gear allowed submerged boats to communicate at ranges of between 30 and 40 miles. On 21 April 1922 A W Johns proposed to incorporate a submerged transmissions (S/T) cabinet which would be used for sending and receiving submerged transmissions. Situated beneath the control room, adjacent to the wireless room, it was set up as a second 'silent cabinet' for the hydrophone operator. The apparatus to be installed in *X.1* was tested at Chatham on 27 July 1922.

Submarine sounding machine

On 10 March 1922 a submarine sounding machine was ordered from Kelvin Bottomley & Baird Ltd of Glasgow. The depth of water beneath the ship could be calculated by leading overboard a cable attached to a sinker. The cable would be carried clear of the hull on a boom. As the sinker descended, the cable would pay out until, on it reaching bottom, the cable would slacken. At that point the seamen manning the machine would read off the figure on the dial at the top which gave the length of wire paid out, in fathoms. They would then refer to a table to ascertain the true depth, taking into account the angle of descent of the sinker at any given speed of the ship.

A 'Kelvite' sounding machine of the period.

Wireless telegraphy

For surfaced wireless transmissions, Johns proposed WT masts suitable for a reliable day range of 1,000 miles. The masts themselves were ordered on 6 April 1922, and would be of the retractable (telescopic) type to reduce underwater resistance. Both were of three-throw design, the forward mast extending from a well set in the front of the conning tower to a height of 35ft 9in and being capped with a T-piece aerial spreader; the rear mast with a similar spreader retracted into the rear hull and was of necessity longer, extending to 43ft 3in. When the masts were extended, the 150ft long three-wire aerial was carried at a height of 68ft above the surface, and ended in a special WT cabinet measuring 13ft by 6ft. As installed, it was intended that the WT set should transmit with a 100 per cent success rate at a range of 500 miles, and that at 1,000 miles, 80 per cent of messages transmitted should be successful. Given the power of shore-based radio communications equipment, reception could normally be assured even at maximum range.

Underwater position indication equipment

On 3 April 1926 the Signal Department memoed that a grenade signal ejector was to be fitted. This device permitted a submerged submarine to indicate its position – for example during exercises – by firing a 'water shot' which would be visible on the surface.

Visual signalling

The after periscope standard at the rear of the conning tower carried a signal mast with a halliard on which signal flags could be hoisted. Behind this was fixed a watertight all-round flashing lamp. The sketch top right shows a potential use of this for flashing

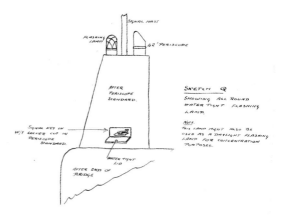

The after periscope standard on *X.1*, and the proposed modification on S/M *X.2*.

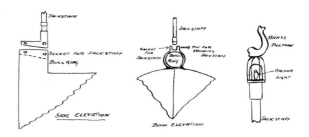

The jackstaff fitting.

Morse Code signals, for daylight concentration manoeuvres. At 'the sharp end', the crew would fasten the jackstaff to fly the Union Flag. This fitting carried a light for use when at anchor, and was topped by the traditional brass dolphin, the famous symbol of the Submarine Service.

A view of *X.1* probably off Portsmouth in September or October 1925 for torpedo trials, showing the WT masts extended.

Mock-up of *X.1*'s upper control room, looking forward.

Mock-up of *X.1*'s upper control room, looking aft.

A drawing by David Hill of the same area as finally constructed, showing the 30ft periscope, and the chart table to the right. The ladder in the foreground connected with the conning tower and the DCT.

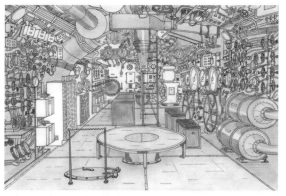

A drawing by David Hill, showing the main control room looking aft. In the centre, the raised platform is used when viewing through the forward 36ft periscope. The steam-driven 'K' class submarines also shared this feature. The circular hatchway in the foreground leads down into the CO_2 machinery space below the control room, a space also occupied by the wireless office and the silent compartment for the hydrophone operator. On the left are valves controlling the main ballast tank vents and further aft on the same side the gyro compass relay panels and an electrical switchboard. The ladder amidships connects with the upper control room and behind the ladder are the gyro compass and a chart table. To the right are coolers for the air-conditioning system, behind which are the hydroplane control wheels, and in the aft corner one of the centrifugal ballast pumps.

Control Facilities

Unlike even the largest U-boats of the Great War, where the commanding officer stood alone in a 'kiosk' during attacks, RN submarine commanders directed operations from the control room under the conning tower, surrounded by the officers and ratings of the control team. Given the size and complexity of *X.1*, her control spaces were larger than normal, but

A David Hill drawing showing the pump room, looking aft. The wooden ladder led down from the foredeck. Whilst at sea this ladder would have been swung upwards and fixed to the deckhead to give more room in the narrow passageway. The watertight door leading aft into the wardroom can be seen at the end of the passageway. To the left in this view is a wooden fuse box and to the right the controls for the forward low-pressure blower.

Periscopes

On 23 March 1922 the periscope specifications were fixed as

Lookout	42ft x 8½ins	(18½ft unsupported)
After (unifocal) (*sic*)	36ft x 7½ins	(14½ft unsupported)
Forward (bifocal)	36ft x 7½ins	(20ft unsupported at the upper control room or 14½ft unsupported at the lower control room)

still appeared extremely crowded. No internal photographs of *X.1* have survived (if any were ever taken), but we can gain an impression of the upper control room from the photographs of the wooden mock-up prepared at Chatham Dockyard. This was used to work out the positions of all the various controls, gauges and communication devices, whilst still leaving sufficient space for the operators to carry out their functions.

As befitted an experimental vessel, *X.1*'s Kingston valves – which controlled her ballast tanks for diving and surfacing – had 20in diameter handwheels made of a 'new aluminium alloy', being 2 per cent nickel/3½ per cent copper/1 per cent magnesium/93½ per cent aluminium.

Barr & Stroud would provide the actual instruments. Blueprint No. 5727 in the Ship's Cover at Greenwich shows the bottom end of Submarine Periscope Type CH9. This measured 42ft from window to eyepiece centre (monocular type).

The binocular power (B/P) scale was 1/2.

On 9 May 1922 Messrs Mechans Limited, of Scotetown Iron Works, Glasgow, produced the following quotations to supply the periscope shafting:

Three-throw types.
35 foot 9 inches, made of copper tube with gunmetal fittings and copper rope would cost £139-15-0;
43 foot 3 inches height above top of fixed tube, made of

steel tube with gunmetal fittings and steel rope would cost £279-15-0;
- both quotes to include delivery.

Steering gear

The helm indicators were to be copied from those examined in surrendered German submarines. A W Johns proposed in a memo dated 19 August 1921 to use AC electrical gear, as on German U-boats. Cannibalised German AC gear was actually fitted in *K.26. U 135* had been used by the Royal Navy for trials, and it was proposed to copy the AC gear tested in this U-Boat.[10] The steering gear itself was to be supplied by Brown Brothers Rosebank Iron Works, Edinburgh, as per the order dated 7 April 1922. Brown Brothers' price appears in an invoice dated 2 May 1922, in the amount of £1,880.

A David Hill drawing of the aftermost compartment, looking forward towards the No 10 watertight bulkhead. This compartment contained the emergency steering position, showing the wheels as rigged for emergency use. Under normal operating conditions they would have been stored elsewhere to allow access to the electric cooking range shown on the right. On the port side is a washing area containing two sinks, a bath and a slop ejector for disposing of food waste. Reportedly the bath was rarely if ever used as such.

The steering gear compartment and *X.1*'s substantial rudder.

Forbes log

A Forbes log was installed in a tank just above the keel aft of frame 79. The ship's speed was given by an impellor which revolved inside a tube, driven by the flow of water past the hull.

Boats

As befitted a vessel costing as much as a light cruiser, and carrying a far larger crew than any previous RN submarine, *X.1* was outfitted with a suitable set of small boats:

- Two 16ft skiff drop keel dinghies, fitted with 5–6bhp petrol motors;
- One 13ft 6in dinghy.

These boats were stowed inboard, under cover, in the superstructure in front of 'Y' turret, and were hoisted in and out by a folding derrick.

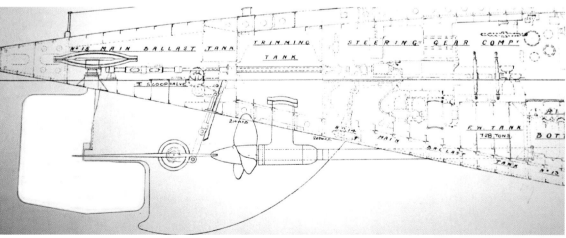

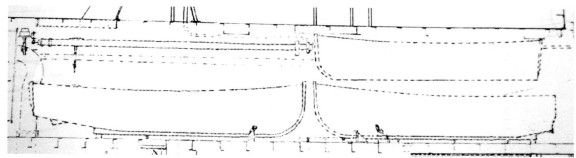

The boat stowage compartment in the rear superstructure.

Complement

As per the original specifications, the crew was to comprise:

7 Petty Officers
16 Stokers
1 Rangetaker
1 Leading Director Layer
2 Gun Layers 2nd class
61 Ratings
plus 7 Executive Officers (including 2 Captains of Turrets)
plus 2 Engine Room Officers
Grand Total 97
On 23 November 1926 the final crew total was minuted as 109 officers and men (including an additional 12 ratings).

Given her experimental rôle, and the highly temperamental nature of her complex propulsion machinery, *X.1*'s complement was to include one Engineering Commander and one Engineering Lieutenant. Normally only depot ships had an Engineering Commander. All other submarines had an Engineering Lieutenant only. Lt W H Bigwood joined her Engineering staff in 1925, and his letters have provided much insight into working conditions on board.

Habitability

In his comments for the projected *X.2*, Lt-Commander Ruck-Keene wrote in October 1928 that the worst congestion was in the Petty Officers' Mess. The Engine Room Artificers' Mess was very

David Hill's drawing of the petty officers' mess looking forward. Ten folding bunks were fitted in this compartment, which was reported to be very cramped when in use. An electric urn was fitted at the after end of the compartment.

David Hill's drawing of the accommodation passageway looking forward to 'A' turret trunking. To the left, two steel pillars add strength to the compartment when *X.1* went deep.

The officers also suffered, as their wardroom was used as a thoroughfare between the control room and the fore ends while at sea. One of several steel support pillars was sited somewhat inconveniently in the centre of the passageway. Meals were taken at an extending table to port, behind which were two small cabins. More happily, a small Spirits Room was adjacent, forward to port. The majority of the crew slept in hammocks.

Cooking facilities were extensive, and situated throughout the ship. Three upper deck galleys were located in the highest point of the superstructure, between the gun turrets, and in addition there were four electric cooking ranges installed inside the pressure hull. Frozen meat came from the main cold store.

To give some degree of shade from the Mediterranean sun, the crew could rig awnings. As befitted such a large vessel, her arrangements for hanging these were quite sophisticated. The sketch below was included in the file of papers proposing the stillborn *X.2*, and gives the overall appearance of the awnings. Note that for *X.2* it was proposed to double up the ridge ropes, and not rely on a single backbone rope as on *X.1*.

cramped and 'the bathing arrangements are atrocious'. As the engine room staff suffered more than most on board *X.1* it is likely they were the most vociferous in their complaining!

Commanding Officers	
1 December 1922	Cdr Robert H T Raikes DSO*
28 January 1925	Cdr Philip E Phillips DSO*
28 July 1927	Cdr C H Allen DSO
29 July 1930	Cdr E C M Baraclough
9 February 1931	Lt Cdr A L Besant
30 December 1931	Cdr J N MacNair
1 March 1933	Cdr J D A Musters DSC
8 December 1933	Lt Cdr C B Barry DSO

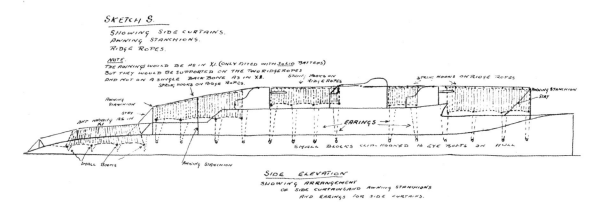

Sketch of the awnings rigged at anchor in hot climes.

David Hill's drawings of the wardroom: above, looking forward; below, looking aft

CHAPTER 7

Trials and Tribulations

A Guilty Secret

With our knowledge of the endless problems which dogged her chequered career, it is no surprise to reflect that *X.1* was conceived and born under something of a cloud.

The Washington Conference which ended in 1922 had resulted in seven treaties, designed to avoid potential future conflicts such as the catastrophic Great War. The unbridled naval race between Britain and Germany was correctly identified as one of the contributory causes of the outbreak of that war, and so the third treaty to be signed, on 6 February 1922, introduced limitations on naval armament. It was agreed by Great Britain, the United States, Japan, France and Italy. Capital ship numbers and replacements were to be strictly limited, and a 'capital ship' was defined as a vessel exceeding 10,000 tons standard displacement (that is, without fuel, ammunition or stores) or carrying a gun with a calibre exceeding 8in.[1]

This treaty, which was to last until the end of 1936, resulted in the construction of the so-called 'Treaty Cruisers', built right up to the maximum 10,000 tons/8in limits. A side-effect was that it also limited new submarine construction to a maximum size of 8in gun armament, if these vessels were not to fall foul of the definitions and be included in the tonnage allocated to 'capital ships'. In the event, only the French built up to the Treaty limit for submarine armament, as we shall see later. One important omission was that the Washington Treaty placed no limitation on the size of individual submarines, although the submarine fleets of each of the signatories were to be governed in terms of their overall maximum tonnage. This clause was to affect the final disposition of *X.1*, as described in Chapter 10.

It was the fourth treaty signed in Washington, which would fatally hamstring the *X.1*. Great Britain, having suffered most at the hands of U-boat crews during the Great War tried to have the submarine banned as a weapon of war.[2] Yet, at that very moment, the Admiralty were pressing ahead with the design of what they intended would be the largest and most powerful submarine ever built. Baulked in their first endeavour, the British delegates in Washington then tried to have the use of submarines against merchant shipping declared illegal. This was understandable since the U-boat blockade had threatened to bring Britain to her knees. But again, it must have been clear to the Admiralty that *X.1*'s gun armament would make her the commerce raider *par excellence*. This second political move on the part of Britain also failed, the assembled Powers agreeing only to pay lip service to the accepted rules of 'stop and search' which had proved so impractical for undersea craft – and which would quickly be discarded once more during the second world conflict.[3]

Given the current political moves, it could seem difficult to justify the Admiralty's desire to go ahead with the construction of *X.1*. The apparent contradictions can be explained if one recalls that, at the close of the Great War, the Royal Navy – while no longer able to adhere to the 'Two Power' standard, was still the largest and most influential naval force in the World. There were those in positions of authority within the Navy who would have held that it was only right and proper for the world's premier naval power to experiment with the latest and most successful weapons systems. It may also be true that there were those who aimed to retain the Royal Navy's technical pre-eminence, precisely in order to circumvent the political aspirations of foreign governments. If the Royal Navy was to be blocked in its development of the largest and latest super-dreadnoughts, then Britain would push ahead with what promised to be the newest type of 'capital ship', the large submarine cruiser.

It was against this international background, and in a universal climate of anti-war revulsion, that the Royal Navy defiantly prepared for the launch of its latest large submarine. The gun turrets themselves were to be installed later, but any competent observer could not fail to notice that she was closely inspired by the Imperial German U-Cruisers, which had been designed expressly for long-distance commerce raiding. As the launch date approached, the authorities became more and more apprehensive of the effect the appearance of this powerful new warship would have.

No cameras would be allowed at the launch, and

Above: The official photograph of *X.1* shortly after her launch. Note the single bow planes. Neither gun turrets, DCT, rangefinder nor periscopes have been fitted at this stage.

Left: Cover of the special commemorative programme.

confiscated. On the day itself, police were on duty to enforce the security clampdown, including a sergeant and constable stationed on the shore opposite the launch slip, and Water Police officers took to the river in boats to prevent any photos being taken from a passing vessel. The actual launch was to be a private Naval, even a Dockyard, affair, but some care was taken in preparing a printed programme to celebrate the event. The ceremony was to be performed by Mrs Kiddle, wife of the Dockyard Superintendent Admiral Kiddle. In the event, *X.1* took to the water without a hitch, at precisely 14.30 hours on the afternoon of Saturday, 16 June 1923, and was soon afloat in the Medway, riding high in her natural element without the weight of her turrets and battery cells.

The *Daily Herald* Affair

The following Monday, 18 June, the *Daily Herald* – a popular newspaper known for its left-wing leanings – announced the launch of *X.1* as the main feature on its front page. She was described as 'a new type of warship, unaffected by the Washington Treaty'. Confusingly, the article then went on to speculate that, since this Treaty limited submarines to 8in guns, it was unlikely she would have 12in or even 13.5in (as had been speculated at the time). It was most likely she would carry 'a pair of 8in'. The paper expressed the fear that she would be the start of a new Naval Race.

notices to this effect were posted at the Dockyard gates. For some time previously, the local press had carried warnings of the strict security which would be in place, and that any cameras seen would be

Only two days later, on Wednesday 20 June, the *Daily Herald* included on page 7 a very small photograph of the *X.1* just after her launch, with the jubilant caption 'An exclusive photograph of the launch of the *X.1* – In spite of elaborate precautions on the part of the authorities the launch of the new super-submarine was photographed. Here is the submersible monster just after taking the water at Chatham'. Retribution was swift.

Rex v Gilbert

M Fitzmaurice, Director of Naval Intelligence, wrote on the next day 'As pointed out by Sir Vernon Hall an unfortunate effect will be produced on the loyal press if this decidedly unpatriotic and provocative action by the *Herald* is allowed to pass unnoticed. I have shown the photograph to an experienced submarine officer who stated that although little or no detail of value was apparent, an expert would at once see from the shape of the hull that the submarine vessel was of a new type.' A search warrant was issued and the services of the City of London Police were obtained, in order to search the premises of the *Daily Herald*, 'to discover and obtain photographs, copies and the printing blocks from which they were produced in the *Daily Herald* of 20th June 1923'. Inspector Gray of the Metropolitan Police, on duty at Chatham, was 'to make all proper enquiries to discover the origin of the photograph'.

It was not difficult to find out from the *Daily Herald* what had transpired, and to track down the culprit. After the first edition for the 20th had been printed, the offending photograph arrived in the post bearing the initials 'S.G.' and an address, '86 Henry Street, Chatham, Kent'. The photograph was passed to Mr Dessurne, Art Editor, who decided to heavily retouch the small image and had a printing block made for the second edition.[4] He assessed the value of this item of news at 17 shillings and 6 pence, but no money had in fact been requested by, nor actually

remitted to 'S.G.'. It was evident the Art Editor had no concept of the design of submarine vessels, for his retouching completely confused the issue, as can be seen below. Nevertheless, the police enquiry was pursued with determination. The sender of the said photograph turned out to be a certain Philip James Gilbert, resident at 86 Henry Street, and he was interviewed by Inspector Gray.

Gilbert, born on 15 September 1899, was actually employed as an Engine Fitter at the Chatham Dockyard, the yard which had built and launched *X.1*, although his duties did not normally bring him into contact with the submarine or any of her fittings. He had begun as a dockyard apprentice at the age of 18 and after eighteen months he had been made a probationary Engine Fitter. After less than three weeks his probation was evidently deemed to have run successfully, and Gilbert was taken on the payroll on 24 January 1921 as a Hired Engine Fitter. His rate of pay was 41 shillings a week, plus war increases of 12 shillings, which Inspector Gray commented was normal for his trade at the time. The Inspector also reported that Gilbert 'appears to be a person strongly impressed by the doctrines of the *Daily Herald*'. He admitted taking the photograph from the foreshore, at a distance of between 350 and 400 yards off, with a small snapshot camera, and sending an enlargement to the *Daily Herald*. Inspector Gray discovered the original negative in Gilbert's possession.

The DNI wrote to the effect that he believed Gilbert to be 'a person of very advanced political opinions' and went on 'in consequence of the publicity given to the precautions against photography and the presence of the general public on the occasion of the launch, he must have known that he was doing wrong in photographing it and forwarding the photograph for publication in a newspaper'. Dessurne was found to be the only person at the *Daily Herald* who had dealt with the photograph, and it was clear that 'the duties of the Art

On the left is the original photograph received by the *Daily Herald*, and on the right, the version which was printed.

Editor of the *Daily Herald* are not of a very important character, and he is a subordinate with no real authority except to pass pictures for appearance in the paper, and thus reduce the space which has to be occupied by the letter press'. He continued '. . . the publishers knew it was desired to avoid all publicity, and they boast of the successful taking [of the photograph] in spite of the elaborate precautions on the part of the authorities'.

Thus the facts were uncovered, and it was left to decide what action the Navy should take. Section 1 (1) (c) and (2) of the Official Secrets Act of 1911, as amended by the Act of 1921, provided that 'if any person for a purpose prejudicial to the safety or interests of the State obtains, collects receives or publishes or communicates to any other person any "sketch" (which includes a photograph) which might be directly or indirectly useful to an enemy, he shall be guilty of felony'. The only defence would have been that such an action was not made for prejudicial purposes – although the *Daily Herald*'s boast went against this. The DNI appreciated that 'the true construction of the legislation would be that it applies to some form of communication with a foreign power'. In order to help the legal authorities decide what to do next, Admiral Kiddle, the Admiral Superintendent of Chatham Dockyard was asked for his opinion of Gilbert. On 21 July Kiddle noted 'His sympathies are towards communist principles and he is a reader of the *Daily Herald* and is sympathetic with its views, but generally speaking he is no more advanced in his views than many others. It is not considered his offence warrants dismissal but is deserving of a week's suspension and a notation that he should not be employed on confidential work'. Gilbert's line manager queried whether a suspension would serve any good purpose. It is clear that he was keen to support his employee who had acted out of what he

had thought was the public interest. He felt that Gilbert's action was dictated by stupidity and a desire for publicity, and merited no more than a severe reprimand. On 24 July Philip James Gilbert himself penned a statement to the effect that he had taken the photograph with a vest pocket Kodak camera. Once back home he had developed the print, and used his Kodak Enlarger to increase the size of the finished print. He claimed he had seen other spectators with cameras. He himself had never expected any pecuniary gain. Finally, he most humbly apologised for the trouble caused by his action, carried out 'without a thought of doing any harm'. These two approaches seem to have convinced the authorities to drop the affair, as at the end of the month the Government Solicitor, Mr C W Loveridge, suggested 'the most politic course would be to administer a severe warning, as proposed by the Engineering Manager, and to note the incident in the Records as proposed by the Admiral Superintendent'. Having had more than his fifteen minutes in the limelight, Mr Gilbert then dropped once more out of sight, and the incident giving rise to such agitation and over-reaction was quietly forgotten.

Commissioning and Early Trials

It is unlikely the crew of *X.1* had any knowledge of this storm in a teacup. They were busy commissioning their highly experimental ship and getting her ready for a series of trials, and they soon had troubles of their own. *X.1* commissioned on 17 December 1923 for trials, although it would not be until almost two years later (23 September 1925) that she would definitively enter service. Before she put to sea, her Official Recognition Silhouette was circulated to Navy ships and departments. The original was drawn to a scale of $\frac{1}{4}$inch = 10 feet.

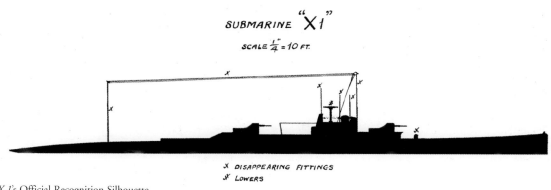

SUBMARINE "X1"

SCALE $\frac{1}{4}$" = 10 FT.

X DISAPPEARING FITTINGS
Y LOWERS

X.1's Official Recognition Silhouette.

The first engine trials

Preliminary engine trials were conducted off the Maplin Sands between 17 and 20 December 1923. At the time the twin gun mountings had not yet been fitted. Such was the anxiety that some foreign power should try to sneak a spy aboard, that the Admiralty Superintendent, Chatham, had sent an urgent telegram to the effect that: 'It is considered that a danger exists of an unauthorised person getting access to the ship by representing that he came officially from one of the firms connected with the machinery of the vessel, and it is suggested that any representative not known to the C.O. or to Dockyard Officers should always carry with them an Admiralty Pass.'

Apparently the old U-boat auxiliary engines gave trouble from the start. It was recorded that engines full ahead to full astern took 30 seconds. Full astern to full ahead took 25 seconds.

On 17 January 1924 Cdr Phillips wrote up the report of the Main Engine surface trials off the Maplin Sands which he had observed two days earlier. *X.1*'s draft forward was recorded as 16ft 3in; aft as 17ft 2in. For her first run, beginning at 08.45, the depth of water was 9 fathoms, with a falling tide, and the sea was smooth with a light wind from the southeast. The actual length of the Maplin Mile was recorded as 6,080 feet.

The results for six runs were tabulated as follows:

Between Dover and the Royal Sovereign Light Vessel, at midnight on 15 to 16 January 1924 the 24-hour full power trials on the main engines commenced. After two hours, the port main engine broke down, with a fractured piston. The piston head and skirt in No. 3 cylinder had separated and the cylinder liner was cracked. The run began again using the auxiliary engines driving the main motors, but was later abandoned as the port main motor shaft ran hot. *X.1* returned to Sheerness on her starboard main motor only, arriving about 16.00 on 16 January.

The next day the Rear Admiral Engineering came on board to examine and discuss the machinery problems. An attempt was made to continue surface running trials with the electric motors, but the port main motor's aft coupling ran hot, so the trials were abandoned. Definitive repairs would take several months, so the ship was paid off into dockyard hands in Chatham, and her crew came ashore.

Commander Philip E Phillips DSO and Bar

On board for trials in January 1924, per his report dated 17 January, P E Phillips was obviously being groomed to take over from Commander Raikes, which he did just over a year later. A further trial run in June 1924 was abandoned due to a variety of minor breakdowns, and just over a week after her crew had returned aboard, they once more found themselves back in RN barracks.

Run	Time	Speed in Knots	Means		RPM Port	RPM Stbd
1 West	4' 37"	13.00	}		295	295
2 East	3' 27½"	17.35	}15.17 }		282	276
3 West	Ran off course, compass out of adjustment		} }			
4 East	3' 27½"	17.35	}15.20	290	287
5 West	4' 19"	13.90	} }		290	286
6 East	3' 37"	16.59	} 15.24 }		292	286

The mean revolutions on the main engines over four hours, between 08.30 and 12.30, were 288. The mean IHP was calculated at 2,640 each shaft or a total shp of about 3,700.

The auxiliary engines were then tested, driving the main motors through the dynamos and the battery, at 200 revolutions. This trial had to be abandoned due to a fire in the aft superstructure. Bags of coal for the galley stoves caught fire from the heat of the auxiliary engine exhaust pipes. Coal fires, once they have been burning for some time, are always difficult to master, and this fire took forty minutes to extinguish. The cause was later ascribed to a defective supply of cooling water to the auxiliary engines' tank, and this had caused the exhaust pipes to overheat.

This time they were to spend a great deal of time on and around their giant vessel, the gunnery team receiving instruction at HMS *Excellent* and on board. Other hands were less fortunate, and spent days cleaning out the three battery tanks. The outer torpedo doors in the bow received attention, and much time was spent on pumping and blowing trials, so critical to the operation of a submersible vessel. Then they embarked on a round of route marches, boat pulling, a week's rifle practice (still referred to as 'musketry drill') and torpedo handling. There was no peace in the peacetime Navy.

Above: Lieutenant P E Phillips on the bridge of HMS/M *D.4*.

Left: On 1 November 1917, when in command of E.52 Phillips attacked *UC 63* in the Dover Straits. Running on the surface at night, his keen lookouts had spotted the German minelaying boat and Lt Phillips had fired his bow tubes. The sole enemy survivor admitted the men on the U-Boat's conning tower were passing the time in chatting among themselves rather than keeping a lookout, and they failed to spot the torpedo which sank them until it was just yards away. *UB 90*, one of the last U-boats to be lost in the First World War, fell victim to Lt Cdr Phillips in *L.12* on 16 October 1918, west of Stavanger.

Another engine trial and another major failure

In September 1924 repairs were completed, and it was decided to resume the main engine trials, *X.1* putting to sea on the 16th. For the next three days it was planned to carry out a 30-hour progressive trial, followed by a 24-hour trial with main engines only. HMS *Sabre*, a destroyer of the 'Admiralty S' class, was detailed to attend on *X.1* throughout the trials at sea. *Sabre* displaced a mere 905 tons – barely a third of the size of her charge.

On 18 September during the 30-hour progressive trial of the main engines, these units were running well up to about 290rpm, when vibration became excessive. It was not possible to exceed approximately 300rpm without developing excessive mean pressure. The loss of lubricating oil was excessive.

On completion of the 30-hour trial the 24-hour full power trial with main engines commenced. After 3¼ hours' running the starboard main engine stopped due to breakage of the governor gear, which also resulted in damage to the vertical shaft driving wheels. The port main engine ran for a further half-hour when it had to be stopped due to the fracture of the engine columns behind No. 8 cylinder. No immediate cause was apparent, and it was felt that the engine would need a complete dismantling to pinpoint the seat of the failure. The main engine evaporators failed due to their being choked with salt. It proved impossible to free the deposits *in situ*. This time, no troubles were experienced with the aluminium pistons, and there was no sign of

A vignette of *X.1* painted by a member of her proud crew.

X.1 during her trials, painted in Scheme II, awaiting the turret windshield tops. Note her single bow planes. She is possibly secured to No. 1 Buoy at Sheerness on 20 September taking on ammunition for her first gunnery trials

overheating. As Commander Raikes laconically reported on the 20th, 'After the breakdown of the main engines, the ship proceeded to Sheerness on her Auxiliary Engines, Generators and main motors.' At Sheerness she embarked ammunition, and her guns were tried out for the first time. Then she returned to Chatham. On returning to harbour the port main engine governor and timing gear was opened for examination, and it was found that all four bolts securing the timing wheels to the layshaft were fractured. This failure was ascribed to inadequate strength of these bolts. Her crew resumed their familiar exodus to RN barracks. This time the hands spent much of their time repainting the ship's casings and sides.

On 7 January 1925 Commander Phillips DSO officially joined the ship, for what was obviously a familiarisation process leading to his ultimate assumption of command. Successful diving exercises shepherded by the destroyer *Shamrock* were carried out in the vicinity of the Tongue Light Vessel. Then on 28 January 1925 Commander Raikes finally left his godchild and handed her over into the capable hands of Commander Phillips.

Views of *X.1* in Home Fleet Grey, at the time of her protracted trials.

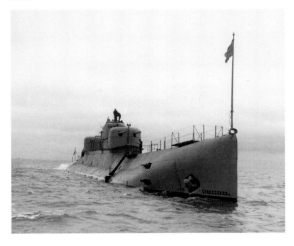

Further trials and further problems

The full power trial was resumed, this time in the company of the destroyer *Tintagel*. On 9 February the trial began at 13.40. Just 20 minutes later it was halted due to the starboard main engine No. 5 exhaust valve box fracturing at one of the holding down lugs. A spare exhaust valve box was fitted, and the trial restarted at 22.00. The main engines ran well throughout the trial, which was completed at 22.00 on 10 February.

The results obtained were:

RPM:	303.5 Starboard/303.7 Port
MEP:	135.7 Starboard/133.5 Port
BHP:	2,208 Starboard/2,169 Port
Fuel consumption:	0.459 lbs per bhp per Hour
Lubricating oil consumption:	0.55 ounces per bhp per Hour.

It was felt that the average speed, of only 14.75 knots, was affected considerably by adverse weather conditions. The revolutions and bhp were lower than anticipated being limited by the Mean Effective Pressures (MEPs) which were up to the pressures considered advisable. On examination after the trial, Nos 6 and 8 starboard cylinders were found to be leaking due to a cracked exhaust valve in No. 6 cylinder and a leak through the water jacket into the air starting passage on No. 8. Spare gear was fitted.

On 12 February the eight-hour trial using main engines and main motors combined began at 00.40. The port main engine was stopped at 01.00 due to heating of the vertical shaft drive. The oil supply was found to be partially choked. Additional lubrication was supplied to the bottom wheel. Two days later, at 06.40 the starboard main engine was stopped due to the forward coupling in the motor room heating up. The trials were abandoned, and the ship returned to Chatham for examination of the coupling. The engineering staff discussed the merits or otherwise of hand-reaming the coupling holes in place of the machining with a hand-held tool which had been used. It was felt that hand-reaming fitted the bolts much more closely and so might mitigate the effects of vibration. The point was disputed, but dropped. It is probable the engineering staff officers were treating a symptom rather than the cause, as Engineering Officer Bigwood felt the problem lay in the rigid couplings used in place of the flexible couplings favoured by the Germans.

In March 1925 further full power trials were conducted, this time using the electric main motors to assist the Engines. The first attempt on the 3rd had to be abandoned when bad weather caused the props to rear out of the water, causing the engines to race. Two days later the trial resumed, but after two hours the main engine vertical camshaft drives were causing problems once more, and the ship returned to Chatham on her auxiliary engines. On 5 March the crew disembarked for reassignment to RN barracks and the familiar round of drills and exercises. *X.1* did not put to sea again for another six months, when she carried out main engine trials off Sheerness, returning to Chatham on 16 September. For the next month she was engaged in extensive torpedo firing trials off Portsmouth.

Another attempt at full power

In the meantime new propellers had been fitted, and renewed full power trials were scheduled for February 1926. It was proposed and approved that the Engineer Captain on the Rear Admiral (S)'s staff should attend the restarted full power trials, and Engineer Captain W H Ham RN was seconded to *X.1* as an observer. Runs were undertaken on the Maplin Measured Mile. On 16 and 17 February at 200 and 250rpm the main engines performed satisfactorily.

On 18 February at 300 revolutions the main motors were put in to assist, and the main engines ran at this speed for half an hour correctly, but when full power was attempted the upper bearing of the vertical shaft of the cam shaft drive on the starboard main engine heated up within a few minutes and the trial was abandoned, 370 revolutions having been achieved on the starboard main engine and 350 on the port main engine. The main engines had been taken through their critical speed of between 310 to 340 revolutions very quickly. Repairs to the defect were immediately undertaken by the dockyardmen who were being carried on board.

On 20 February a full power trial was restarted at 12.00 with main engines at 370 revolutions for 25 minutes, when the trial had to be abandoned owing to the brushes on both forward main motors and on the starboard after main motor jumping on the commutators causing excessive sparking. A speed of 18.5 knots was achieved on this short trial run. No damage of importance was done to the main motors.

Over the following days Commander P E Phillips reported:

- *New brush springs are needed for the main motors.*
- *Leaks in the gun trunk glands are to be fixed at Chatham.*

- *The trials have proved the new propellers to be a great improvement.*
- *On the Starboard Auxiliary Engine the bolts securing the frame have become slack and the cap of No. 4 Main Bearing is fractured. This engine needed the crankshaft removed and re-aligned.*
- *The hand-turning of the Auxiliary Engines is very slow. It takes 15 minutes by hand by three men. An estimate is to be sought for the cost of providing power turning gear. A suggestion was made that some power gearing taken from withdrawn 'K' class boats may be suitable.*

On 4 March 1926 further trials were run between the Galloper Light Vessel and the Outer Gabbard. A few bolts leaked in the gun trunks. A very little water came in through both glands. The cause needed investigating but the ship was considered seaworthy for diving purposes. It was felt the cause probably lay in the joint of the rotating coaming, as the glands themselves would tighten up as the pressure increased. The main engines apparently ran satisfactorily, Engineer Bartlett recording that at 12.00 they achieved a maximum of 7,784bhp at 374rpm, giving a speed of 18.55 knots. He felt that 390 revolutions would achieve 19.2 knots. However, the trial was stopped at 16.00 due to a defective fuel suction pipe on the starboard main engine.

On return to port the machinery was carefully checked, and once more substantial damage was discovered, as detailed in a report dated 12 March 1926. Examination showed the studs securing the lay shaft bearings were fractured. The full weight of the lay shaft and cam shaft driving wheels were thus bearing on the fuel pump bearings. Under the excessive vibration this caused, the fuel suction pipe had fractured. It was felt that, if this fracture had not occurred, very serious damage would soon have resulted to the camshaft driving wheels. Examination of the latter showed considerable tearing of the faces of the teeth on the bronze wheels. There were a considerable number of small pieces of metal found in the casings. In a footnote to the main report, dated 9 May 1926, it was proposed to obtain camshaft wheels made of improved materials. One cylinder was opened up and no defects were found. There were some minor problems elsewhere. In particular the coupling between the thrust shaft and the port motor was suspect.

The ex-U-Boat auxiliary engines were another matter altogether. Close examination found the following defects:

- An exhaust valve spring on the Port Auxiliary Engine had fractured.
- Three exhaust valves were seized up.
- The webs supporting the valve seats had partly cracked through. These would need welding.
- Induction valve springs on both the Starboard and Port Auxiliary Engines were found to be broken.

The comment was made that these auxiliary engines were satisfactory for charging purposes but it was 'doubtful they will survive long runs at Full Power'.

Given the sad state of the auxiliary engines, the Engineering Report commented: 'It was thought unwise for a submarine to discharge her batteries for surface running. Rather the batteries should be rested and kept for their principal object of propelling the submarine submerged.' The Rear Admiral (S) concurred with this opinion on 19 March. To counter this Commander Phillips proposed that the propellers be recut to attain a speed only slightly less than the present full speed, using main engines alone. On 18 March the Superintending Electrical Engineer replied that no redesign of the propellers could compensate for a 25 per cent loss of the designed power.

A week later, Rear Admiral (S) W H Haggard wrote:

The Auxiliary Engines, being old, are showing signs of wear. Discharging batteries on the surface is not a good idea. As already stated, X.1 is an experiment. Originally intended to maintain 21 knots, after more than five years it appears we must be content with a certain speed of 16½ knots on main engines only. Valuable experience has probably been obtained with her development so far she must not be looked upon as a complete failure, and it is hoped that much more experience and many lessons from her torpedo and gunnery and W/T installations etcetera. It has already been established that her method of control under water, for example, is infinitely superior to that of any other submarine. It is recommended that electric drive be abandoned and that the best speed with main engines is to be accepted.

A First Foray Overseas

Despite all these problems, it was decided that *X.1* should venture out on her first long sea transit, a round trip to Gibraltar and back. Commander Phillips was entreated in his sailing orders 'In the event of seeking shelter should adverse weather be encountered it is most undesirable that you should enter a foreign port'. And this with an experimental submarine with extremely temperamental and fragile main and auxiliary engines . . .

She departed from Chatham on 2 April 1926, and took the opportunity to carry out deep diving trials *en route*, with the dramatic results recorded in Chapter 6. Gunnery trials continued during the return trip. Constructor Commander Mr A G W S Stanton went along as an observer, and on his return prepared a detailed report, elements of which have been included in previous chapters. In connection with the main engines, he recommended the construction of 12-cylinder diesel engines to produce 4,500bhp. *X.1* set out on the return journey to Chatham on 27 May 1926. Back in the UK, the forward gun trunk gaskets were replaced, and the auxiliary engines given a long refit to try to suit them for further service.

Trips to the cold waters off Scotland followed, then more machinery refits. In January 1927 *X.1* carried out satisfactory speed trials on the Maplin Measured Mile, and she was ready for her first overseas posting. It was possibly during this last refit that she began to shed her dark overcoat, like a young albatross coming to maturity, and took on her light grey on the superstructure and upper hull, in preparation for eventual posting to the Mediterranean Station.

The Mayers Scandal of 1927

X.1 featured heavily in the 'spy' scandal concerning retired Commander Colin Mayers. Not only were top-secret plans of the ship found in his possession, but it is clear that many of the techniques pioneered by *X.1*, such as the use of active Asdic, were intimately known to the Commander, and might feature in any of his planned future commercial activities.

Retired Naval Commander Colin Mayers, lately commander of the submarine *M.2*, was arrested at Euston Railway Station Hotel on the night of 16/17 March 1927, and was charged under Section 2 of the Official Secrets Act, 1911. The facts as presented to Naval Intelligence and MI5 suggested that he was in the pay of a foreign power. When Mayers' home in Barrow was searched the next day, among the cache of secret documents discovered in his possession was a plan of *X.1* and details of trials which would have involved *X.1*, such as submarine Asdic and the tactical functions of fleet submarines. Remanded at Bow Street Police Court (but surprisingly released on bail by the magistrate) Commander Mayers appeared in

the Central Criminal Court on 7 April 1927, charged with passing confidential information to the Japanese Naval Attaché in London.

Born in Demarara, British Guiana to mixed-race parents on 4 February 1891, after service with the 1st Submarine Flotilla in an old 'B' class boat, Colin Mayers had served on the Grand Fleet's staff during the Great War as an expert on the Dutch language, presumably in case fleet actions involved deliberate or accidental incursions into Dutch territorial waters, before commanding the submarines *L.11*, *M.3* and lastly *M.2*. After his attachment to the submarine base at HMS *Dolphin*, Fort Blockhouse, Commander Mayer's duties had been to train submarine crews, but also to investigate and report on all new and experimental gear fitted to submarines for trials at Fort Blockhouse. He was once described by a senior officer as 'knowing more about modern submarines than any officer in the Navy'. In a glowing reference provided by Admiral Max Horton in August 1926, Mayers was described as being called upon for advice and remarks on reports by submariners in other flotillas 'and abroad'. He had showed exceptional ability and an astonishing grasp of every technical detail, and had been entrusted with rewriting and revising the official

Commander Colin Mayers in uniform. In August 1916 the young Lt Mayers had been captain of the old submarine *B.3* of the 1st Submarine Flotilla, Firth of Forth.

Submarine Instructional Manual. His own speciality seemed to have been W/T and sonic submerged communications. Admiral Horton ended with the regret that Commander Mayers' forthcoming retirement would be a sad loss for the submarine service. For in 1926 Colin Mayers, seemingly smarting about being passed over for promotion, had contacted several firms about possible employment outside the Navy, including Vickers, Sperry of New York, Electric Boat of Groton and Mitsubishi in Japan.

Backed with his formidable references, it was simple for him to obtain a position at Messrs Vickers at Barrow in Furness. Placed on the retirement list at his own request, effective from 26 January 1927, he became an adviser to Vickers Submarine Service at the beginning of February, and moved to Barrow with his wife. It seems that he still hankered after foreign appointments, however, and this was to lead to his downfall. The day before his retirement, the Admiralty was informed from a 'delicate and reliable source' of the astounding revelation that, a fortnight earlier, Commander Goro Hara of the Japanese Naval Office in London had handed Mayers a shopping list of naval information required by the Japanese, and was prepared to pay the sum of £300 for this information.

On 12 March staff at Fort Blockhouse discovered that certain sets of official plans were missing. As Mayers had been the last person to have access to these plans his last commanding officer diplomatically wrote to him asking if he could suggest where the missing documents might be filed. In the meantime, Admiralty Intelligence and MI5 began close surveillance of the seemingly wayward ex-officer, tapping his phone line and intercepting his mail. From his passport records they circulated the following description:

Height	5 ft 5½ inches
Forehead	Broad
Eyes	Brown
Nose	Straight
Mouth	Small
Chin	Square
Complexion	Clear
Face	Full

Distinguishing features Small scar on nose and slight enlargement of rim of left ear.

After his arrest, the search of a cupboard in Mayers' home revealed that he had retained the following official Naval documents relating to:

- Plans of *X.1* and the patrol submarine *O.1*

- Counterattacks of A/S vessels
- Submarine Asdic
- Tactical functions of Fleet Submarines
- Submarine automatic inboard ventilating gear trials
- Manuals for four different submarines
- Rough plans for the US submarine *V.2*
- Blueprints of the *M.3*, *H.23*, *L.25*, *H.27* and *L.12*
- Plans to convert the *M.3* to a minelayer
- Photos of *U 126*
- Proposals on converting the M-Class boats to carry seaplanes [i.e. the eventual *M.2*]
- A small plan of a one-man submarine christened the 'Devastator'[5]
- Copy of a memo on possible conversion of *M.3* to carry midget submarines[6]
- Reports on tactics etc
- Lecture Notes
- Assorted documents market 'SECRET' or 'CONFIDENTIAL' [and, most damningly,]
- Two sheets of paper with the names of Japanese officers.

The phone taps and mail interceptions had thrown up a healthy – or perhaps unhealthy – correspondence between Commander Mayers and his Japanese contacts in London. It was discovered that he had continued his close friendship with Petty Officer Goldsmith at Fort Blockhouse, obviously with the intent that the P/O would continue to feed him the latest information on submarine developments. Finally, a brother officer admitted that he had found a large file of papers which Mayers had planned to have despatched to himself at Vickers in Barrow, containing copies of papers on submarine Asdic installations and experiments. The officer had burned the documents. When he told Mayers of this by phone, the Commander had seemed mightily relieved. His fate would seem to have been sealed. The authorities would be cheated of their prey, however.

At his trial, Commander Mayers was adamant that he in no way intended to pass on secret information to an existing or potential hostile country. With only circumstantial evidence on this, the Admiralty withdrew the more serious charges, and Mayer was charged with minor offences under Section 2 of the Official Secrets Act, i.e. unlawfully retaining documents which he was no longer permitted to possess. In the circumstances it was impossible for Mayers to do anything but admit to such a charge. He was found guilty, and was bound over.

The inevitable upshot was that Vickers immediately divested themselves of the services of the errant Commander. He was later to consider legal action against them for breach of contract, but the PRO file has no record of the eventual outcome of this, besides the Admiralty's wish to avoid further embarrassing publicity on the matter. It seems that the Commander still hankered after continuing his training and support function, and he offered his services as an instructor for submariners at the Imperial Japanese Naval College. In this he was to be sadly disappointed, as Commander Hara was doubtful: the Japanese 'took advice only from the Germans and the Italians, but never from the British on submarines'. Finally, on 24 April 1930 the Japanese Admiralty would – as reported by the same 'delicate and reliable source' – turn him down as unsuitable for the post of instructor 'for reasons of character'. In the meantime the Vice President of the Electric Boat Company confirmed that a note from 'the late unlamented Mayers' had been 'duly filed in the waste paper basket'. His confiscated passports (for some reason he had two – itself a cause for suspicion) were only returned after Commander Mayers had given his word of honour to the Admiralty to the effect that he would not pass on secret information to foreigners. Presumably he then fled the country which had accused him of preparing to betray it. The last, pathetic, note on file concerning ex-Commander Mayers is a memo dated 16 December 1943 from Captain Courtney Young of MI5, reporting that 'Mayers is employed by Metro-Goldwyn-Mayer as an electrician and lives in Los Angeles'. There was, he continued, no evidence of espionage or related activities and he had had no connection with Squadron Leader Rutland.[7] We are left to ponder on a possible family connection which gave poor old misguided Mayers this humble employment. And so he disappears from our story, and from history.

Analysis of the Mayers affair

The tragedy of the affair, which impacted heaviest of all on Mayers himself, is that apparently he was not driven by malicious intent, but merely trying to make a living outside the Navy, which he felt had passed him over, by employing his considerable talents elsewhere. Submariners – who by their very nature were independently-minded, and with a wartime tradition of individuality in dress habits and discipline matters – could be their own worst enemies when it came to advancement inside the peace-time 'Silent Service'.

Mayers' skills lay in technical analysis and training. His Staff duties would not have given him much opportunity to indulge in heroic actions. As a 'technical expert' he may have been one of the last victims of the traditional Navy suspicion of 'engineering' officers. He could be accused of naivety in offering his services to the Japanese, but it is by no means clear how much the newly-perceived threat posed by the Japanese Navy in the eyes of the Admiralty had actually percolated down to officers of Mayers' rank. Historical precedents would all have pointed to the fact that the Japanese Navy continued to be one of our closest allies.[8]

After flirting disastrously with French designs, the nascent Imperial Japanese Navy had firmly decided to copy the British model. We supplied them with their successful early pre-dreadnoughts, which had given them the edge over Russia, and the heavy guns of their first home-built dreadnoughts. The magnificent *Kongo* class battlecruisers were a Vickers design, and the lead ship was built in Barrow. In the early 1920s, retired Lieutenant Commander Frederick Bernard Fowler, RNAS, who pre-war had founded the Eastbourne Aviation Company, led a team of pilot instructors to teach the Japanese Navy how, of all things, to operate torpedo bombers and fighters from the deck of their first aircraft carrier, the diminutive *Hosho*. The design of *Hosho* herself owed much to the plans of HMS *Argus* which the Royal Navy had freely provided to Admiral Iida in 1918.[9] And up until the early 1930s, the Imperial Japanese Navy continued to be the best customer for rangefinders produced by Barr & Stroud. Little surprise, then, that Mayers innocently believed he could continue to work with the Japanese.

Unfortunately, reading between the lines, it is possible that Mayers' non-British parentage may have gone against him, at a period when class distinctions were still set in stone, especially within the main state institutions. Police investigations discovered that one of his parents was Dutch, although the file showed a question mark as to which one. By his name it is likely that it was his father who was of Dutch nationality, probably from neighbouring Dutch Guyana. It is likely he was also Jewish.

The ultimate outcome of the Mayers affair was that Britain lost the services of a talented submarine officer, who might have made a significant impact on the tactics of the Submarine Service during the Second World War, especially if he had had the opportunity to examine the tactics and attitudes of Japanese submariners through close working contact with them.

CHAPTER 8

A Cushy Billet

Meanwhile, at the end of January 1927, *X.1* joined the Mediterranean Fleet. Her log entries describe the daily life of a peacetime submarine crew, continually practising for war.

X.1 had been conceived at a time when the Admiralty was planning for a possible future confrontation with the growing power of Japan in the Far East. The natural location for the giant raider would therefore have been the China Station. However, in 1921, there was no large dockyard in the Far East which could tend to the giant's teething problems with her propulsion units, never mind the host of other experimental features built into her. The China Station itself was centred on Shanghai, and repair facilities there would not be secure. Furthermore, the experimental vessel would be under the constant gaze of the Japanese contingent in the international port. An alternative would have been Kowloon Dockyard in Hong Kong, but the security problems would still exist, and the Yard's capabilities were restricted. At the beginning of the 1920s, Jellicoe and Beatty had both argued for a substantial naval base at Singapore, and in 1923 Stanley Baldwin's government gave the go-ahead for work to start. Two years later the base naval personnel counted just seven officers and twenty-five ratings, and in the cash-strapped 1920s and 1930s progress was painfully slow. The Singapore naval base was not to be officially opened until 1 February 1938, more than a year after *X.1* had been cut up for scrap.

Given the experimental nature of *X.1*'s troublesome main engines, it was logical to base her where she could exert maximum influence on potentially hostile powers, while remaining close to established repair facilities with a strong engineering tradition. The natural choice was thus Malta. The restricted waters of the Mediterranean, however, would be a difficult war station for the large *X.1*, which was highly visible from the air in the clear water, even without the drawback of leaving a trail of fuel oil from her leaking external tanks. On the other hand, the Mediterranean Fleet was where the legendary Nasmith had done such good work with the deck gun of *E.11* in the Black Sea, so *X.1* would carry on the traditions of one of the men who was instrumental in her design as a surface combatant.

The second major drawback, of course, was that the full cost of maintaining, nursing and repairing the giant submarine fell squarely on the peacetime resources of the Mediterranean Fleet, as can be read between the lines of the damning memo by Captain (S) Thompson which was to effectively cut short *X.1*'s service career.

'Why not our own magazine'

It was at Gibraltar that the first edition of the 'MAGAZINE. *X.1*.' was produced, probably between 11 and 19 March 1927, while the ship was in for repairs to the starboard generator and the main engines.

As her anonymous editor proudly proclaimed: 'We have our own canteen and our own library. We give our own sports, whist drives, dances, socials, we

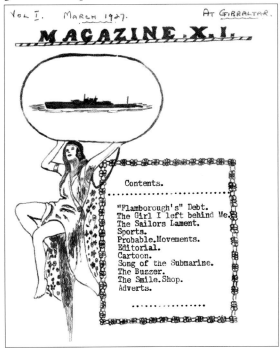

The front cover, with the contents typed in black, which would seem to have been added after printing. Note the charming vignette of the ship held aloft by a maiden dressed in what was a most alluring outfit for the time.

enjoy amenities that no other submarine anywhere has ever possessed. We have our own barber, boot repairer, and lemonade purveyor. Why not our own magazine.' One copy of this document is carefully preserved in the archives of the Submarine Museum in Gosport. The typescript is complemented by hand drawings and handwritten articles, and the whole has been run off on a standard mimeograph machine, in the attractive purple-blue ink of the period.

"Flamborough's" Debt.

Extracts from the magazine

For a day and a night and a day the wind howled without intermission from the grey south east. For twenty hours the seas, cold, green and bearded with smoking white, had pounded the 'Flamborough's' glistening flank. Those seas had had a thousand miles of gale-swept ocean in which to gather speed for they had come straight from ice-sheathed tusks of Kerguelen to hurl themselves at last upon the cowering cargo tramp. Severn miles to loo'ard they crashed in awesome thunder on the rock-rimmed coast of South Africa, a coast that is ever eager to receive what the sea has conquered and to make that conquest sure. A lee shore it is when the black south-easter blows, a lee shore that offers no refuge for the sea victims for over six hundred miles, and the bones of half a hundred good ships bear witness to its hate.

The mate clung tightly to the rail of the bridge, his skinned figure glittering like a statue in the watery sunlight. His face was lashed and smarting with the agony of the spindrifts hail, he was soaked to the skin in spite of his oilskins, and his wrists showed angrily red with salt water boils under the rasping cuffs.

The 'Flamborough' wallowed heavily in the trough, for her course took her almost beam-on to the seas, turning her gleaming decks to the foe and disappearing to the bridge in the bursting cloud of foam that heralded the next monster.

It struck her as might a giants hand, and the whole hull boomed like a colossal drum through the blow, the well-decks were buried under surging green now, and the high foc'sle loomed dimly through the driving sprey like a guant, scarred rock. For a moment evan the yelling of the wind was eclipsed by the thunder of that avalanche; the, Miraculously as it seemed, the embattled ship shook herself free of the tons of water that had burst aboard her and climbed stiffly to the summit of her would'be destroyer.

'Flamborough' was a dogged fighter, as the brass plate down on the well-deck told. Both skipper and mate had been of the company who had fought with her, in the days when the ragged red duster aft had given place to the white ensign of the Royal Navy. She had been a ship of hidden terror then, spoken of in whispers by white faced officer's who watched from the Zeebrugge Mole for submarines which did not return.

'Develish weather!' howled the mate. 'Wind fifty an hour at least!'.

'Why dosent—old man—turn—face it?' yelled the newcomer.

'Better ask him! Charthouse—been there—since yesterday evening'.

'She'll-roll-over-if-this-goes-on!'

'Must-keep-on-course! not-enough-coal-otherwise!' cried the mate. 'Chief-says-just-make-East-London-as-it-is! We'er edging-into it as much-as we dare-now! G'bye-an' don't get-washed-overboard' Course North eighty six east by compass. Seals point abeam distance severn miles and there's nothing in sight'. He was wrong there was something in sight. A lean grey something that rose and fell helplessly in the hollow of the sea disappearing intermittently in a bath of foam, above which reeled her drunken masts and whitened funnels, a rag of sail on her main mast and the wire that stretched, bar-taut, from her bows, told all that they needed to know.

'She's broken down and riding to a sea anchor! Trying to keep her head to the wind, but its too much for her', said the mate, and swore. 'She's blowing away like a hay barge. My God, She's a warship! . . . Hear that?.'

Dulled by the distant and much choked by the wind, there came to their ears the unmistakable boom of a gun.

Leaving the junior in charge the mate went for the skipper, whom he met on the ladder, a flimsy sheet of paper in his hand. He drew the mate into the shelter of the chart house. His face was expressionless and hard as iron beneath the dripping peak of his cap.

'She's the 'Acacia' he snapped. 'Broke her tail shaft and drifting ashore'.

'She's wired for tugs from Port Elizabeth, and two of them are coming full speed. But they cant be here under eighteen hours. She'll be in the breakers in three, the way she's going! and we'er the only ship within a hundred miles of her. With her tow rope aboard of her and full steam on we might just hold our own till the tugs come-but it'll use all our coal! that is unless the wind drops-and if it comes to this-if we send her our hawser, we'er committing suicide. If we don't she's done for! '

They stood in silence now, staring out over the cruel expance to where the little warship fought her hopeless battle. Their minds had slipped back five years, to a certain grim scene off the Irish coast. the 'Flamborough' lay with her nose cocked drunkenly in the air and the sea's breaking around the four inch gun on the poop, whence arose a thinning cordite haze. Two hundred yards away whitening patch of scum on the water spoke of a shot that had gone well home and a submarine that had fired her last torpedo. The story is known wherever seamen forgather, and I need not detail it here. You who would know more may find it in the records. There you will read of how the men of the Q ship 'Flamborough', allowing themselves to be torpedoed in order to lure the enemy to share their end, waited while the ship sank beneath them and the seas washed higher and higher around their consealed guns, till at last the U boat broke surface and the prize was their's. You will read of the messgae that came to Queen Town-the most pathetic message that the ether has ever carried to an anxious Admiral:

'Flamborough slowly sinking.
Regretfully wishes you good-bye'.

Read on, and you will know that she did not sink, that a little sloop-of-war put out at top speed and reached her just in time to tow her to safety. The sloops name does not appear in the records, But on the memories of the two in the wheelhouse it was inscribed in letters of fire. A sinking ship, in those days of relentless underseas war, was nothing less than a death trap to her sisters, for there might be other submarines lying in wait for those who would come to her help. But 'Acacia' had not hesitated. Was 'Flamborough' to hesitate now?.

'Mr Ellis!' ordered the Captain tonelessly. 'get up the six inch hawser and stand by with a heaving line, Im going down to her'.

'Very good, Sir', replied the mate, and clattered down the ladder to carry the death warrant into effect. He knew, and the skipper knew, that by the time the tugs arrived the 'Flamborough's' bunkers would be swept clean; he knew, as clearly as though the moment had already come, that unless the wind

moderated those tugs could not save them both, and that no other help could arrive in time. But a warship was more valuable to the Empire than a tramp, and she carried a hundred men to their twenty four. It was a simple sum in proportion, and the gale yelled the answer in howling malice as he stumbled aft along the streaming decks.

Dawn broke in a grey and pitiless sky, bringing no comfort to the weary officers who clustered on the 'Acacia's' bridge. The Captain turned his leaden eyes to the tumultuous breakers astern, and he saw that were very close.

To windward sky held no promise; rather it seemed that the forces of the gale had redoubled. The 'Flamborough' toiled at her hawser, pounding into the grey backs and crumbling them into milky ruin about her. The wreckage of them, borne down by the wind, crashed upon the warships bridge screens like endless shrapnel. From her funnel poured smoke of her labour, and presently the 'Acacia's' captain saw that sparks and an occasional glow of flame had begun to mingle with that smoke. It arrested his puzzled attention, for neither coal nor oil fuel could wholly account for this. Then it was that the 1st Lieutenant, his glass levelled on the dim seen hull ahead, Exclaimed in sudden excitement.

'They are cutting away their boats, Sir;' he cried, and the Captain, following his gaze with his own glass. saw that he spoke the truth. The davits on the 'Flamborough's' port side were empty, and he who had seen the 'Kent's' boats burned at the Falklands, knew only too well the meaning. He ran down the ladder to the wireless, and two minutes later the tramp's Captain frowned at the message in his hand.

'Please explain why you are burning your boats' it ran. 'If short of coal cast off hawser, or I shall do so myself'. For the Navy, too, knew how to die.

Back came the answer at once.

'Flamborough' to 'Acacia' Did you cast off when you towed us into Queentown ? Am burning wood to increase pressure. Am not short of coal, tugs in sight!'

'The Flamborough' good lord, of course! This was the ship that . . .

Meanwhile, had he but known it, the tramps bunkers had been empty for an hour, and the furnaces had swallowed all but the last of the boats. Every other available bit of woodwork had gone into them long before, and the axes rang now on their sole remaining chance of life.

'Here comes the tugs, thank God!' breathed the warship's Captain, and presently 'Acacia' took the pull of their hawser and began to move forward at last, plucked from the very breakers. 'Flamborough' loomed mistily to port now, her wire reeled in and her blunt bows bursting a path through the bluaked seas as, exuberant in her new freedom, She fought steadily off-shore. But even as her grimy flag dipped in answer to the sloops salute, the smoke thinned at her funnel and the beat of her propeller slackened . . . slackened . . .

Her anchors plunged away dragging their chains roaring through the hawse pipes. But no anchor that was ever made could have held her without the help of the engines in such a gale and on such a shore, and they gave her but a momentary respite.

On her bridge a tight lipped officer swung over his telegraph lever and the bells below clanged their last message.

Then, wearily, as though her long struggle had tired her beyond the telling, she fell away into the trough, and around her helpless balk the seas leaped in boiling triumph. One moment she loomed in full sight, high and black and ugly yet with a strange and stately dignity, as a giant comber lifted her. Then she vanished forever in the spouting chaos that rimmed the cowering land.

'Flamborough's' Debt was paid.

The Sailor's Lament: To the Tune of
The Bonny Banks of Loch Lomon

❖ ❖ ❖ ❖ ❖

On yon little table, and on yon oily deck,
On the lockers each side of the table,
Where I and my messmates dished up the dirty crocks
And we must scrub out the blooming doss house.

Oh! you can scrub the mess shelf
And I'll do the floor
And perhaps you'll be finished before me.
But I don't really care; cos' its our stand off next,
And all of the messmates come before C.

Twas there I was wrong because the ship went to sea
And my watch next day had the morning
So it was my turn again, to scrub the doss house clean,
And I've not yet given over moaning.

Oh! you can clean the tin gear and
And I'll clean the brass
Knives, forks, and spoons we'll do last.
I'd as soon be on the dole, as in this oily home
So thank ————— we never joined for ever.

❖ ❖ ❖ ❖ ❖

Mary had a little watch
    Fixed upon her garter
        And always when I asked the time
            She knew what I was ar'ter.

SPORTS.

Football
Matches played since arrival
at Gibraltar ....

'X.1.' v Princess Margaret	Lost 5. 4.
'X.1.' v H.M.S. Conquest	Won 2. 1.
'X.1.' & K.26 v Submarines	Draw 0. 0.
'X.1.' & K.26 v Submarines	Won 0. 1.
'X.1.' v R.A.M.C.	Lost 3. 2.

Inter Part Matches.   Ist Flotilla.

Gunnery v Stokers Draw 1. 1.   Post : Pro 2. 1.
Torpedo v Daymen 1. 6.

The Following Matches are arranged

Saturday 19th Submarines v Conquest & Cyclops
Monday 21st Submarines v R.E.s

The ship is expected to leave Gibraltar on March 29th. Arriving at Philipeville on April 1st.

Note on Philipeville

<u>Historical note.</u> The site of Philipeville is that of Rasicade, once a phenician town, but founded by the Romans in 45.B.C. It belonged to Rome under the Empire, and was known as the Colonia Veneria Rusicade. The chief harbour in the Gulf formerly Astharet, but was superseded by that of Philipeville constructed 1860, at a cost of 20 Million francs.

<u>The Town</u> Situated on the Gulf of Stora about 2 kilos. from the mouth of the Safsaf. It is surrounded by a wall now of very little military value. The business part of the town is situated in a valley. The sides of which are covered with flats and villas. The population is 24,000 of which 17,000 are Europeans.

<u>Exchange.</u> It is usual to arrange for one of the banks to send off a representative to the ships. Money should only be changed in this manner or at a bank.

<u>Hotels.</u> Foy, Grand, and Hotel de France, all situated on the Place de Marque. None of them are very good.

<u>Theatre.</u> The theatre Municipal in the Place de Commerce stands on the site of a Roman Temple. It is used as a cinema.

In compiling this magazine the editor hopes to secure the support of all on board 'X.1.' In addition to ourselves it is hoped that several copies will be disposed of amongst the 1st Flotilla and posibly other ships. The intrinsic value may be negligible; but it is the only magazine that has ever been printed (apologis) in a submarine. It is unique and as a curio may find a limited circulation outside the ship. continuance of publication, however will need to rest entirely on the circulation and support maintained aboard.

We have our own canteen and our own library. We give our own sports, whist drives, dances, socials, we enjoy amenities that no other submarine anywhere has ever posessed. We have our own barber, boot repairer, and lemonade purveyor .

'Why not our own magazine.

Whatever our present expressed or private opinions there is probably not one amongst us who in later years will not be proud of his association with 'X.1.'

The prestage of the ship now will at that time mean something to you (us). Will you increase that prestage ? You can assist<u>by purchasing your own</u> copy of this magazine on the first of each month, and deposit your efforts, which should be original and kept private at the ship's office for perusal by

The Editor

THE SONG OF THE SUBMARINE.

I can rise, I can dip, Im a wonderful ship,
    And I roll like a tub in a gale;
I can quiver and plunge, and leak like a sponge;
    I can slither and slide like a whale.
     . . . .
I can glide like a bird, but its rather absurd
    to see me sedately at anchor;
For once on a trip they allow me to 'lip'
    and I chased a U boat and sank her.
     . . . .
I can twist like a screw, and between me and you,
    My slewing is said to be 'some'
Just a turn of the rudder, a tremble, a shudder,
    and round a sharp corner Ive come.
     . . . .
In a Battle ship hunt I am well to the front,
    And Im not very slow to begin it;
You can take it from me, when we fight on the sea,
    Submarines are sure to be in it.

Magistrate (*to Prisoner,*): 'Whats your name, your occupation, and what are you charged with?.
Prisoner: 'My name is Sparks. I am an electrician by trade. And I am charged with battery.'
Magistrate: 'Constable, put this man in a dry cell!

THE BUZZER.

It's a secret – and he keeps it!
Yet he lets a hint or two
Come falling like the truth
Of a place thats far away.

. . . .

And it isn't quite of Chatham
And it isn't quite of here.
And we've never yet discovered
Where the story had its truth.

. . . .

And it isn't quite of Philipeville.
And it isn't quite of Malta.
But the thoughts of all are one
In the thoughts of going Home.

. . . .

The Buzz has swept the messdeck
In a hush we pause to hear
There's something Big with promise
In the message that we hear!

❖ ❖ ❖ ❖ ❖

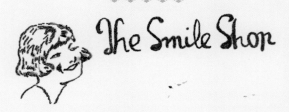

The Smile Shop

Sufficient Unto The Day

'Boy' think of the future'.

'I cant; its my girls Birthday, And I must think of the Present'.

. . . .

With gracefull feet, a damsel sweet,
Was tripping the light fantastic.
All at once Tore for the Dressing room Door,
You can never Trust elastic.

. . . .

Mother (suspiciously) 'Has Tommy been singing that horrid song the Boys have taught him ?'

Daughter (regretfully): No, the little wretch would only whistle it.'

. . . .

'She screamed for help when I kissed her.'

'What did you do ?'

'Gave her a second helping.'

. . . .

Equal to her requirements

<u>Old Lady</u> : 'He's certainly a very fine parrot, But does he swear ?'
<u>Bird Seller</u> 'No Lady, but he's a Bright Bird and He'd learn in no time.

. . . .

IT was growing Dark, And the small boy, groping on the pavement, Was weeping noisily. An Old man came along and paused in dismay.

'Dear, Dear, What is all this about.
Whats the trouble, My Boy. He asked the Youngster kindly.

'Ive gone and lost one penny!' Wailed the Boy.

The Old Man felt in his pocket.

'Well Don't cry ' he said. 'If you Don't find it before Dark, Here's a match .'

. . . .

Little Girl : 'Please is this the lost property office.'

Clerk : 'Yes'.

Little Girl : Well Im lost.

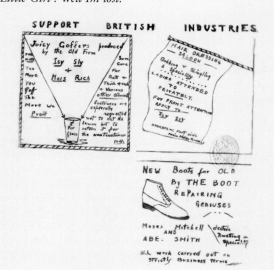

Mediterranean Service

Trips around the bay, hands to bathe, water polo, picnic parties, plus the usual *X.1* routine of cleaning, painting, chipping, and exercise! The crew of *X.1* were certainly among the best trained, and certainly the fittest, members of the Submarine Service. They had had multiple opportunities to carry out complex and regular training drills, and they spent a great deal of their time on route marches, rifle practice, boat pulling and the like, to say nothing of cleaning, scraping and painting their large vessel. Not for them the cramped environment of long sea voyages in the small submarines of the day . . .

X.1's cruises in the Med

A key part of *X.1*'s duties in the Mediterranean was 'showing the flag'. The ship's Log lists the seven voyages she undertook on that station, but we are left to fill in the gaps in the log with the usual routine of shore leave, watch duty and tourist excursions. Two important elements were showing solidarity with the Greeks who felt vulnerable after their trouncing by the renascent power of Turkey in the early 1920s, and keeping a watch on the growing naval strength of Italy. On 29 March 1927 *X.1* left Gibraltar for her new base at Malta. *En route* she called at Philippeville in French North Africa, an event mentioned in the very first edition of the ship's magazine.

Her first specific cruise began on 6 July 1927 when she departed Malta for a tour of the Greek islands. She arrived in Navarino Bay the next day and the crew spread awnings for a stay of four days. On 11 July she departed for Port Iero, Mitylene, and the 26th found her at Salonika, where Commander Allen took over from Captain Phillips. On 29 July she sailed under her new captain to Skiathos, narrowly missed colliding with the German freighter *Stettin*, and arrived on 1 August. Just three days later she was *en route* for Argostoli and a longer stay. On 10 August her crew took part in a regatta, and on the 16th they departed for Malta, arriving on the 18th.

Her third cruise began on 13 March 1928, when she sailed for Gibraltar for exercises and the shale oil trials. On 5 April she departed for Valencia, arriving two days later. The crew landed for shore leave in Valencia on 8 April, and six days later she left Valencia for Malta.

Cruise number four saw a return to the Greek islands. On 14 July 1928 she left Malta for Suda Bay in Crete, to take part in the regatta organised for the 16th. On 19 July she sailed for Spezzia, and on 31 July she departed for Skiathos. The final port of call

Lieutenant Gilbert H Roberts joined *X.1* for gunnery trials in the Mediterranean in early 1927. When attached to HMS *Glowworm* of the Danube Flotilla, he had taken the parole of ex-Emperor Karl of Austria-Hungary during his journey into exile. He was an established gunnery specialist who at HMS *Excellent* had helped write manuals for the new 16in and 8in guns coming into service. Before joining *X.1* Gilbert Roberts had taken a submarine CO's course at Fort Dolphin to prepare himself for his new environment. Invalided out of the Service in 1939 suffering from TB, he was recalled to the Navy in March 1940 and went on to establish the Western Approaches Tactical Unit, which was a crucial element in defeating Hitler's U-boats. The photo shows Captain Roberts in 1943 at the Tactical School, Liverpool.

was Argostoli, where she arrived on 11 August, and her crew took part in a two-day regatta on the 16th and 17th of that month. Five days later she sailed for Malta.

Her fifth trip took in several Italian ports. She sailed from Malta on 7 September 1928 and arrived in Messina the following day. Eight days later she sailed for Brindisi where she arrived on 18 September for a five day stay. The 25th saw her at Ancona, and on 3 October she sailed for the Brioni Isles. October 12th saw her *en route* for Fiume, the port which had

X.1 secured alongside the faithful depot ship HMS *Cyclops*. *Cyclops*, the former merchantman SS *Indiabarrah*, bought by the Navy in 1905 for use as a fleet repair ship, became a submarine depot ship in 1922. Displacing 11,300 tons, she could make 11.75 knots and was armed with six 4in guns. Surviving the Second World War, she would be sold for scrap in 1947.

A fuzzy snapshot showing *X.1* tied up alongside her smaller compatriots. The last of the giant 'K' class boats, the much-modified *K.26*, is to starboard, dwarfed by the cruiser, and five small 'L' class boats to port.

Tied up alongside *Cyclops*, with the bulbous bow of *K.26* to port.

Relaxing on board HMS *Cyclops*, summer 1927.

Another view of *Cyclops*, from the bow, showing her flock.

Returning to Grand Harbour (showing the paint scheme she carried for return to the UK).

A map of the Mediterranean in 1929, produced by one of *X.1.*'s potential opponents, the Italians.

Bathing at Malta with two *Queen Elizabeth* class battleships in the distance. The crew are using *L.27*'s stern as a pier.

Bathing Beauties show a leg.

Bathing at Pembroke Ranges, Malta.

briefly been seized by the fascist forces of the Italian poet and patriot Gabriele D'Annunzio, and a week later she departed for Giavosa. On 28 October her Italian trip ended when she left for Malta, arriving two days later.

Her sixth cruise took her back to the Greek islands. On 27 June 1929 she left Malta for sea exercises, then two days later headed for Dragamesti. On 10 July she sailed for Navarino, but early in the morning of the 11th she suffered an explosion in No 1 Battery which necessitated her return to Malta the following day.

Her last Mediterranean excursion took place during her return journey to the UK via Gibraltar beginning on 8 March 1930. After exercises with *Cyclops* in Pollensa Bay, on 11 March she called at Pollensa and Palma. Only one picture of members of *X.1*'s crew at play in the Med survives. However, one of the submarines which accompanied her on several cruises was *L.27*, whose crew contained a keen amateur photographer. He has left us an anonymous record of submariners at play during peacetime.

Practising for war

On those apparently rare occasions when *X.1*'s main engines and all the other essential equipment were running well – and sometimes when one or both main engines were actually unserviceable – *X.1*'s crew went to war, in peacetime . . .

During her brief Mediterranean service she carried out:

- Ten anti-ship attacks on battleships, aircraft carriers and destroyers, firing a total of forty-one practice torpedoes.
- Thirty-six mock attacks on ships, both submerged torpedo and gun-action from submerged.
- Sixteen surface full-calibre shoots, including shore bombardment.
- Twenty-one surface sub-calibre shoots, including shore bombardment.
- Eleven anti-submarine and submerged exercises with destroyers, submarines and her own depot ship.
- Three Lewis gun/anti-aircraft shoots

To say nothing of the dozens of drills for the above actions, carried out without involving any other vessels or actual firing of torpedoes or guns.

This total represented far more 'actions' than most

Typical tourist shots:

The Sea Mill at Argostoli.

Locals at Skiathos.

Lt Commander Philip Ruck-Keene of *X.1* and Simpson at Skiathos.

Wine, Women and Song. A happy picnic group,

Regatta at Argostoli or Suda Bay.

Finish of the cutter race, seen from the bridge of *L.27* showing *L.20*'s conning tower and 4in gun

Boats coming alongside after the cutter race. In the left foreground is a collapsible dinghy as carried by submarines. On the horizon to the right is the aircraft carrier HMS *Hermes*.

L.27's cutter crew await a tow.

Mock gun attack dated September 1928. *X.1* carried out two surface gun attacks on *Cyclops*, on the 18th and 24th of that month. Note the raised DCT roof.

Submerging after mock gun attack. Despite the propaganda to fool the Japanese, *X.1* could get her hull under in thirty seconds.

Commander Allen had made a name for himself in *E.42* in 1918. On 23 April Scheer sortied the High Seas Fleet preceded by the battle-cruisers, to attack the Scandinavian convoys. *En route* the battlecruiser *Moltke* suffered a major breakdown: one of her starboard propellers became detached, the blades of the driving turbine overspeeded and stripped, and an auxiliary condenser was damaged when a flywheel disintegrated. Scheer called off the sortie, and while *Moltke*'s crew effected emergency repairs, she was taken in tow by *Oldenburg*. Scheer broke radio silence, and among the RN units directed to intercept them was *E.42*, commanded by Lt Allen, who was ordered to take up position in the northern section of the Bight. The crew on *Moltke* had confined the damage and had slipped the tow when the line of warships passed in front of *E.42*. Allen fired four torpedoes at the German ships and the last torpedo hit the unfortunate *Moltke*. Despite taking on more than 2,100 tons of water, and with her port turbines running under water, the crippled battlecruiser succeeded in limping into the Jade, while German destroyers unsuccessfully counter-attacked *E.42* for an hour. Undamaged, she returned to Harwich. Awarded the DSO for this heroic action, in July 1921 Allen became Commanding Officer of *L.18* in the 2nd Submarine Flotilla. On 13 June 1926 he was promoted to the rank of Commander, and took charge of *X.1* on 28 July 1927 at Salonika. Commander Allen retired from the Navy in July 1953 and was made a 'Retired Captain' at that date.

Commander Allen and his crew at Malta.

submarines actually undertook in several active tours of duty during wartime. Little wonder that her systems and machinery gave more than their share of problems. The poor vessel was being well-used. Unfortunately her prototypical layout and non-standard equipment did mean that she was far more costly to maintain than one of the old 'clockwork mice', the Great War 'L' class boats, and even most of them were thoroughly worn out long before the Second World War began.

Distinguished Visitors

Such was the draw of 'the world's largest submarine' that even when locked up in drydock she was popular with a string of distinguished visitors . . .

Born on 18 November 1882, and after service in the Imperial Russian Navy, the German Baltic Landewehr, and the Latvian General Staff, Captain Archibalds Grafs Keizerlings (left) became Commander of the Naval Squadron in June 1924. Promoted Admiral in 1927, he retired in September 1931. On the Soviet takeover of the Baltic States in 1939, Admiral Keizerlings moved to Germany, where he passed away on 5 December 1951. Captain Keizerlings' command included the tiny submarines *Ronis* and *Spidola*, built in French shipyards the previous year. Displacing only 390 tons on the surface they were among the smallest submarines in service in 1927. The two broad gold bands on his sleeve, plus the two gold diamonds, may indicate his recent promotion to the rank of Admiral.

Archibalds Grafs Keizerlings

The photograph of Admiral Keizerlings, Commander of the Latvian Navy, with Commander Allen – who was to assume command of *X.1* the following month – is dated June 1927. At the time the *X.1* was in

dockyard hands, in No 1 Dock, Dockyard Creek for a refit including the main and auxiliary engines, the underwater fittings and batteries.

From the buttonholes worn by both officers it is possible the occasion was the visit of the Duke and Duchess of York, who left Malta on board HMS *Renown* on 20 June. *X.1*'s Log makes no mention of Keizerlings coming on board, but it is likely that he was shown Commander Allen's next command from the dockside. The photograph was probably taken on board her depot ship, *Cyclops*. The original caption states that the photograph was taken 'after lunch (fourteen vodkas!)'.

HM The King of Spain

On 9 November 1927 the ship was in dockyard hands in Malta for a refit. The Log entry states:

10.15   H M The King of Spain visited the ship.
10.40   H M The King of Spain left the ship.

The Monarch in question was King Alfonso XIII, and to mark the event he presented the ship's company with a signed photograph of himself wearing naval uniform. This photograph is a treasured part of the Gosport Submarine Museum's collection of papers on *X.1*.

High-ranking Admiralty visitors

At first, Their Lordships took a paternal interest in their troubled child. *X.1* was regularly inspected and put through her paces by the Captain (S) of her current Flotilla. In addition she received on board the following important visitors:

On 15 July 1924, in No 1 Basin, Chatham Dockyard, the Civil Lord of the Admiralty visited the ship. Two days later it was the turn of the First Lord of the Admiralty.

Five months later, on 7 December 1924, the First Lord returned, accompanied by the Commander-in-Chief, Nore for what the Log notes was an 'unofficial visit'.

On 19 and 20 January 1925 Rear Admiral (S) visited her at Portsmouth. The next day the C-in-C came on board, followed by the Blockhouse Training Class. Three days later it was the turn of the Admiralty Superintendent. On 28 January 1925 the Rear Admiral (S) was on board during exercises.

On 23 February she was back at Chatham, where the C-in-C visited the ship. Two months later, on 13 April and again on 23 April, the C-in-C returned for two further 'unofficial' visits.

To H. M. Submarine · X.1.
Alfonso
Malta · Nov 1927

Like his father Alfonso XII, Alfonso XIII was keen on sailing his royal yacht, the *Giralda*, and it is likely that such a voyage entailed a stop at Malta. The Spanish Navy had worked closely with British shipbuilders ever since 1908, when Vickers, Armstrong and John Brown had secured a 24.5 per cent share in the shipbuilding and armaments firm SECN (Sociedad Española de Construcion Naval) set up to rebuild Spain's shattered navy after the disastrous Spanish-American War. British Naval Architect Sir Phillip Watts designed four large cruisers for Spain based on RN designs. It was therefore natural for Alfonso to wish to view current Royal Navy vessels such as *X.1*. Alfonso XIII, King of Spain between 1886 and 1931, was born on 17 May 1886, the posthumous son and successor of Alfonso XII. His mother, Maria Christina (1858–1929), was regent until 1902. In 1906, Alfonso married Princess Victoria Eugénie of Battenberg, granddaughter of Queen Victoria of Great Britain. An attempt was made to kill the couple on their wedding day, the first of several assassination attempts. Although Alfonso enjoyed some personal popularity, the monarchy was threatened by social unrest in the newly industrialised areas, by Catalan agitation for autonomy, by dissatisfaction with the constant fighting in Morocco, and by the rise of socialism and anarchism. After keeping Spain out of the First World War, in 1923 Alfonso, who was disillusioned with parliamentary government, supported General Miguel Primo de Rivera's establishment of a military dictatorship. With Primo de Rivera's fall from power in 1930, discontent was running high in the country. The municipal elections of 1931 showed an overwhelming republican majority, so on 14 April 1931 Alfonso declared he would suspend the exercise of royal power, and went into exile. A few weeks before his death in Rome he renounced his claim to the throne in favour of his third son, Juan. Alfonso passed away on 28 February 1941.

Sir David Beatty was born in Howbeck, Cheshire on 17 January 1871, and entered the Royal Navy at the age of 13, serving with distinction in the Sudan from 1896–8 and in China during the Boxer Rising of 1900; even at this early stage Beatty marked himself out as a bold, aggressive officer, succeeding in becoming the youngest officer for a century to achieve flag rank at the age of thirty-nine, the last such being Lord Nelson. He was made Rear Admiral in 1910 and served as Winston Churchill's Naval Secretary from 1911–13, after which he was appointed Commander of the Grand Fleet's Battlecruiser Squadron in 1913, a position he held at the outbreak of war in August 1914. Intended as a swift-moving reconnoitring force, the squadron's role was to locate enemy forces and to subsequently hold them at bay until the arrival of the main force. Following up success at Heligoland Bight in the first month of the war, Beatty scored a further victory with an action at Dogger Bank in January 1915. Beatty's name however is most associated with the greatest naval action of modern times, at Jutland in May 1916. His dashing leadership of the battlecruisers, which both inflicted and suffered grievous damage, led the German High Seas Fleet into the jaws of the British Grand Fleet. Their eventual narrow escape might be classed as a tactical victory, but on the strategic level the High Seas Fleet would never again dare to confront the Grand Fleet in a major surface action. With Sir John Jellicoe, in overall command of the action at Jutland, blamed for the lack of a decisive British success, the dashing Beatty was seen by some as his natural successor. He was accordingly appointed Commander of the Grand Fleet in November 1916 following Jellicoe's promotion to First Sea Lord, although his rapid promotion caused controversy within the Royal Navy. Admiral Beatty was a firm supporter of the convoy system which helped defeat the U-boat offensive. Following the armistice declaration, on 21 November 1918 Beatty received the surrender of the German High Fleet, off the coast of Scotland at Rosyth. The tally comprised ninety ships plus a further eighty-seven U-boats. Appointed First Sea Lord in 1919 and awarded a grant of £100,000 by Parliament in recognition of his services, Beatty held the position until his retirement in 1927. Subsequently granted a peerage, Earl David Beatty died on 11 March 1936. Among many other honours from a grateful country, he had a variety of gooseberry named after him.

On 11 September the C-in-C was back, this time in an official capacity, and twelve days later the Admiralty Superintendent of Chatham Dockyard carried out an inspection.

When she called at Invergordon in October 1926, the C-in-C Atlantic Fleet visited her, on the 11th.

A month later, the C-in-C Portsmouth visited her when she sailed there, on 10 November. Two days later, the Rear Admiral (S) called.

On 4 May of the following year, at Malta, it was the turn of the C-in-C Mediterranean Fleet. Nine days later, *X.1* carried out a full-calibre shore bombardment under the gaze of the Vice Admiral commanding the 1st Battle Squadron.

The Log Entry for 21 February 1928 notes laconically 'Admiral of the Fleet Earl Beatty visited the ship.'

On 20 August 1928 she hosted the Vice Admiral, First Cruiser Squadron, and demonstrated a surface gun action from submerged. Later the same day she took an RAF party from HMS *Courageous* for a demonstration dive.

Back home again, on 5 May 1930 the First and Third Sea Lords inspected her at Chatham. Her last VIP visitor was to be the Rear Admiral (S), who inspected her on 13 October 1930.

No doubt many of these visits were prompted by curiosity and a desire to see the world's largest submarine. However, it is probable that in 1930 the Sea Lords and Rear Admiral (S) wanted to see for themselves the state of the ship, following the recommendation by George P Thompson, Captain (S) commanding her Flotilla at Malta, that *X.1* should be reduced to reserve status.

CHAPTER 9

A Litany of Failures

Only four days after arriving in the Mediterranean, *X.1* suffered an explosion in a battery while carrying out underwater speed trials. Repairs cannot have taken very long, as just five days later she resumed the trials. It was to be only the first of a new series of misadventures.

Her starboard generator and, once again, the main engines received repairs at Gibraltar in March 1927, before she departed for Philippeville, no doubt to the relief of the long-suffering dockyard workmen at Gib. In May 1927, her rangefinder was lifted out at Somerset Wharf in French Creek, Malta. The reason is not specified in the log, but earlier that month she had carried out a series of full-calibre and sub-calibre shoots, including a shore bombardment. It could be that the instrument required calibrating or routine servicing. The next time the rangefinder is mentioned in the log entries was 27 February 1929, when it was stated as being remounted. Several photographs taken during this period show *X.1* without it, even though she was carrying out regular full-calibre and sub-calibre shoots during the same period. Perhaps it was classed as too secret to expose to prying eyes on *X.1*'s regular summer cruises? A month later she was in dockyard hands for a refit of the main and auxiliary engines, her underwater fittings and batteries, in Number 1 Dock.

All went well for two months, but leading the 'L' class boats in formation off Skiathos for exercises, the port main engine broke down with a bent con rod. She continued on the power of her starboard main engine and carried out the exercises. Securing alongside *Cyclops* at Argostoli, long notice was given for repairs to the port main engine, but the log notes that these in fact took only two days!

On her return to Malta, on 5 September 1927, she once more entered Number 1 Dock for further refits, and remained in dockyard hands until 28 December. On 6 January 1928 *X.1* proceeded to sea for full-power trials, interrupted for three days by a minor fault with the port main motor. When the trials recommenced, after only three minutes at full power the vertical drive to the overhead camshaft on the starboard main engine broke down. This is the failure which has been reported as *X.1* fracturing a

propeller shaft, which in fact never happened. Back in dockyard hands until 12 March 1928, she sailed for Gibraltar the next day.

The Shale Oil Experiment

On one of the few occasions when *X.1* was behaving herself, as the Mediterranean Fleet's 'experimental' submarine, she was used as a pilot vessel for a seemingly bizarre project.

Her log laconically records that on 22 March 1928, at Gibraltar, *X.1* received 22 tons of shale oil from the oiler *Prestol*. As a major strategic initiative in case of wartime petroleum shortages, this must have been regarded as a sensitive subject. Accordingly, there are no remaining records of the trials in *X.1*, other than a scathing comment by Engineer Lieutenant Bigwood, who was horrified at the attempt to run *X.1*'s diesel engines on what he described as 'boiler fuel'. It was patently not a success and was never repeated.

Oil shale is a relatively hard rock, called marl, containing an organic substance which is chiefly kerogen. The rock itself can be burned directly in a power plant as fossil fuel, as is done in Estonia. Properly processed, the kerogen contained in the rock can be converted into a substance similar to petroleum. To do this it needs to be heated to a high temperature, which converts the organic material to a liquid. Further processing produces an oil of medium-grade quality. By-products include significant quantities of sulphur and other valuable minerals. The heat and water required for the refining process are substantial, and given the availability of cheaper crude oil, shale oil is produced in only small quantities. It remains, however, a significant source of fossil fuel for the time when crude oil begins to run out. During the early 1900s the US Geological Survey studied the enormous reserves of oil shale in the USA, and the government established the Naval Petroleum and Oil Shale Reserves, which for much of the twentieth century served as a contingent source of fuel for the nation's military – primarily as a reserve supply of fuel oil for naval vessels.

The British Empire contained significant reserves

X.1 exercising diving stations in Grand Harbour, Malta.

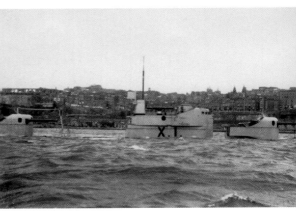

Such a straightforward exercise would have struck terror into the crew of a 'K' boat.

of oil shale, notably in Canada and Australia, so it was natural that the Admiralty would seek to test shale oil as a substitute fuel source. Despite *X.1*'s 'experimental' nature, however, it would seem to have been overly optimistic to expect her temperamental main diesels to be the most appropriate test-bed for this oil. Of lower quality than diesel oil, shale oil is of a higher viscosity than the bunker fuel oil fed to steam boilers, but for best results it still needs pre-heating to allow it to be pumped and injected. In the event, there was to be no shortage of higher-quality petroleum oil, and the experiments, fortunately for *X.1*'s hard-pressed engine room staff, were short-lived.

More Mishaps

In May 1928 *X.1* was back in dockyard hands yet again, refitting the vertical drive to the port main engine. The only mishap noted was the loss overboard of one motor boat starting handle, a minor incident compared with the saga of the main engines and the tribulations yet to come, but a major inconvenience for anyone trying to start the motor boat!

She remained in dockyard hands until 16 June, and three days later *X.1* proceeded to sea for exercises with the fleet. These were cut short when she needed to return to harbour for a new generator. Then the crew had to fit a spare armature to the midships air compressor. Two days later it was felt advisable to check on all her compressors, and she went back into dockyard hands for a full refit of her aft and midships air compressor sets. Repairs took until 13 July, following which *X.1* sailed to rejoin the Fleet at Suda

Bay, arriving just in time for her crew to take part in the regatta. A propeller shaft sealing gland received attention from divers at Messina on 15 September, but the next day *X.1* sailed for Brindisi with the Fleet. A minor defect in the port main engine *en route* to Malta on 29 October 1928 was fixed while she proceeded on the power of her starboard main engine.

As if all the previous work was not enough, *X.1* paid off into dockyard hands on 3 December 1928 for her annual refit, in Number 1 Dock, Malta. The work continued until the middle of March 1929, when she proceeded to sea for main engine trials on the Measured Mile. To the obvious disappointment of all, on examination of the overhead camshaft drives on both main engines, the ball bearing races were found to have broken, and the gear teeth were badly worn. She proceeded to sea for one 'gun action from submerged' exercise, probably to try to impress Captain George P Thompson, the new Commanding Officer, Submarines, Malta, who had taken control the previous December. Then she went straight back into dockyard hands. Despite her log noting that 'Owing to main engines being out of action the ship is not considered "ready for sea"', that did not stop her crew from leaving harbour on her electric drive to carry out a director test, underwater manoeuvres and two sub-calibre shoots.

In May 1929 she was moved to No. 8 Dockyard Creek, only to have the crankshaft on the old German port auxiliary engine break on the 21st. June 1929 saw engine trials, then the round of gun and torpedo firing resumed, with a cruise to Marsa Scirocco to join in a Fleet exercise off Navarino. Only two weeks

This is possibly the infamous dive of 6 January 1930, when the aft trim tank burst, necessitating a hurried return to the surface. Despite the mishap, *X.1* DID rise again, unlike too many of her older siblings . . .

later, however, *X.1* suffered a second battery explosion, and returned in disgrace to Malta. The Log noted that 127lbs of meat taken on board to feed the crew during their cruise was condemned and 'thrown overboard'. No environmental protesters in those days! Repairs took until 2 December. During the repairs the dockyard workers managed to run *X.1* aground off Conspicua Slips, which necessitated a further five days' repair work on the outer torpedo doors in the bows.

Finally on 4 January 1930 *X.1* put to sea again, but disaster struck only two days later. Carrying out diving trials to check on her trim following repairs, the aft trimming tank burst open. *X.1* blew her main ballast and surfaced safely, but apart from the ruptured tank, damage had been caused to the aft bulkhead and the steering and aft hydroplane controls. She was towed into No. 4 dock in disgrace. Repairs took until 6 March 1930, when *X.1* proceeded to sea for trials and to swing the compass. The next time she sailed from Malta she was never to return.

Deliberate Misinformation

In the meantime, on 27 August 1929 George P Thompson, Captain (S) 1st Submarine Flotilla HMS *Dolphin* at Malta, wrote a damning report on *X.1* to the Commander-in-Chief, Mediterranean Station.

'Proposals Regarding the Future Employment of H M Submarine X.1'
An overview of the vessel since her commissioning in December 1925.

X.1 was constructed not to represent any definitive type of submersible, but as an experimental vessel to prove that a submarine can be of great size yet still retain good submerged qualities.

In this she has amply justified her construction: submerged control is good at all speeds.

Time to dive to periscope depth of 2 minutes 30 seconds is very satisfactory.

But the Main Engine Vertical Drive has continually given trouble, and except on one occasion on 1 January 1927 X.1 has never been able to reach full power without a breakdown.

Now after replacement of the old drive after failure of a new spur wheel gearing, the safe speed of X.1 is between 12 and 13 knots. This speed is not to be exceeded until a new design of camshaft drive can be fitted.

Because of frequent breakdowns X.1 has been in dockyard hands for a total period of well over 2 years of the 3½ years in commission.

Already £33,000 has been spent in dockyard labour since joining the Mediterranean Fleet in 1927.

X.1 has been ready for sea for only five weeks.

The German engines are bad due to their age.

Her experimental layout has meant that some joints etc. require major dismantling work just to reach them.

Her living conditions are unsatisfactory, very cramped. All complain of the heat in the Mediterranean.

Point 8. It is recommended she be placed in reserve at the end of the financial year.

Furthermore, if the action in Paragraph 8 above were combined with an announcement to the world that X.1 had been a failure and was being withdrawn from service, it might well have the effect of discouraging other Powers, such as France and the USA (who are now building or about to build similar types) and thus serve our country's best interests from a broad point of view.

Her top hamper and great size make her unsuitable for operations with the Fleet.

X.1's true function is that of a cruiser submarine to which type she approximates. But this type would appear to be one of which the British Empire stands least in need. We should look to control communications with surface ships. The enemy will use cruiser escorts for his trade and transports.

The tactics of engaging surface targets is unsound in principle, although her armament and the small part of the pressure hull exposed above the surface should occasionally enable her to achieve useful results.

I suggest she be used as an experiment to produce fleet minelayer and other submarine types.

This was a truly damning assessment of the ship: £33,000 spent on repairs – which had still not guaranteed her reliable operation – must have represented a significant proportion of his total maintenance budget for the whole Flotilla. In other words, the Mediterranean Station was being expected to fund development work – and this at a time of worldwide economic depression.

Captain Thompson's comment about the crew suffering from excessive heat on the Mediterranean Station hit on the second most frequently mentioned problem with *X.1*, after her engines. The French prototype *Surcouf* suffered similar problems, but in her case the situation was partly alleviated by the extension of the magazine cooling arrangements to provide air-conditioning in the crew's quarters. It is not inconceivable that *X.1* could have been fitted with an air-conditioning plant if she had survived long enough to be refitted in a US Naval Yard, to say nothing of an ice-cream making machine for use in the Pacific.

Here was the deliberate misinformation which was supposed to dissuade our naval rivals from copying the features of *X.1*. In this way, even through the manner of her demise, *X.1* would be of service to her country – in dissuading potential enemies. Unfortunately neither France not the USA – nor, of course, the Power not mentioned, Japan – would ultimately be dissuaded by this subterfuge.[1]

It appears that Captain Thompson had given no thought to the suitability of *X.1* for service with the Far Eastern Fleet, where her size and top hamper would not have been such an obvious handicap as in the shallower waters of the land-locked Mediterranean. However, if her habitability was bad by Mediterranean standards, her crew would have suffered even more in the Tropics. His assessment of the British Empire's need for surface ships to control trade was feasible as long as it held overall local superiority. The tragedy of a war on several fronts severely weakening the Royal Navy's presence off Malaya in late 1941, would have been impossible for him to foresee. He gives away his submariner nature by the strange comment '*X.1*'s true function is that of a cruiser submarine to which type she approximates', since in fact she represented THE archetypical 'cruiser' submarine. Again, Captain Thompson's penultimate comment about *X.1*'s surface gunnery capabilities seems oddly contradictory. But he was an experienced submarine officer brought up in the tradition of the 'Silent Service' which held that a submarine's best defence was her invisibility, and her best tactic, stealth. *X.1*'s dramatic *modus operandi* in surface action was thus anathema to him.

X.1 photographed from an aircraft off Malta, showing what a huge target she made from the air. Before the inadequacies of Italian level bombers were so cruelly revealed, Captain (S) had always to consider the threat of Mussolini's air arm. In the glassy calm seas of the Mediterranean, a patrolling aircraft could make out the shape of a submerged submarine at depths of as much as 100ft. On HMS/M *Upholder*'s second patrol on 12 February 1941, the crew noticed to their discomfort that the forward casing some 25ft below the surface was clearly visible through the periscope.

Preparing to be taken in tow by *Cyclops* as an exercise on 10 March 1930, and flying the appropriate signal of two black balls ('Not Under Control'). Although this scenario was a very real possibility at any moment given the fragility of *X.1*'s main engines, in fact she still had two other means of propulsion at her captain's disposal, so towing was never needed.

Close alongside *Cyclops*, with the towing cable – sent over by line-throwing gun – being made fast. Her faithful depot ship was about to escort *X.1* on her way out of the Mediterranean and back to home waters. Perhaps the exercise was timely . . .

Home in Disgrace

Before leaving Malta, *X.1* had one last annoying trick to play on the long-suffering dockyard maties – she lost overboard her wardroom galley funnel (the H-shaped pipe seen in photos of 'A' turret), and divers had to suit up and go down to recover it.

The faithful *Cyclops* shepherded her safely as far as Gibraltar, from whence *X.1* departed the Mediterranean on 25 March 1930 for the UK, never to return. She sighted the Eddystone at 09.15 on 29 March, stopped for a day in Plymouth, called via Sheerness to unload her ammunition, and finally arrived home in Chatham, where she had first taken to the water, on 15.40 on the afternoon of 1 April 1930. An appropriate date . . . The crew were given Foreign Service Leave and the empty ship remained secured alongside the North Wall of No. 2 Basin.

June of 1930 saw a wedding, and July a funeral, the latter for the unfortunate Leading Seaman Coleman who died as a result of a motorcycle accident. Towards the end of July Commander Baraclough took over from Commander Allen, who eighteen months later would countersign *X.1*'s Log entries in his capacity as Commander (S) of the Reserve Half Flotilla. The new commander's first task was to prepare the ship for her appearance in the Navy Week the following month.

But first a mundane duty in connection with the Navy Day beckoned. On 30 July a scale model of the 'County' class cruiser HMS *Kent*, built by the firm of Basset-Lowke, secured alongside *X.1* to charge the batteries of the model. Powered by electric motors, the scale *Kent* would be manned by naval personnel during a display which would include blank firing her guns. The overnight battery charge was completed the following morning, and at 12.30 members of the Press visited *X.1* to prepare their write-ups on the monster submarine.

Revealed at Last

Chatham Navy Week opened on Saturday 2 August and continued the following Monday. *X.1* was open to visitors every afternoon of the week, the final visitors leaving at 19.20 the following Saturday. Following up on the event, the *Illustrated London News* of 23 August 1930 came up with a cutaway drawing, headed 'A Cruiser of the Depths – Details of Britain's Giant "Hush-Hush" Submarine Revealed for the First Time'.

The basic configuration is reasonably well depicted, but the hull is drawn foreshortened and far

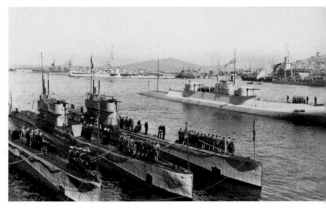

X.1 arrives at Gibraltar. Note the mixture of Home Fleet ships in dark grey finish and those from the Mediterranean Fleet in pale grey.

less slender than in the real *X.1*, the deck area is far too wide, and the turret tops are squared off. The Asdic turret forward of 'A' turret has been omitted, and the gunnery director tower is described as a 'conning tower'. The artist has depicted the secret rangefinder as a simple surface type with no periscopic fittings inside the control room. Obviously, if our previously secret submarine was to be publically declared a failure, some details were still to be kept under wraps. At about the same time, the postcard firm of Salmon issued a colour postcard of *X.1*, also lacking the Asdic housing. Here is a much-simplified *X.1* ploughing through the waves and keeping station with a cruiser in Home Fleet dark grey. Behind the scenes, however, all was far from well with the 'new' star.

Salmon Postcard Ref 3683.

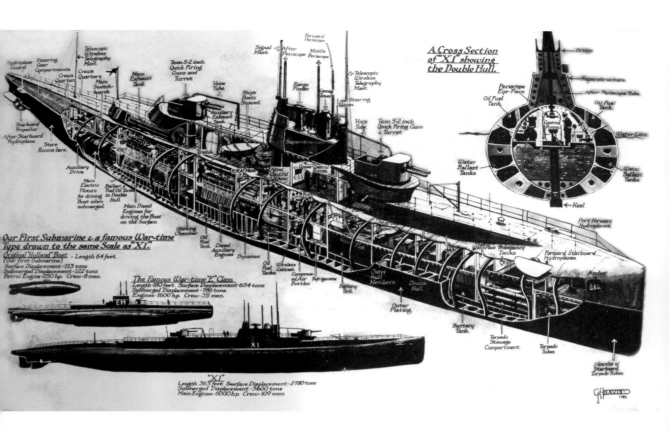

FOR COMPARISON WITH THE DRAWINGS OF THE BRITISH SUBMARINE "CRUISER" "X I" (GIVEN ON A DOUBLE-PAGE IN THIS NUMBER): THE U.S.S. "V 5" GOING AT SEVENTEEN KNOTS DURING HER RECENT TRIALS—A PORT-SIDE VIEW.

It is interesting to compare this new giant submarine "cruiser" of the United States Navy, illustrated above, with the British "X I," of whose interior construction we give, on pages 332 and 333 in this number, the first detail drawings sanctioned by the Admiralty. A note supplied with the above photographs of her new American rival states: "The 'V 5,' one of the largest submarines of her type in the world, recently underwent her speed tests and trials off Provincetown, Massachusetts. The 'V 5' has a cruising radius of 15,000 miles, carries 7 officers and 81 men, and could stay at sea 60 days without refuelling or calling at a port for supplies. She will go through her official Navy trials in October." The following particulars of this and a sister ship are given in the latest edition of Jane's "Fighting Ships" under the heading of Fleet Submarines—Cruiser Type, of the U.S. Navy: "'V 5' (1929), 'V 6' (1929). Laid down at Portsmouth and Mare Island Navy Yards, respectively, May 10 and August 2, 1927. Machinery for both vessels at New York Navy Yard. Displacement: 2760—3960 (standard) tons. Dimensions: 371 by 33½ by 16 ft. Diesels of 5447 S.H.P.—17 knots. Estimated cost: hull and machinery, $5,350,000; armament, $1,020,000." The American "V" boats are nearly as large as the French submarine "Surcouf," now being completed at Cherbourg. Our "X I," however, was the pioneer of submersible cruisers.

Comparisons with the latest US Navy cruiser submarine.

CHAPTER 10

An Unlucky Fall

After the exposure and excitement of Navy Week, not much happened in the life of *X.1* until October 1930, when she conducted basin trials and then went to sea for engine trials. Annoyingly, both main engines developed minor faults which caused her return to Sheerness on the starboard main engine. In November the familiar sequence of events was repeated: basin trials followed by putting to sea for main engine trials. This time one of the old German auxiliary engines overheated, followed inevitably by overheating of the camshaft drive on the starboard main engine.

More dockyard work was followed by more basin and sea trials. Then on 3 February 1931 *X.1* suffered a major breakdown. During main engine trials off Sheerness the No 3 piston in the port main engine temporarily seized and caused serious damage to the cylinder. The ship's log notes an 'explosion' in the crankcase, but it is more likely that the con rod and possibly the piston broke through the casing. In any case there were some injuries among the engine room staff, though luckily no fatalities. *X.1* returned to Chatham in disgrace on her remaining main engine and the port main motor, for another round of repairs, and an enquiry into the accident took place three days later.

A steady stream of crew members began transferring to other duties, until only a third of the original crew remained. It was during this period that a fire broke out on board. It started in the port main engine room and took nearly 25 minutes to extinguish. More dockyard repairs and basin trials followed, and on 30 March 1931 *X.1* sailed for Portsmouth and her date with destiny.

On 9 April Lt Commander Besant took over from Commander Baraclough, and the veteran vessel settled into a comfortable round of inaction, which dramatically ended on 26 June. At 11.00 on that fateful day *X.1* was moved into No 15 Dry Dock in Portsmouth. It appears that the dockyard mateys used insufficient shoring to prop up the giant submarine. The pumps were started to empty the basin when the lunch break siren sounded and the workmen all decamped to the canteen, and then the inevitable happened. At around 13.30 *X.1* fell over on her port

Securing *X.1* before reflooding the dock to try to right her.

side, assuming a 40-degree list.[1] Acid spilt from the batteries was the cause of a fire in the auxiliary engine room, which took 45 minutes to extinguish.

The damage looked worse than it was. When refloated she retained a slight list to port, but the main hull was watertight. The outer plating of the port compensating and fuel tanks was buckled in several places, and this would have been the ideal opportunity to replace the riveted fuel tanks with welded ones. But the damage was the last straw for an

Views of the unfortunate *X.1* fallen over in the flooded No 15 Drydock, Portsmouth, before the efforts of her crew to bring the ship upright.

X.1 from ahead.

X.1 from astern, after refloating but before righting. A 'County' class heavy cruiser is in the next dock.

exasperated Admiralty. The 'old' ship, aged beyond her years, had been a drain on scant resources for too long, and this was the straw that finally broke the camel's back.

Decline into Oblivion

The giant submarine was once more an embarrassment. She was not repaired, and in December 1933 she was laid up in Fareham Creek, Portsmouth. The 'living death' of the Care and Maintenance Routine followed. The sad details are evident from her final Log entries.

On 15 November 1935 a revised Scrapping and Replacement Programme was published. It proposed that *X.1* be scrapped immediately should the international tonnage limitation on submarines be removed.

On 8 April 1936, with *X.1* already in dockyard control, an official request to scrap her was made.

In October 1936 *X.1* was struck from the active list.

In December 1936, without any publicity, she was towed quietly to Thos Ward's yard at Milford Haven and was broken up. No recognisable part of her has ever come to light, and no photos of her demise exist.

CHAPTER 11

Only the British were Fooled

Captain (S) Thompson's hopes fell on deaf ears abroad. The US Navy, the French Marine and the Imperial Japanese Navy were busy building and proving submarine cruisers of their own, and thus the 'black propaganda' served only to fool the British public into believing that large submarines, and especially cruiser submarines, were 'A Bad Thing', and not worth persevering with.

United States' Cruiser Submarines

Narwhal class

These boats were the US versions of the U-Cruisers, as their hull design shows. Designed for long-range

ocean cruising, they were as long as a *Fletcher* class destroyer, but with a greater displacement: 2,915 tons on the surface. Submerged they displaced all of 4,050 tons, of which no less than 732 tons was accounted for by their fuel load. This gave the boats a maximum range of 18,000 nautical miles at the modest speed of 8 knots, falling to 8,500 miles at 15 knots. Underwater they could manage only 8 knots maximum, about average for these monster craft, at which speed the batteries were exhausted in only 10 miles. Their main gun armament consisted of two 6in/53-calibre weapons in single mounts fore and aft of the conning tower. *Nautilus* and *Narwhal* were easily identifiable by the raised midship gundeck surrounding the conning tower. Four single 21in

Nautilus at sea in the 1930s, showing what an enormous target she represented for any prowling aircraft. Like *X.1*, her sole anti-aircraft armament at the time was two rifle-calibre machine guns.

USS *Nautilus* Specifications

Displacement: 2,987 tons surfaced/ 3,960 tons submerged

Length: 371ft; **Beam:** 33ft 3in; **Draught:** 16ft 11in

Twin screws: MAN diesels 5,450bhp = 17 knots surfaced/ electric motors 2,540hp = 8 knots submerged

Range: 18,000nm @ 8 knots surfaced/10nm @ 8 knots submerged

2 x 6in/53-cal guns; 2 x .30 cal machine guns;

6 x 21in torpedo tubes (4 forward, 2 aft) with 20 torpedoes

1942: Plus 4 external 21in tubes (2 forward, 2 aft) with 4 torpedoes

Crew: 90

Narwhal on trials. This photograph appeared in the *Illustrated London News* at the time the *X.1* was revealed to the British public.

Narwhal in the Navy Yard at Pearl Harbor during the Japanese attack. Her machine gunners claimed a share in destroying at least one Japanese plane. Ironically, they were kept sleeping at action stations the previous night as a punishment for a recent misdemeanour, and were therefore among the first navy gunners in action that fateful morning.

Nautilus in drydock at Pearl Harbor in March 1942, being modernised, dwarfing the adjacent fleet boat of the *Grampus* class.

external torpedo tubes were fitted beneath this deck in 1942.

USS *Nautilus* was built at the Mare Island Navy Yard, California. Commissioned in July 1930 as USS *V-6* (SC-2), she was renamed *Nautilus* in February 1931 and redesignated SS-168 in July 1931. Prior to the Second World War, she mainly operated in the Pacific, based at Pearl Harbor and at San Diego. Modernised between July 1941 and April 1942, her first war patrol included the Battle of Midway, during which she attacked a Japanese aircraft carrier that was at that time identified as *Soryu* but was more probably *Kaga*. Later during the same patrol, while off Japan she sank the destroyer *Yamakaze*. The photograph of the last moments of *Yamakaze* slipping beneath the waves, taken through her periscope, remains one of the classic images of the Pacific submarine campaign. *Nautilus* then began an active career as a transport submarine, a role for which her large size made her especially useful. She landed Marines to raid Makin Island, in the Gilbert Islands in August 1942; put scouts ashore at Attu, in the Aleutians, in May 1943; again landed Marines in the Gilberts in November 1943 and carried out several missions in the Philippines area in May 1944–January 1945. During this time *Nautilus* also conducted anti-shipping and reconnaissance patrols off Japan, in the Central Pacific and in the Solomons area, sinking and damaging several Japanese ships. Ordered home after her fourteenth war patrol, she arrived at Philadelphia, Pennsylvania, in May 1945 and was decommissioned the following month. *Nautilus* was sold for scrapping in November 1945.

Narwhal used her deck guns in anger for the first time on 15 July 1942, bombarding an airfield on Matsuwa. She created a diversion to allow three fleet submarines to exit the Sea of Japan. In December 1942 she shelled and sank a small Japanese freighter. Her next shore bombardment mission was to fire fifty-six shells at petrol storage facilities on Bula Ceram Island. During her return to base she shelled a Japanese barge and a tanker.

In all *Narwhal* conducted fifteen successful war patrols and engaged in nine secret drop and pickup missions in the occupied Philippine Islands. After her eventful career she was decommissioned on 23 April 1945 and sold for scrap the following month. Her two 6in deck guns are mounted on permanent display at the Submarine Base in Groton, Connecticut.

USS *Argonaut*

A third large vessel, *Argonaut* (the former *V-4*), was built as a minelayer. Combining the features of both the U-Cruiser *U 140* and the ocean minelayer *U 117*, *Argonaut* featured the high flat-sided bow design of the U-Cruisers, but her minelaying equipment was of

Argonaut at sea.

a novel type: sixty mines were stored in two aft compartments, and hydraulically-powered worm shafts moved the mines into rotating cages. These offered the mines up to the inner doors of her stern minelaying tubes. The system was complex and noisy underwater, and very slow in operation, so that the resulting minefield tended to become widely spread out. It did, however, avoid the often fatal problem inherent in the German method of carrying mines in vertical tubes, and releasing them *beneath* the submarine. The Royal Navy had come to the same conclusion with their conversion of *M.3* to a minelayer, which led to the successful *Porpoise* class used in the Second World War.

Originally planned to have a cylindrical hangar for a floatplane mounted horizontally on deck, as pioneered with *S-1*, she never carried an aircraft. The

US Navy's method of launching and recovering aircraft was novel, in that the parent boat would submerge to awash to allow the plane to float off and on the deck. The use of such a small and necessarily flimsy aircraft, without a catapult launch system, would have strictly limited its usefulness in all but the most glassy of calm seas – as the Kriegsmarine discovered with their small folding Arado prototypes.

Argonaut participated with *Nautilus* in the Makin Island raid in August 1942. Whilst in transit to Brisbane, on 10 January 1943 *Argonaut* was directed to attack a heavily-defended Japanese convoy of five freighters. Firing torpedoes in a submerged attack, her presence was signalled by the premature explosion of one torpedo, which drew down the wrath of two *Kagero* class destroyers, the *Isokaze* and the *Maikaze*, which easily detected and bracketed their huge

Photograph of *Argonaut* showing her stern minelaying doors.

USS *Argonaut* Specifications
Displacement: 2,710 tons surfaced/4,164 tons submerged
Length: 381ft; **Beam:** 33ft 9in; **Draught:** 15ft 3in
Twin screws: Diesels 3,175bhp = 13 knots surfaced /electric motors 2,400hp = 8 knots submerged
Range: 18,000nm @ 8 knots surfaced/10nm @ 8 knots submerged
2 x 6in/53 cal guns; 2 x .30 cal machine guns;
4 x 21in torpedo tubes (all forward) with 16 torpedoes
Mines: 60
Crew: 89

opponent with depth charges. A passing US Army aircraft witnessed her demise, when her bow was blown to the surface by exploding depth charges, and the two destroyers, armed with six 5in guns apiece, pumped shells into her until she sank back out of control and was lost. Her commander did not attempt to surface and use his two 6in deck guns to shoot it out with her attackers. Possessing none of the sophisticated gunnery equipment installed in *X.1*, her chances of success against two modern fleet destroyers on the surface would have been minimal.

The *X.1* (and also the Type XI U-Cruisers) carried a heavy surface armament to defeat warships, but only in order to remove escorts from around vulnerable convoys. The American boats, while carrying a heavy gun armament, seemed to suffer from a lack of well-defined user strategy, and appeared as simply copies of the Great War U-Cruisers, without any attack strategy having been devised for their wartime employment. This was all too evident during the Second World War, when the three boats were employed on transport missions, including the giant minelayer *Argonaut*, which never laid a single mine in anger.

Surcouf

Surcouf was the cruiser submarine which most closely approached the design of *X.1*, in that she was the only other submarine to carry a heavy surface armament in a revolving twin turret.[1] The ultimate corsair submarine, as her name implied,[2] in her day she was the largest submarine in the world.

At the beginning of the 1920s, France was anxious to regain her status as a major naval power. During the Great War French industry had concentrated on meeting the needs of the Army, facing the Imperial German forces on land. The Navy was forced to cancel most of its planned major warships, and many vessels already in service were laid up and had their armament removed for land service. In a similar way to the British Admiralty, the French Navy saw the large submarine as a means of restoring France's naval hegemony at a time of financial cutbacks and international disarmament initiatives. *Surcouf* was planned as the first of six sister-ships, to form two divisions of three submarines each. Each division would attack surface ships – presumably convoyed merchant vessels with naval escorts – in a triangle formation, surfacing simultaneously. However, as with *X.1 Surcouf* was to remain a sole prototype, due no doubt in part to the operational difficulties which would have become obvious during her trials, but also because France in the 1930s had other more pressing financial priorities.[3]

The starting point for *Surcouf* was the last design of large German U-Cruisers to be commissioned. In common with the other naval powers considering cruiser submarines, the French had noted the performance of the large German U-Cruisers of the *Deutschland* type. As part of her war reparations, France had obtained *U 139*, the only boat of her class to have actually carried out a war patrol – under the command of the U-boat ace von Arnaud de la Perrière – and renamed her *Halbronn*. The French Navy was impressed by her armament, armour protection and surface stability. However, they failed to draw lessons from the fact that *U 139* remained a very clumsy submarine underwater. One further drawback the French were soon to discover was the fragility of *U 139*'s diesel engines, which never produced more than 50 per cent of their nominal rated horsepower. In this way their experience paralleled the Royal Navy's problems with the auxiliary engines of *X.1*.

Multi-gun designs with two twin and even triple turrets were proposed. However, the design of the submarine which was ultimately to emerge as *Surcouf*

Surcouf in her initial form, before the conning tower was raised, sporting the attractive Dark Prussian Blue finish for overseas submarines which she received in 1933.

owed much to the parallel concept of a 'bombardment submarine' – to be used against enemy communications and shore installations as much as against opposing vessels. In this respect *Surcouf* had more in common with the 'M' class than with *X.1*, and at one stage – Project 'J' – it was proposed to arm her with a single 12in gun as used in the pre-dreadnought battleships. Her twin 203mm (8in) turret guns were the largest calibre permitted under the terms of the Washington Treaty – otherwise she would have come under the definition of a 'capital ship'. No other navy anywhere built submarines with guns of this size between the wars.

The derivation of the new submarine's name was interesting. Obviously she would be used for '*guerre de course*', and therefore choosing the name of the most famous French corsair was highly appropriate. Again, in 1937 the port of Saint-Malo where she was built was to celebrate the centenary of Surcouf's death, and finally Admiral Darlan, a gunnery expert, had a house there. Her top-secret launch on 18 November 1929, with no cameras allowed, had provided a moment of high drama. The dignitaries had assembled, the band was playing the Marseillaise, and the order was given. The giant vessel refused to move down the slip, however, and began to rock ominously from side to side, as if she was about to fall over. The dignitaries hurriedly moved, the band stopped playing, and then *Surcouf*, resignedly, slipped backwards into the water as planned, when the band hurriedly re-commenced the Marseillaise. Some observers took this as a portent of things to come.

Surcouf's armament

Surcouf appeared a strangely unbalanced design, with her huge 8in gun turret, which could shoot far further than the rangefinder could see. Two large guns do not allow for effective ladders to be shot and quickly bracket a moving target. The large, spacious turret and the gun barrels were watertight, which unnecessarily complicated construction and operation. The muzzles were closed by hinged tompions worked by an endless screw, and the barrels pivoted in a ball mounting. The guns could be loaded underwater with shell and bagged charge, but could not be trained until on the surface. Watertightness of the revolving trunk was achieved solely by the weight of the turret bearing down on a rubber ring, with a locking bolt to prevent unwanted movement and shear damage to the ring. To bring the turret into action, its pivot was jacked up 20mm by oil pressure, freeing the base from contact with the sealing ring.

There appears to have been no other positive form of watertight seal. This *ad hoc* arrangement may have contributed to the reported inaccuracy of the 8in guns.

Surfacing in calm weather, fire could be opened in three and a half minutes from the command to surface being put into effect. In rough weather this time could become almost five minutes . . . The rate of fire achieved was only four rounds per gun per minute, instead of the five intended. The 8in guns were reported to suffer from abnormal dispersion as to range, although fire was controlled by a mechanical computer similar in operation to the Admiralty Fire Control Clock. This latter problem may have been the result of the basic lack of surface stability. A major drawback compared with *X.1* was that the 4m-base rangefinder was not used when submerged – it could only be brought into action once its base had cleared the surface.

Although it was possible to hoist a precarious crows-nest on top of the rear periscope, for all practical purposes the range of the turret guns was severely limited by the low height above water of the rangefinder – the designed maximum sight range of the rangefinder was 12,000m. This could theoretically be extended out to 16,000m by spotting through the auxiliary periscope. Longer ranges would require the use of the aircraft for spotting, but since she carried no catapult there was no guarantee the aircraft could be used in all circumstances and sea states. Using the rangefinder alone, in practice it was found impossible to spot fall of shot further out than 7,000m. The rangefinder and fire control position proved to be sited too near the muzzles of the guns and was usually unsighted by gunsmoke on opening fire. Two surprising omissions were the lack of any manual sighting arrangements on the mounting itself, and the inability of the fire control apparatus to engage shore-based targets – which should surely have been its principal *raison d'être*. Strangely enough, although the 8in guns had a maximum elevation of 30 degrees, they were unable to depress below the horizontal. This would have rendered the turret inoperative in the event of a list on the opposite side to the target, and if the boat listed more than 8 degrees the turret could not be trained at all. Also, the ability to bring the main armament to bear on a target astern of the conning tower was strictly limited. During initial gunnery trials it was discovered that, firing the turret on aft bearings could cause deformation of the flimsy bridge structure through blast effects. Finally, although the magazine held an

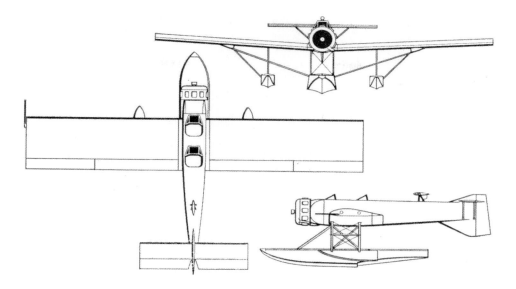

The MB-41.1 was a two-seater observation aircraft, with a single central float and two small stabilizing floats, that could be dismantled for storage inside the cylindrical hangar behind *Surcouf*'s conning tower. Assembly normally took up to thirty minutes from cracking the watertight door to lowering the aircraft into the water by crane. One prototype, the MB-41.0, and two production MB-41s were built. The aircraft which she carried on escaping to England in 1940 was disembarked at Devonport and damaged in a German air raid. Neither the aircraft nor its pilot were aboard when *Surcouf* sailed on her final voyage.
175hp Salmson 9Nd air-cooled radial engine, with removable 2-bladed propeller. Maximum speed: 118mph; range: 249 miles.

impressive load of 600 8in rounds, a severe limitation on sustained action was the fact that ammunition only sufficient for fourteen salvoes was held in readiness for loading. Further fire would have required accessing additional rounds from more distant storage . . . And if she rolled or listed more than 15 degrees either side the large 8in projectiles could become dislodged from the upper storage racks. For all its impressive size, the twin 8in gun turret on *Surcouf* was in no way capable of matching the volume of rapid, accurate and sustained fire which *X.1*'s smaller guns could produce.

One positive feature was *Surcouf*'s reasonable (for the early 1930s) anti-aircraft armament of two 37mm Model 25 high angle guns (firing 4lb projectiles) and two twin 8mm Hotchkiss machine guns, used in conjunction with a hand-held 1m-base rangefinder. Surprisingly, during her American refit, her two 37mm semi-automatic AA guns were not replaced by fully automatic weapons. She could have carried a pair of 40mm Bofors, but even the 20mm Oerlikon which was then being mounted in such large numbers on every American warship was not mounted. The hand-loaded 37mm Model 25s would have been completely ineffective against any determined

Japanese aerial assault on the island of Tahiti where she was finally despatched as a guardship.

In addition to her special mixed torpedo armament, including 400mm tubes intended to sink merchant ships, *Surcouf* was well-stocked with demolition charges to sink her prey. She was also fitted out to carry up to forty prisoners, being the crews of merchant ships she apprehended and sank. Both prototypes of her large launch, intended to carry an eleven-man boarding party and a crew of three, and to be craned into the water using one of the gun barrels as a jib, were complete failures in any seaway, and she would have been forced to rely on smaller naval pinnaces with outboard motors.

Surcouf's tactical shortcomings

After six years of construction and commissioning, and following exhaustive testing, the *Surcouf*'s principal drawbacks in a surface gun action were painfully obvious to the French Navy:

- The delay in bringing the guns into action on surfacing was too long.

Surcouf in Holy Loch after her seizure and handing-over to the Free French.

Surcouf Specifications

Displacement: 3,304 tons surfaced/4,318 tons submerged

Length: 110m; **Beam:** 9m; **Draught:** 7.18m

Maximum pressure hull thickness 22mm; conning tower and upper deck armoured up to 40mm

Diving depth: 80m

Twin screws: Sulzer diesels 7,600bhp at 330rpm = 18.5 knots surfaced/electric motors 3,400hp = 8.5 knots submerged

Range: 10,000nm @ 10 knots, 6,800nm @ 13.8 knots surfaced/70nm @ 4.5 knots submerged

Armament: 2 x 203mm (2 x 1) guns with 600 rounds; 2 x 37mm sub-calibre exercise barrels with 900 rounds;

2 x 37mm Model 1925 semi-automatic anti-aircraft guns with 1,000 rounds;

4 x 8mm Hotchkiss Model 1914 machine guns on twin mounts, with 16,000 rounds;

6 x 550mm torpedo tubes plus 8 reloads and 4 x 400mm torpedo tubes plus 4 reloads;

One Besson MB-41.1 scout floatplane

Complement: 8 officers, including a doctor and a pilot, plus 111 other ranks

Wine storage: 5,200 litres

- The rangefinder's low height restricted the practical range of the turret.
- The spotter aircraft was of necessity small and therefore fragile and vulnerable. The absence of a launch catapult was a serious drawback, but the small aircraft needed calm weather to land again. The helicopter offered much improved capabilities, and the firm of Breguet was tasked with creating a suitable prototype – which was never completed due to the military collapse of France in May and June 1940.

What is clear from the photographs is that, the one thing *Surcouf* had was 'presence'. And not just from her enormous gun turret. The French had popularised the concept of streamlining, notable examples being the nineteenth-century 'coupe-vent' locomotives of the PLM, Camille Jenatzy's electric 'torpedo' which captured the world speed record for land vehicles in 1899, and the famous Bugatti Railcars. So it was natural for *Surcouf*'s designers to incorporate '*carénage*'. There was not much that could be done with the chunky, Labœuf-style hull and underwater fittings, but above deck her huge gun turret was encased in a streamlined external shell, which blended into the sinuous curves of her conning tower, ending in the aircraft hangar cylinder at its rear end. After initial trials even her rangefinder had received a streamlined casing – submerged it would have induced resistance, to say nothing of underwater noise. In addition, when not in use it was normally aligned fore-and-aft to further reduce drag.

For more than fifty years French designers had built psychology into their warships – the 'fierce face' look typified by the series of pre-dreadnought French ironclads such as the *Hoche* of 1890, with her piled up superstructure, exaggerated tumblehome, and enormous fighting masts. Such ships were intended to overawe a potential enemy before firing a single shot. *Surcouf* certainly followed in this tradition, and her planned transfer to Tahiti would have boosted morale in that isolated Free French outpost. She would have been a 'threat in being' similar to that posed by large Kriegsmarine units based in Brest and Norway during the Second World War.

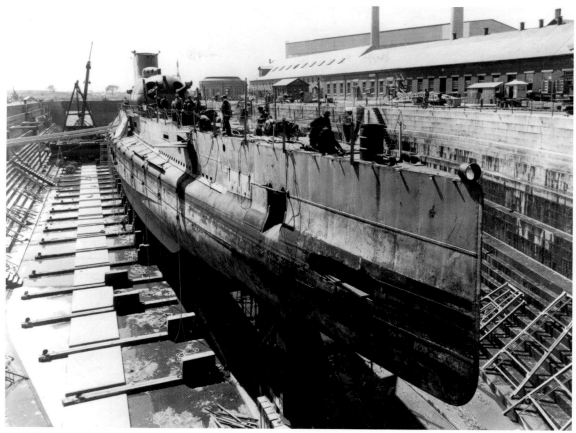

Surcouf undergoing a major refit in No 2 Dry dock at Portsmouth Naval Yard, New Hampshire, September 1941. If *X.1* had survived just a few more years, this is where she could have been re-engined.

Her pre-war commissioning and career were far from painless, but on the outbreak of hostilities in September 1939 *Surcouf* was brought up to combat readiness. The outwardly dangerous expedient of using submarines as convoy escorts – during which many highly imaginative stories of *Surcouf* torpedoing Allied ships grew up – made much more sense when one considers *Surcouf*'s surface combat potential. During calm weather her aircraft could patrol around the convoy. In theory her guns could outrange the 15cm guns carried by merchant raiders, and a larger surface unit would be vulnerable to submerged attack from her torpedoes. In fact, Capitaine de Vaisseau Claude Huon has suggested that *Surcouf*'s presence as part of the escort actually saved Convoy KJ-2 from attack by the 'pocket battleship' *Deutschland* in late 1939. Alerted to the possible presence of *Surcouf* by German Naval Intelligence, Kapitan Wennecker turned away from the convoy when one of his lookouts spotted a silhouette resembling a surfaced submarine at 21.27 on the night of 9 October.

Having fled to England with her main engines not fully tested after major repairs, *Surcouf* was one of the vessels seized by the British during Operation 'Catapult' in July 1940, which resulted in considerable loss of life, and the repatriation to Vichy France of most of her crew. In 1941 she was re-commissioned by the Free French Naval Forces with a scratch crew of mainly young Breton fishermen, virtually none of whom had ever been to sea in a submarine before, never mind one as complex and fragile as the *Surcouf.*

The threat of her 8in guns must certainly have been a leading consideration in the bloodless submission of St Pierre and Miquelon in December 1941. However, the rumours of a hushed-up firefight between *Surcouf* and US forces despatched to restore the *status quo* in those islands must be relegated to the

Postage stamps featuring Surcouf. *The larger airmail stamp commemorates the twentieth anniversary of the seizure of St Pierre et Miquelon by a Free French naval force supported by the guns of* Surcouf. *The smaller stamp remembers her last captain, Cdt Louis Blaison.*

status of a myth, as there is little evidence that *Surcouf* could hope to defend herself on the surface against destroyers. Tragically, *Surcouf*'s disappearance from the scene was much more dramatic than that of *X.1*. She departed Bermuda at 15.00 on 12 February 1942, routed to Tahiti via the Panama Canal, where she was expected on or around the 19th. *Surcouf* never arrived, and it was presumed she was accidentally rammed and sunk by an American freighter on the night of 18 February – although other reports have her sunk in error by US Army Air Force bombers operating out of Rio Hato.

Surcouf in retrospect

Official French reports catalogue a list of major problems. It would appear that, in stark contrast to *X.1*, *Surcouf* failed to some degree in all three aspects of her design – as a submarine, as a gunnery platform and as a vehicle. She was clumsy underwater and took too long to surface, lacking large quick-blow tanks in her bows as were deemed essential in *X.1*. The novel arrangement of mounting her main battery cells on trolleys for rapid removal was a failure inasmuch as it did not permit them to be held sufficiently rigidly in place, leading to frequent battery spills. The major drawbacks in her gunnery department – her basic *raison d'être* – are detailed above.

It appears her riveted hull was not really strong enough to carry the enormous weight of the turret, and worked in a seaway. Being top-heavy she often rolled sufficiently to allow acid to spill from her batteries, and this led to numerous electrical fires. Finally, and most crucially, *Surcouf* seemed fated to share with *X.1* an unreliable propulsion plant. Her main Sulzer two-stroke supercharged diesel engines, although far from trouble-free, did manage to carry her across the Atlantic on several occasions, which

one is tempted to think would be beyond the capabilities of *X.1*'s Chathams. Her electric motors, on the other hand, must be regarded as failures, suffering from a design defect whereby shaft lubricating oil was blown into the armature windings by the forced ventilation system. Like *X.1* her external ballast tanks usually leaked diesel oil, but unlike *X.1* this problem was ultimately resolved by welding up the tanks. *X.1*'s rudder is recorded as having jammed only once in service, whereas *Surcouf*'s rudder actually broke up on one occasion.[4]

Reports written by Royal Navy officers attached to this orphan vessel, and by officers ashore charged with her upkeep and maintenance, are full of critical comments. She appeared top-heavy (not surprisingly) and could roll up to 40 degrees each side. This caused acid to spill from her batteries, starting small fires in electrical wiring. Heavy seas at one time damaged her superstructure, and temporarily jammed her turret. Her inexperienced crew often mismanaged dives, and diving drills were infrequent and laden with tension. On at least one occasion she got out of control and dived below her designed operating depth. Cut off from her home dockyards and spare parts stores her maintenance was a continuing struggle, and on her last fatal voyage she sailed with one main motor burnt out and awaiting repairs. RN Liaison Officer Sub Lt Roger Burney RNVR reported before the start of that voyage that, of her sixteen hydrophone underwater microphones, only seven still worked.

Like *X.1*, *Surcouf* was to remain an only child, although French pride ensured she was always held in high regard and assured of a place in the submarine battle-line. Also a ship of pathos, her story was to end ultimately in tragedy, leaving many questions behind her, including how she would have performed had she reached the Pacific Theatre. The dramatic end to her wartime career, and the many myths and rumours which have persisted ever since her disappearance on 18 February 1942, make her every bit the 'mystery submarine' equal of *X.1*.

Japanese Boats

In contrast to all the other major naval powers, Japan built significant numbers of submarines with a very large displacement. With an eye on extended action across the expanses of the Pacific, the primary Japanese need was long range, and the concomitant ability to carry supplies and munitions for long patrols. Habitability seems to have come a poor third in Japanese submarine designs, leading to increased combat fatigue and reduced effectiveness compared with their American opponents in the Second World War.

Many of the Japanese boats carried floatplanes for reconnaissance duties, and copying the example of the ill-fated *M.2* they launched their aircraft by catapult. The Japanese had also copied the U-Cruiser design, having purchased detailed plans from the

German shipyards. The 'KaiDai' or 'Large Admiralty Type' boats were derived from the *U 139* (apart from *I-51* which was built to British plans), and were designed for long range patrol duties. The only 'submarine cruisers' *by designation* were the double-hulled 'JunSen' Type (Jun Sen = Submarine Cruiser), with two 5.5in deck guns and light armour plating on the hull and conning tower, copied from plans of the *U 142*. *I-7* and *I-8*, the third variant of this type, reached the high surface speed of 23 knots. The eight units in three variations were built from 1923 to 1938, and in terms of the overall Japanese submarine programme were a relatively insignificant element. The giant long-range Japanese boats *I-351* and *I-352* ('Sen-Ho') were completed at a late stage when no deck guns were available, so they were bizarrely armed with four 3in trench mortars instead. Their design role was that of advanced base for seaplanes and floatplanes, carrying aviation fuel and bombs.

Although of a size and possessing many of the attributes of true blue-water cruisers, these large Japanese boats differed in one significant aspect from their counterparts in other navies. They were long-

The large submarine *I-8*, docking at a French port after her long journey from Japan. For her role as blockade runner, her aircraft-handling arrangements have been removed, and she carries an unusual twin 5.5in gun mounting.

range patrol submarines, but their primary targets were to be enemy warships, not merchantmen. For this they relied almost exclusively on their excellent 21in oxygen-fuelled, wakeless torpedoes. Their respectable deck armament was rarely used, and almost never against warships. The later Japanese boats tried to make up for Japan's loss of aircraft carriers by turning into submersible flattops, carrying the aerial battle to strategic targets deep inside US-controlled waters. By this transformation they turned away from the role of commerce destroyer which was the *raison d'être* of the cruiser submarine.

Type 'A' and 'AM' (for 'Modified') boats were intended as flotilla leaders, for patrol submarines of the KaiDai or Type 'B' classes. The 'AM' boats had an extended hangar to contain not one small observation floatplane, but two Seiran floatplane bombers. On their final mission to Ulithi, to attack the US invasion fleet, the two Type AM boats *I-13* and *I-14* carried two standard 'Myrt' reconnaissance aircraft to scout for their larger sisters.

The Type 'A Modified' boats were ultimately diverted to take part in the Panama Canal attack, supporting the giant *I-400* 'Sen-Toku' ('Special Duty') class boats each carrying three *Seiran* attack aircraft. These latter vessels were the largest submarines built before the nuclear era, submersible aircraft carriers designed for Admiral Yamamoto's planned surprise attack on the Panama Canal (and also possible 'dirty bomb' nuclear attacks on the US West Coast). When the attack on Panama was put on hold, all the submersible aircraft carriers were ordered to stand by for the final assault in the Japanese Home Islands, when they were to launch their bombers in suicide attacks on the US invasion fleet, taking the Allies by surprise from the rear.

Another view of *I-8* being welcomed by her Axis allies, taken from the roof of the receiving U-boat pen as she is guided into her berth inside.

Watanabe E9W1, known to the Allies as 'Slim'. Inspired by the Parnell Peto delivered to Japan, this tiny foldable reconnaissance biplane was carried aboard large patrol submarines in a watertight cylindrical hangar. It was in service from 1938, when it patrolled the seas off China, directing its parent submarine to vessels attempting to break the Japanese blockade of the Chinese coast, right up until July 1942.

A total of thirty-five were built, including prototypes. Replaced by the E14Y1.

300hp Hitachi GK2 Tempu 11 9-cylinder radial engine; Maximum speed: 144mph; endurance: just under 5 hours at cruising speed of 92mph.

Yokosuka E14Y1 floatplane, known to the Allies as 'Glen'. A total of 126 of this type were built. Carried by the large patrol submarines *I-9* to *I-11* and *I-15* to *I-35*, the E14Y1 carried out many reconnaissance missions, including one over Pearl Harbor ten days after the Japanese attack. An E14Y1 was the only aircraft to carry out an attack on the American mainland, when in September 1942 one of these tiny aircraft, launched from the *I-25* dropped two incendiary bombs on a forest in Oregon in an unsuccessful attempt to start fires.

340hp Tempu 12 9-cylinder radial engine. Maximum speed: 153mph; endurance: just over 5½ hours at cruising speed of 104mph.

Aichi M6A1 *Seiran* (Mountain Haze). Unknown to the Allies during the Second World War, it received no codename. This modern attack bomber of relatively high performance was carried aboard the *I-13* and *I-14*, as well as the monster *I-400* Class boats. Ostensibly designed to attack the Panama Canal, it is likely they were intended to carry out a 'dirty bomb' nuclear attack against the American West Coast in 1945. Eight prototypes were followed by twenty production machines, several with retractable wheeled undercarriages for training.

1,400hp Aichi Atsuta 32 12-cylinder liquid-cooled engine. Maximum speed: 295mph; cruising speed: 184mph; range 739 miles; one 1,760lb bomb.

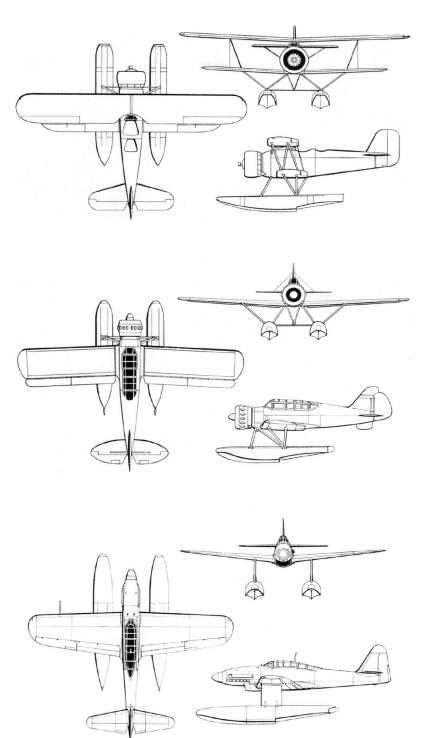

I-14, the surviving Type A Modified aircraft carrier, after the Japanese surrender. Photo taken from the submarine depot ship USS *Proteus*.

Above: Japanese submersible aircraft carriers, in US Navy hands at Guam in November 1945, while *en route* to Pearl Harbor.

Right: *I-14* berthed outboard of *I-400* and *I-401* alongside the *Proteus*. The giants are being de-stored by their Japanese crews, under US Navy supervision. The stench from the latrines and the rotting foodstuffs was noted, as was the large number of stowaway rats.

Large Japanese Submarines Specifications

Hull Numbers	Completed	Displ surface/subm	Power/Surface Speed	Range	Armament
JunSen (Submarine Cruisers)					
I-1, I-2, I-3, I-4	1924–8	2,135/2,791 tons	6,000bhp = 18 knots	24,400nm	2 x 5.5in; 6 x 21in TT
I-5	1931	2,243/2,921 tons	6,000bhp = 18 knots	24,400nm	1 x 5.5in; 6 x 21in TT; 1 floatplane
I-6	1934	2,243/3,061 tons	8,000bhp = 20 knots	20,000nm	1 x 5in DP; 6 x 21in TT; 1 floatplane
I-7, I-8	1935–6	2,525/3,538 tons	11,200bhp = 23 knots	14,000nm	1 x 5.5in; 6 x 21in TT; 1 floatplane
KaiDai (Large Admiralty Type)					
I-51	1924	1,390/2,430 tons	5,200bhp = 20 knots	20,000nm	1 x 4.7in; 1 x 3in; 8 x 21in TT
I-52	1925	1,500/2,500 tons	6,800bhp = 22 knots	10,000nm	1 x 4.7in; 1 x 3in; 8 x 21in TT
I-53, I-54, I-55, I-58	1925–6	1,800/2,300 tons	6,800bhp = 20 knots	10,000nm	1 x 4.7in; 8 x 21in TT
I-56, I-57, I-59, I-60, I-63	1927–9	1,800/2,300 tons	6,800bhp = 20 knots	10,000nm	1 x 4.7in; 8 x 21in TT
I-61, I-62, I-64	1927–9	1,720/2,300 tons	6,000bhp = 20 knots	10,800nm	1 x 4.7in; 6 x 21in TT
I-65, I-66, I-67	1931	1,705/2,330 tons	6,000bhp = 20.5 knots	10,800nm	1 x 3.9in; 6 x 21in TT
I-68, I-69, I-70, I-71, I-72, I-73	1933–5	1,785/2,440 tons	9,000bhp = 23 knots	14,000nm	1 x 3.9in; 6 x 21in TT
I-74, I-75	1936–7	1,810/2,564 tons	9,000bhp = 23 knots	10,000nm	1 x 4.7in; 6 x 21in TT
I-76, I-77, I-78, I-79, I-80, I-81, I-82, I-83, I-84, I85	1941–3	1,833/2,602 tons	8,000bhp = 23.1 knots	8,000nm	1 x 4.7in; 2 x 25mm; 6 x 21in TT
Type A (Flagships for Submarine Flotillas)					
I-9, I-10, I-11	1939–41	2,919/4,149 tons	12,400bhp = 23.5 knots	16,000nm	1 x 5.5in; 2 x 25mm; 6 x 21in TT; 1 floatplane
I-12	1943	2,934/4,172 tons	4,700bhp = 17.7 knots	22,000nm	1 x 5.5in; 2 x 25mm; 6 x 21in TT; 1 floatplane
Type A Modified (Submersible Aircraft Carriers) 'Kai-ko-taka' design					
I-13, I-14	1944	3,603/4,762 tons	4,400bhp = 16.7 knots	21,000nm	1 x 5.5in; 7 x 25mm; 6 x 21in TT; 2 *Seiran* bombers
Type B1 (Cruiser/Patrol Submarines) 'Otsu-gata' design					
I-15, I-17, I-19, I-21, I-23, I-25, I-26 to I-39 (Total of 20 boats)	1939–42	2,589/3,654 tons	12,400bhp = 23.6 knots	14,000nm	1 x 5.5in; 2 x 25mm; 6 x 21in TT; 1 floatplane
Type B2 (Cruiser/Patrol Submarines)					
I-40, I-41, I-42, I-43, I-44, I-45	1942–3	2,624/3,700 tons	11,000bhp = 23.5 knots	14,000nm	1 x 5.5in; 2 x 25mm; 6 x 21in TT; 1 floatplane
Type B3 (Cruiser/Patrol Submarines)					
I-54, I-56, I-58	1943–4	2,607/3,688 tons	4,700bhp = 17.7 knots	21,000nm	1 x 5.5in; 2 x 25mm; 6 x 21in TT; 1 floatplane
Type C1 (Cruiser Submarines/Special Attack Boats) 'Hei-gata' design					
I-16, I-18, I-20, I-22, I-24	1938–9	2,554/3,561 tons	12,400bhp = 23.6 knots	14,000nm	1 x 5.5in; 2 x 25mm; 8 x 21in TT
Type C2 (Cruiser Submarines/Special Attack Boats)					
I-46, I-47, I-48	1943	2,557/3,564 tons	11,000bhp = 23.5 knots	14,000nm	1 x 5.5in; 2 x 25mm; 8 x 21in TT
Type C3 (Cruiser Submarines/Special Attack Boats)					
I-52, I-53, I-55	1943	2,564/3,644 tons	4,700bhp = 17.7 knots	21,000nm	2 x 5.5in; 2 x 25mm; 6 x 21in TT
Sen-Toku ('Special Type Submarines')					
I-400, I-401, I-402	1944	5,223/6,560 tons	7,700bhp = 18.7 knots	30,000nm	1 x 5.5in; 10 x 25mm; 8 x 21in TT; 3 *Seiran* bomber aircraft

Japanese tailpiece: the remains of Cruiser *I-1* sunk off Guadalcanal by the New Zealand corvettes *Moa* and *Kiwi*. High and dry on a reef just offshore, *I-1* displays her 'shark's nose' bow copied from the plans of the *U 142*, which would also appear on the US Navy's cruiser submarines. Forced to the surface by the two small corvettes, *I-1* fought a running gun battle at night. Surprisingly, she scored no hits with her forward 5.5in gun (the aft gun had been removed to make room for a landing craft for her resupply mission). The New Zealand gunners were, for their part, unable to penetrate the thick hull of the Japanese boat, and she was finally disabled by ramming.

Raeder's Z-Plan

Imitation is the sincerest form of flattery. *X.1*'s gunnery armament, thick hull plating and, to some

extent her engineering plant, had been inspired by the *U 141*. In a repeat of history, the twenty-four Type XI U-Boats included in Grand Admiral Raeder's ill-fated Z-Plan of 1938 mirrored the *X.1*'s gun armament, were to be protected against surface shell hits, and would also have had a multi-engined layout. Could it be more than just coincidence that the type number allocated was X followed by I?

One major departure was that they were planned to carry a scouting seaplane, as did *M.2* and *Surcouf*, but this time inside the main hull itself in a cylindrical hangar set vertically between the conning tower and the forward turret. This 'Ubootsuge' or 'U-Boat eye' would have built on the valuable experience gained by the German surface raider *Wolf* in the Great War, when she had deployed her '*Wolfschen*' ('Wolfcub') seaplane to such good effect. However, given the marginal water- and airborne performance of the Arado AR 231 seaplane prototypes and the lack of a catapult, it is likely that the aircraft would have been supplanted in service by the Focke-Achgelis Fa 330 rotary-wing observation kite. This machine was a simpler means of providing an observation platform, and could be more easily jettisoned in the event the parent boat needed to crash-dive. The slow-moving kite would, however, have made a significant radar echo, pointing to the presence of the U-boat beneath. Provision of airborne observation facilities was

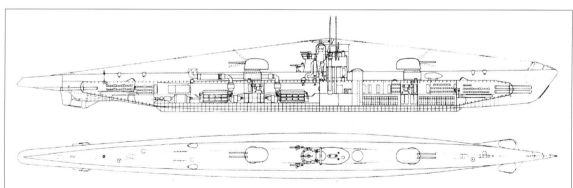

Profile and plan of the Type XIB, the final design dated 13 April 1939. These U-Cruisers were to bear the numbers *U 113*, *U 114* and *U 115*.

Type XI U-Cruisers

Displacement: 3,140 tons surfaced/3,930 tons submerged

Length: 115m; Beam: 9.5m; Draught: 6.2m

Twin screws: 8 x 2,200bhp diesels (total 17,600bhp) = 23 knots surfaced/electric motors 2 x 1,100hp (total 2,200hp) = 7 knots submerged

Range: 15,800nm @ 12 knots surfaced/50nm @ 4 knots submerged

Armament: 2 x twin 12.7cm LA guns with 250 rounds per gun; 2 x 3.7cm SA Flak guns with 2,000 rounds per gun; 1 x 2cm Flak; 6 x 53cm torpedo tubes (4 bow, 2 stern) with 12 torpedoes; one aircraft or towed kite

Crew: 110

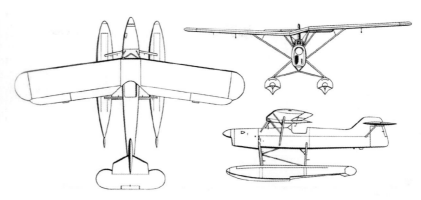

Plan of the single-seat Arado AR231. Note that the wings were staggered vertically, in order to allow one to fold over the other. It is possible this asymmetrical arrangement gave rise to its poor flight performance, but the need to crane the small and fragile aircraft onto the water for take-off was a definite drawback in all but the calmest of sea states. The small photo shows the aircraft stowed.

Hirth HM 501 6-cylinder air-cooled engine; Maximum speed: 106mph; cruising speed: 81mph; range 310 miles. Six built for evaluation, not proceeded with.

evidence of the fact that the U-Cruiser was designed to operate in a 'blue water' environment, the kind of deployment dear to German Navy strategists ever since the earliest days of the High Seas Fleet.

The multi-engined layout required the German designers adopt a 'double-hull' design with two half-cylinders, similar to the engine room of the Japanese *I-400* class boats. The conning tower and upper hull were to offer resistance against 13cm (5.1in) projectiles, and the finalised design employed Chief Engineer Hans Vogel's arrangements for fighting a surface gun action in the awash state, buoyancy being assured by additional buoyancy chambers added low down in the sides of the boat.

The Kriegsmarine was never to receive any Type XI U-Cruisers. Britain's declaration of war on 3 September 1939 doomed the ambitious German U-Cruiser construction plans as well as those for the battleships designed to follow the *Bismarck* and *Tirpitz*, and the Kriegsmarine would never seriously rival the Royal Navy as its predecessor had tried to do.

The original parameters for the Type XI included access to the rangefinder compartment and turrets while still beneath the surface, and it is likely that the design problems encountered in attempting to make the twin turrets watertight were what fatally delayed the whole project until it was too late. In this respect, *X.1*'s free-flooding mountings and perfected hull sealing glands were a simpler and thus much better solution to the problem.

CHAPTER 12

Reflections and Epilogue

X.1's main propulsion machinery was weak, and unless she was taken in hand for drastic modernisation, she could never be trusted on long voyages in hostile waters, far from the support of a waiting dockyard. However, the vessel suffered from a list of other problems as well, not all of which resulted from the main and auxiliary engines.

- Her compressors wore out less than five years after she was launched, though this may have been due to the extensive use they were put to, and the high pressures they were designed to handle.
- She suffered two explosions in her batteries, thus demonstrating that the sealed ventilation system was far from ideal.
- On different occasions, various items of equipment such as the gyro compass, the aft hydroplanes and the steering gear failed.
- The fuel ballast tanks were never oil-tight, and the hydraulic rams for raising the DCT roof leaked oil.
- Worst of all, the after trim tank actually burst under pressure in the course of a test dive on 6 January 1930.

Sabotage?

This surprisingly long list of recurring defects makes one wonder what was going wrong with quality control of the vessel and her fittings. Such a list might make a modern researcher ponder on the possibility of industrial sabotage – after all one of the Chatham engine fitters had sent the launch photo to the very same left-wing newspaper which, several days before on the occasion of her launch, had posed the question of whether *X.1* was intended as the start of another arms race.

And there is the incident on 10 February 1931. Just one day after forty-seven ratings and three officers were drafted out of the ship, reducing her to one-third complement, a fire mysteriously broke out in the main engine room. Was this sabotage by a disaffected crew member who had been passed over for the draft to other submarines? We shall never know.

Penury

Bare facts may point elsewhere. Great Britain was not short of ideas in the early 1920s, but the country was financially destitute after having financed the Great War. Hence the almost pathetic way in which available second-hand fittings were proposed for *X.1* to reduce the overall cost – some 'wonder weapon' to begin a new arms race! – such as her torpedo tubes, air bottles, battery cells and, most notoriously, the old U-boat diesel generator sets.

Unfortunately it is sad to state that one must, reluctantly, question the standards of maintenance and inspection prevalent in the Navy Dockyards which had to handle the ship. Time and again she left dockyard hands after a scheduled regular refit, only to have some minor or major catastrophe occur only days later . . . This seemingly careless attention culminated in the embarrassing tumble she took on 26 June 1931 in drydock!

Of course, with hindsight again, one can imagine the reluctance of harassed dockyard management to expend scarce money and even scarcer trained workmen on what most submariners (apart from her own crew) regarded as a monstrous 'white elephant'. In that case it is not surprising that she was accorded a low priority, even straightforward repairs taking months at a time. And all this against the background of the modern world's first great financial crisis. At a time when Britain was forced to suspend construction of the great prestige liner *Queen Mary*, how could the authorities justify spending scarce money on the orphan *X.1*? Or was this symptomatic of the gradual decline of Great Britain as a leading industrial power?[1]

Were the novel ideas put forward by *X.1*'s designers and protagonists too far ahead of the already outmoded British industrial base which would have to build and maintain the ship? The first country to industrialise, Britain was already falling behind her newer rivals in industrial capability. There had been previous examples of shoddy ship construction and poor quality control. Most notorious was the theft by Tyneside workers of the cork magazine insulation for the monitor HMS *Glatton* which led directly to her loss in Dover Harbour in September

1918.[2] From the high point of the Great War, RN submarine design and construction had fallen so far behind the standards of other nations by May 1940, that the U-boat men who examined HMS *Seal* after her capture during a minelaying sortie into the Kattegat were surprised at the obsolescence of much of her equipment and fittings, compared with their own boats. They did re-use her telephone buoy equipment, but *Seal* herself was not used by the German Kriegsmarine, suffering the ultimate insult of being broken up for scrap in 1941. It was against this background of declining industrial strength that the men of the Royal Navy's Submarine Service fought so bravely in the Second World War, and with such stunning success against German and Italian warships.

What Might Have Been

X.1's main engines may have been too fragile and her auxiliary engines practically worn out when first installed, but all these faults could have been rectified, if the political will to do so had existed. The later 'River' class boats, which were being designed at the very time that *X.1* was falling from favour, were to be fitted with high-powered supercharged 10-cylinder diesels of the required output for *X.1* – 5,000bhp – and it is sad no-one ventured the opinion that *X.1* might be re-engined. Her auxiliary engines could have been replaced with standard Admiralty diesel generator sets as fitted to the 'T' class boats, and producing 1,250bhp each. The amount of opening-up involved would have appeared drastic, but relatively minor compared to the gutting and total reconstruction – virtually from the keel up – of the battleships *Warspite*, *Valiant* and *Queen Elizabeth*, plus the battlecruiser *Renown*.[3] Presumably by that time she had cost so much in maintenance costs and unjustified hopes that any such idea would have been dismissed. Also, the 'Chathams' had been the pride of the Yard when constructed. Presumably the old 'State Versus Private Enterprise' competition which had proved so disastrous in the *R.100/R.101* airship rivalry may have had some influence?[4]

If only she had survived in service until the outbreak of the Second World War she might have been sent to the USA to have her unreliable engines replaced by, say, four sets of the latest diesel engines fitted to the new breed of US boats. Thus rejuvenated, the Old Lady could have been sent to the Pacific to meet the foe she had been designed to beat! At the same time Mare Island could have outfitted her with an air-conditioning plant for tropical service . . . Her leaking external tanks should have been welded up, as per Commander Raikes' original suggestions. Many other RN submarines were so modified before the war. The ideal opportunity to carry out this work would have been when her crumpled port-side ballast tanks needed repair after the drydock fiasco of June 1931.

HMS *Thames*, first boat of the 'River' class. The 'River' class, ordered in the 1929 Programme, were to have 2 x 10-cylinder diesel engines producing 5,000 BHP each. The first vessel, *Thames*, was launched on 26 January 1932 and commissioned at the end of that year. Displacing 2,165/2,680 tons, she reached a top speed of 21.5 knots, and her two later sisters were even faster. So, large high-powered diesels could be designed and built successfully at the time.

Service in the Pacific

Let us imagine a whole flotilla of a dozen 'X' boats, operating out of the new Singapore Naval Base. Would the Japanese have attacked in the face of such a powerful deterrent force? There could have been no need to send out the fatally-unbalanced Force Z at the end of 1941. And the names to be given to this Phantom Flotilla? The most appropriate name beginning with 'Ex' had of course been already allocated to HMS *Excellent*. *Eagle*, *Enterprise* and *Emerald* were already allocated to ships built or building. Alternative names – many of which would later be given to RN warships, or which had already served afloat – could include *Excalibur*, *Excelsior*, *Exciter*, *Exmoor*, *Exmouth*, *Expert*, *Explorer*, *Express* and *Exeter*. Then we have the closely associated *Escapade*, *Eskdale* and *Eskimo*, with the possibility of *Earnest*, *Electra*, *Eden* and *Eclipse* making for a wide choice of good names. *Echo* would have been most inappropriate for a submarine.[5] And it would be too cruel to consider the nicknames which could follow even minor mishaps, such as '*Expensive*', '*Expletive*' or '*Execrable*'.[6]

However, this Far Eastern scenario would have worked only in hindsight, and hindsight always gives us 20/20 vision. Who in the 1930s could have predicted that the Japanese air forces, with their myopic pilots and bomb aimers, flying poor under-powered copies of superseded Western designs, could be capable of sweeping the Allied navies out of great swathes of the Pacific in 1941–2, and would even force the weak British fleet-in-being to flee to the very periphery of the Indian Ocean? This was the strategic vacuum into which a flotilla of *Excalibur*s[7] could have ventured. After all, when RN surface ships were driven from much of the central Mediterranean by overwhelming Axis air power in 1941–2, it was the submariners based on Malta who had made the major contribution to severing Rommel's supply lines between Italy and North Africa. The *Excalibur*s could have fulfilled the same role in the defence of Malaya and Singapore . . . But they were never to be built. Therein lies the true tragedy of the *X.1*. She and her stillborn prodigy might have delayed the loss of face and precipitous fall of the Empire on which the sun had never set . . . Allowing of a structured and federalist approach to de-colonisation, instead of the indecent haste in which dependent colonies were simply cut adrift financially, politically and morally.

Epilogue

Obviously, the Mark IV torpedoes landed from *X.1* would have found their way onto other vessels, and would have been among the more than 500 fired in anger in the Second World War. Her twin 5.2in gun mountings would have made a valuable contribution to coastal defence during the desperate months of summer 1940, when obsolete warship guns were brought out of storage and hastily mounted at likely invasion spots. There were never enough guns, however, and the twin 5.2in mountings, with the revolving trunk removed and replaced by a central pivot bolted to the girders of the turntable, would have been ideal for anti-shipping use, in local control, worked by hand, and fed from rear expense magazines.

Unfortunately, although the Gun Logs record that four of the original six 5.2in guns were still in existence in late 1940, they were never proposed for coast defence use. This is sad, but understandable if in fact the complete mountings, including gun cradles, had been cut up with the ship. To preserve the turrets might have indicated that they had performed to design specifications . . . so they were cut up with *X.1*. Each individual barrel had no means of training or elevation outside the mounting proper, so the bare barrels would eventually have been – in the terminology of the day – reduced to 'produce'. However, it has been reported that some of the earliest experimental aircraft rocket projectiles used obsolete '5.2in' shells as their heads during the first trials. If these were stocks taken from *X.1*'s magazines and replenishment stores, then the old ship did actually contribute in a significant way during the Second World War – from beyond the grave, so to speak.

Appendices

Appendix A: Extracts from *X.1*'s Log Books

Note: Repeated routine tasks are mentioned in summary or only initially. **Breakdowns and accidents are highlighted in bold.**

ADM173/13219		December 1923
17/12/23	08.00	*X.1* moved into North Lock, Chatham.
	09.00	Commissioned by Captain R H T Raikes. Lt Cdrs H L Fitzpatrick and G A Garmons-Williams; Eng Lt Cdr B J Wilkinson; Lts R G Murray, G F K Hill and J H Lewes.
	10.43	Left North Lock.
	12.10	Secured to No 7 Buoy at Sheerness. Commenced swinging the ship with a tug for adjustment of the compasses. The following officers and officials joined the ship for surface trials: Eng Captain Ham; Eng Cdrs Spriddle, Ham, Robertson and Turner; Cdr Cartlie, Lt Cdr Maxwell, Lt Milner, Mr Bassett, Mr Jackson and the GEC Representative.
	13.15	Discharged to 'Blenheim' – sick – 1 AB.
	14.45	Started Charge.
	15.30	Finished swinging ship.
	16.45	Broke Charge. Hands cleaning ship and as required.
	19.10	Commenced Charge.
	19.30	Broke Charge.
	21.00	Rounds correct.
18/12/23	06.30	Hands preparing for sea.
	08.40	Slipped from Buoy. Preliminary Trials in the vicinity of the Measured Mile, Maplin Sands.
	09.12	Streamed Forbes Log.
	12.20 to 12.30	Carried out Stopping and Starting Trials.
	13.59	Started Charge.
	15.00	Tested Kelvin's Sounding Machine.
	15.29	Broke Charge.
	16.15	Secured to No 7 Buoy, Sheerness. Started Charge.
19/12/23	07.28	Slipped from Buoy.
	08.11	Streamed Forbes Log.
	10.15	Started working up to Full Power.
	10.30	Commenced Full Power Trial.
	10.48	**Stop Both: Main Engine Defects.**
	12.30	Proceed under Port Engine, for return to Sheerness.
	13.00	Started Charge.
	13.10	Broke Charge.
	16.15	Secured to No 7 Buoy, Sheerness.
20/12/23	09.00	Rove ship's rope.

	10.00	Slipped from Buoy.
	10.08	Fouled Flying Boat.
	10.11	Proceeded as required up harbour.
	11.20	Secured in North Lock, Chatham.
	13.10	Ship shifted to North Wall, No 3 Basin. Hands employed returning stores and mess traps and bedding.
	18.00	Ship's Company proceeded to RN Barracks. Ship in charge of the Care & Maintenance Party.
21/12/23		In charge of Care & Maintenance Party, with Sentries posted. Hands employed as required.
22/12/23		In charge of Care & Maintenance Party, with Sentries posted. Hands employed as required.
	10.00 to 22.30	Discharging the Battery.
	22.35	Started Charge from the Shore.
23/12/23		Care & Maintenance Party.
24/12/23	09.30	Paid Ship's Company. Crew to proceed on 10 days Christmas Leave, less the members of the Care & Maintenance Party.
	13.45	Broke Charge.
25/12/23 to 31/12/23		Care & Maintenance Party. Commenced & Broke Charge each day.

ADM173/13220		**January 1924**
03/01/24		Ship's Company returned from Shore Leave. Hands employed as required, cleaning ship.
04/01/24		Care & Maintenance Party on leave till 08.30 Monday.
09/01/24	11.25	Ran main motors.
	11.40	Stopped main motors.
	14.15	Ran main motors.
	15.00	Stopped main motors.
	17.00	Started Charge from the Shore.
10/01/24		Two more main motor tests. Tested Sounding Machine and lost one lead for the same.
11/01/24	12.15	Ran main engines.
	12.45	Stopped main engines.
	13.15	Ran main engines.
	14.55	Stopped main engines.
	17.15	Ran Port Auxiliary Engine.
	18.00	Stopped Port Auxiliary Engine.
12/01/24	12.45	Ran Starboard Auxiliary Engine.
	14.20	Stopped same.
	15.55	Ran Port Auxiliary Engine.
	16.04	Stopped same.

	16.55	Ran Starboard Auxiliary Engine.
	17.15	Stopped same.
13/01/24	09.00	Ran Starboard Auxiliary Engine.
	09.15	Stopped same.
		Hands embarking stores and mess traps and bedding, and preparing the ship for sea.
	11.25	Ran Starboard Auxiliary Engine.
	11.55	Stopped same.
	18.40	Started Auxiliary Engines and a Charge.
	21.00	Broke Charge.
		Ship's Company quartered aboard.
14/01/23		Various Admiralty and Dockyard Officers boarded the ship for the trials. Draught of water: Forward 16' 6"; Aft 17' 3".
	09.28	Slipped tug. Proceeded on main motors.
	13.47	Streamed Log and carried out Trials with main motors.
15/01/24	08.30	4/5 Power Trial of main engines.
	12.30	Working up to Full Power.
	12.45	Commenced Full Power Trial, Revs 315.
	13.40	**Stopped both main engines for Defects off Folkestone.**
	15.30	Proceeded on main engines.
	16.00	**Stop both for Defects.**
	16.57	Proceeded on main motors (Series Parallel).
	18.40	Auxiliary Engine Trial.
	19.34	**Fire on the upper deck.**
	20.14	Fire extinguished.
16/01/24	00.15	24 Hour Full Power Trial. Between Dover and the Royal Sovereign Light Vessel. Revs c. 315.
	02.37	**Stop Port main Engine – defective. No 3 Piston seized. Piston Head and Skirt parted. Liner cracked.**
	07.13	Proceeded on main motors.
	07.25	Auxiliary Engines Trial.
	08.00	**Stopped Port main motor. After bearing heating up.**
	12.10	Returned to Sheerness on Starboard main motor only.
	16.00	Secured to Buoy at Sheerness.
	20.00	Discharged sick to 'Blenheim' 1 AB.
17/01/24	11.05 to 12.15	Engineer Rear Admiral on board for conference.
18/01/24	07.23	Slipped, proceeded on main motors.
	08.37	**Port main motor after bearing hot.**
	14.15	**Port main motor after bearing hot.**
	19.50	Secured to No 2 Buoy at Sheerness.
19/01/24	07.14	Slipped for main motor Trial.
	08.07	Finished Trial.
	09.26	In collision with barge *Suez*.
	09.30	Proceeded up river. Lost overboard: one gangway Ladder Bracket.
	10.45	Secured in North Lock, Chatham.
	13.00	Hands returning stores, mess traps, bedding etc.

21/01/24		Ship was shifted from North Lock to the North Wall of No 1 Basin.
23/01/24		Ship Paid Off into dockyard hands.

ADM173/13221		**June 1924**
02/06/24	09.00	Ship commissioned for further trials with the same officers and ratings.
03/06/24	07.08	Slipped from Buoy at Sheerness, and left harbour on main motors.
	07.20	Proceeded on main engines.
	07.26	Streamed Forbes Log.
	08.00	Engine Trials on the Maplin Measured Mile and up Barrows Deep.
	09.55	**Defect on main engines. Lug fractured on Exhaust Box of Starboard Main Engine.**
	10.32	Stopped both main engines. Out Engine Clutches. Proceeded on main motors.
	11.10	Started both Auxiliary Engines.
	12.05	Three Hour Auxiliary engine Trial.
	13.40	**Steering Motor burnt out.** Connected up Hand Steering.
	13.45	Defective bearing on Starboard Dynamo.
	20.35	Secured to No 8 Buoy at Sheerness.
06/06/24	15.31	Slipped from Buoy for the Maplin Sands Measured Mile.
	17.20	**Starboard Auxiliary Engine defect – After Pedestal Bearing defective.**
	17.32	In both Main Engine clutches. Preliminary trial carried out with main engines.
	21.35	Secured to No 8 Buoy at Sheerness.
07/06/24	11.30	Received 10cwt of coal. Lost one lead for the Sounding Machine.
10/06/24		Returned to Chatham.
	08.10	Secured in North Lock.
	13.00	Secured in No 1 Basin. Hands returning mess gear and bedding.
	15.30	Ship's Company returned to RN Barracks, excluding necessary watchkeepers sleeping aboard while in commission.
12/06/24	13.00	Trimming Trials in No 1 Basin.
16/06/24		Guns Crews to Instruction at Gunnery School.
17/06/24		Guns Crews to Instruction at Gunnery School.
18/06/24		Into No 7 Dock – Pumped out Dock.
19/06/24		Guns Crews to Instruction at Gunnery School.
20/06/24		Hands employed disembarking ships stores for return to Barracks. After Turret's Crew to Instruction.
22/06/24		Guns Crews employed aboard, preparing for Gunnery Equipment Trials.
23/06/24		Dressed ship with Masthead Flags for Prince of Wales' Birthday.
	09.30	Flooded Dock.
	10.00	Gunnery Equipment Trials. Pumped out the Dock.

30/06/24		Hands working about the Guns.

ADM173/13222	**July 1924**

08/07/24		No 1 Battery tank was cleaned out.
09/07/24		No 2 Battery tank was cleaned out.
10/07/24		Work carried out on the Bow Shutters. Worked the Aft Hydroplanes by hand.
11/07/24	14.00	Cleaned No 3 Battery Tank. Flooded the Dock.
14/07/24	02.00 07.30	Lt Geoffrey Frank Kenyon Hill died of septicaemia at RN Hospital Chatham. Undocked, and moved ship to East Wall of No 1 Basin.
15/07/24	14.30	Dockyard Flooding and Pumping Trials. Civil Lord of the Admiralty visited the ship.
16/07/24	09.45	Moved ship to underneath No 1 Sheer Legs. Pumping Trials.
17/07/24	 13.45 to 14.45 14.00	Flooding and Blowing Trials in the Dockyard. All hands to the funeral of Lt Hill. Half-masted Colours. First Lord of the Admiralty visited the ship.
22/07/24	11.00	Hands (After Turret) under Instruction at the Gunnery School. Ship moved to North Side of Basin near to the Battery Shed.
25/07/24		Pumping and Blowing Trials.
25/07/24		Pumping and Blowing Trials.
28/07/24		No 1 Turret Crew and Control Parties to drill at Gunnery School.
29/07/24		Aft Turret's Crew to drill at Gunnery School.
30/07/24	08.30	Ship's Company on Route March.
31/07/24		Lt G Grantham joined the ship.

ADM173/13223	**August 1924**

05/08/24	Hands employed boat pulling.
06/08/24	Hands on Route March.
07/08/24	Hands employed boat pulling.
08/08/24	Hands working on torpedo gear.

09/08/24		Hands to Sheerness Rifle Range for one week's Musketry Course.
11/08/24		Embarked torpedoes and prepared for Torpedo Trials.
12/08/24		Embarked torpedoes and prepared for Torpedo Trials.
18/08/24		Some ratings attended Gas School.
19/08/24		Some ratings attended Gas School. Pumping and Flooding of Tanks.
20/08/24		Some ratings attended Gas School. Pumping and Flooding of Tanks.
21/08/24		Replaced cells in No 2 Battery.
25/08/24		Fore Turret Crew to Gas School.
29/08/24	10.50	Ran Port Main Engine.
	11.00	Stopped the same.
	11.15	Ran Port Main Engine.
	11.35	Stopped the same.
	12.30	Hands exercised at Diving Stations.
	13.30	Ran main engines.
	14.30	Stopped the same.
30/08/24	11.05	Ran main engines.
	11.40	Stopped the same.

ADM173/13224		**September 1924**
01/09/24	12.00 to 12.30	Exercised Diving Stations.
02/09/24	12.00 to 12.30	Exercised Diving Stations.
03/09/24	12.00 to 12.30	Exercised Diving Stations.
04/09/24	12.00 to 12.30	Exercised Diving Stations, and Dockyard Trials of foremost Pump.
05/09/24	11.20	Ran main engines.
	14.30	Stopped the same.
06/09/24	08.15	Ran Port Main Engine.
	08.25	Stopped the same.
	10.30	Ran Port Main Engine.
	11.50	Stopped the same.
08/09/24		Main engines and Auxiliary Engines running. Tested new Centrex Pump.
09/09/24		Main engines and Auxiliary Engines running. Tested new Centrex Pump.
10/09/24		Main engines and Auxiliary Engines running. Tested new Centrex Pump.
11/09/24		Diving Stations Exercise all morning.

12/09/24		Trimming in the Basin. Main Engine Trial.
13/09/24		Hands provisioning and storing ship for Trials.
16/09/24	13.45	Streamed Log.
17/09/24		To sea for Engine and Motor Trials.
	20.10	Secured to No 1 Buoy at Sheerness.
18/09/24		30 Hour Progressive Trials of main engines.
	12.00	255 Revs.
	15.37	270 Revs.
	22.35	200 Revs.
19/09/24	05.15	255 Revs.
	15.35	Commenced 24-Hour Full Power Trial.
	18.33	**Stopped Starboard Main Engine. Speed Governor disintegrated.**
	19.00	240 Revs on Port Main Engine.
	19.08	**Port Main Engine stopped – Crack developed in the main column at the after end of the Port Main Engine.** Proceeded on main motors. Speed 9 Knots.
20/09/24	09.22	Secured to No 1 Buoy at Sheerness.
22/09/24		Cleaned Magazines ready to receive ammunition.
23/09/24		HMS *Excellent*'s Gun Trial Party arrived. Hands prepared for Gun Trials.
24/09/24	09.00	Commenced Gun Trials.
	12.25	Finished firing. Hands to dinner.
	13.20	Recommenced firing.
	15.25	Finished Gun Trials.
25/09/24		To Chatham, East Wall of No 1 Basin. Ship's Company discharged the bedding. Ship's Company returned to RN Barracks.
29/09/24		Inclining and Trimming Trials.

ADM173/13225	**October 1924**

07/10/24	Hands attended Medical Lecture at RN Barracks.
16/10/24 to 19/10/24	Hands painted out the fore end . . .
20/10/24	. . . and then the rest of the ship.
21/10/24	. . . and also worked about the Cable Gear.

ADM173/13226		**November 1924**
25/11/24		Signal School carried out W/T Trials.
26/11/24		Signal School carried out W/T Trials.

ADM173/13227		**December 1924**
		Hands painted the Casings all month.
01/12/24		Dressed ship with Masthead Flags on the occasion of Queen Alexandra's Birthday.
07/12/24	13.00	First Lord of the Admiralty and the C-in-C Nore visited the ship unofficially.
31/12/24		Slipped from the North Wall to No 7 Dock to paint the ship's side.

ADM173/13228		**January 1925**
06/01/25		Dock flooded for Basin Trials.
07/01/25		Embarked boats. Carried out Engine Trials. Commander Phillips DSO joined the ship.
09/01/25		Trimming Trials in the centre of the Basin.
10/01/25		Ditto.
12/01/25		Ditto.
13/01/25		Proceeded to Sheerness.
14/01/25		Diving in the vicinity of the Tongue Light Vessel. HMS *Shamrock* in company.
	10.45	Dived.
	12.35	Surfaced.
	13.07	Dived.
	13.20	Surfaced.
15/01/25		Repeat Diving Trials.
	18.45 to 19.45	**Stopped Starboard Auxiliary Engine due to worn camshaft bearing.**
17/01/25		At Spithead.
19/01/25	11.30	Rear Admiral (S) visited the ship.
	16.00	Captain Raikes left the ship at Fort Blockhouse – sick.
20/01/25	11.15 to 11.40	Rear Admiral (S) visited the ship.
21/01/25	10.30 to 11.15	C-in-C visited the ship. The Blockhouse Training Class visited the ship.
24/01/25	10.00	Admiral Superintendent visited the ship. Captain Raikes rejoined from the Sick List.

27/01/25		From Portsmouth to Spithead. Diving Exercises with HMS *Shamrock* in company.
28/01/25	09.25 to 17.10 19.00	Diving Exercises with HMS *Shamrock* in company. Rear Admiral (S) on board. Captain Raikes left the ship. Commander Phillips took over command.
29/01/25		At sea.
30/01/25		Returned to Chatham.

ADM173/13229   **February 1925**

09/02/25	 14.02 22.00	To sea for trials in company with HMS *Tintagel*. **Fractured Exhaust Box on Starboard Main Engine.** Commenced 24-Hour Full Power Trial.
10/02/25	22.00	Completed 24-Hour Full Power Trial. Anchored in Margate Roads.
12/02/25	23.18	To Galloper Light Vessel. Working up speed to Full Power as required.
13/02/25	00.30 01.00	Commenced 8-Hour Full Power Trial, Motors assisting main engines. **Defect on Port Main Engine. Vertical Drive Shaft ran hot.**
14/02/25	05.32 06.32 06.35 07.45	Proceeded on main engines. Working up to Full Power. Started Auxiliary Engines. Commenced Full Power 8-Hour Trial, Motors assisting. **Starboard Forward Motor Coupling ran hot.** Returned to Chatham. Hands returned personal gear to Royal Naval Barracks and returned to Barracks.
23/02/25	11.15 to 11.45	C-in-C visited the ship.

ADM173/132301   **March 1925**

02/03/25		Basin Trials with main engines.
03/03/25	12.35 13.09	Commenced 8-Hour Full Power Trial with Motors assisting the Engines. Trial abandoned due to the weather conditions causing racing. Returned to Sheerness.
04/03/25	23.55	Half Ahead on main engines.
05/03/25	00.15 01.00 03.01	Working up to Full Power. Commenced 8-Hour Full Power Trial with main motors assisting main engines. Stopped both main engines. **Vertical Drives defective.** Returned to Chatham Hands returned to Royal Naval Barracks.
06/03/25		Began Charging using Auxiliary Engines.

14/03/25	Starboard Watch to Sheerness for one week's Annual Range Course.
23/03/25	Hands painted casings.
25/03/25	Worked the periscopes and rangefinder.

ADM173/13231	**April 1925**
	Charging using Auxiliary Engines.
	Hands cleaning and painting/Make and Mend Clothes/Sunday Routines & Church Services.
13/04/25	C-in-C visited the ship unofficially.
16/04/25	Auxiliary Engine and Main Engine tests.
17/04/25	Main motor tests.
18/04/25	Party to Sheerness Rifle Range for one week.
23/04/25	C-in-C visited the ship unofficially.
27/04/25	Competitors for Rifle Meeting to Sheerness.
	At the end of April – Shifted berth three times.

ADM173/13232	**May 1925**
	Charging using Auxiliary Engines.
	Hands cleaning and painting/Make and Mend Clothes/Sunday Routines & Church Services. Inspection of cables and chain lockers.
07/05/25	Into No. 7 Dock.
18/05/25	Hands to Gas School and Seamanship Class.
19/05/25	Ditto.
20/05/25	Ditto.
21/05/25	Ditto.
22/05/25	Ditto.
25/05/25	Dressed ship for Empire Day.
26/05/25	Dressed ship for the Birthday of Queen Mary.

ADM173/13233	**June 1925**
	Hands attended Instructional Classes at the Royal Naval Barracks.

03/06/25		Dressed ship for the Birthday of H M The King.

ADM173/13234		**July 1925**
		In Dockyard Hands for the whole month.
10/07/25	09.00	Hands employed preparing the guns for lifting, embarking torpedoes and preparing for undocking.
23/07/25		Ship moved to underneath No. 3 Sheerlegs.

ADM173/13235		**August 1925**
05/08/25		Torpedo Party carried out Torpedo Equipment Trials with HMS *Vernon*'s officers.
11/08/25	11.30	Sheerlegs Lighter alongside to hoist in the rangefinder and the after guns.
	12.20	Chief of Staff to C-in-C Nore on board.
14/08/25	13.35	Hands employed stripping breechblocks.
18/08/25	15.17	**C2 Panel burnt out causing a slight fire in the Control Room.** The fire was extinguished with a pyrene extinguisher and the ship was ventilated.
27/08/25	11.10	S/M *K.26* secured alongside.

ADM173/13236		**September 1925**
		Batteries were regularly topped up.
03/09/25		Hands employed scrubbing deckboards.
09/09/25		Basin Trial of main engines.
10/09/25		Ditto.
11/09/25		Hands embarked stores.
	10.45	C-in-C visited the ship.
13/09/25		Proceeded to Sheerness.
14/09/25		Main Engine Trials.
15/09/25	11.40	Admiralty officers arrived on board.
		Reducer Motor Generator binding carried away. The Dockyard undertook repairs.
	14.44	Main motors assisted main engines.
16/09/25		Returned to Chatham.
17/09/25		Hands disembarked.

	11.30	Ship on blocks.
18/09/25	09.45	Ship afloat.
22/09/25		New Armature of Reducer Motor Generator fitted on a new bed. Hands embarked stores.
23/09/25		Admiral Superintendent of Chatham Dockyard inspected the ship.
24/09/25		To sea.
25/09/25		Proceeded to Portsmouth.
26/09/25		Arrived at Portsmouth.
28/09/25	18.00	**AC Motor Generator of the Sperry Gyro Compass Field burnt out**. Fixed by the ship's staff.

29/09/25		Torpedo Firing off the Isle of Wight and Portsmouth.
	At 40 feet depth	09.18 Fired one torpedo.
		09.58 Fired two torpedoes.
		10.52 Fired one torpedo.
		11.21 Fired one torpedo.
		13.15 Fired two torpedoes.
	At 42 feet depth	13.40 Fired one torpedo.
		14.24 Fired two torpedoes.

ADM173/13237		**October 1925**

01/10/25		Torpedo Exercises.
	11.38	Dived to 60 feet.
	At 60 feet depth	11.40 & 11.42 Fired two torpedoes.
		12.46 & 12.47 Fired two torpedoes.
		14.53 & 14.54 Fired two torpedoes.
		15.23 & 15.26 Fired two torpedoes.

02/10/25		**Strained focsle bollard.** Repair to be a Dockyard job.

06/10/25		Torpedo Trials.
	At 40 feet depth	09.54½ & 09.56 Fired two torpedoes.
	At 80 feet depth	10.57½ & 10.58 Fired two torpedoes.
		11.23½ & 11.28? Fired two torpedoes.
		13.00½ & 13.02 Fired two torpedoes.
		13.33 & 13.34½ Fired two torpedoes.
		14.02 & 14.04½ Fired two torpedoes.

08/10/25		Torpedo Trials.
	10.40	Dived to 100 feet.
	At 100 feet depth	10.42 & 10.44 Fired two torpedoes.
		11.31 & 11.34 Fired two torpedoes.
		12.06 & 12.08 Fired two torpedoes.
		13.35 & 13.37 Fired two torpedoes.
		14.02 & 14.05 Fired two torpedoes.
		14.43 & 14.44 Fired two torpedoes.

13/10/25		Surface Torpedo Firing.
		Fired nine torpedoes (and lost one).
	15.40	**Steering Motor broke down and Steering out of action due to a bearing running.**
15/10/25		Dived to 40 feet using HMS *Ross* as target.
	11.48	Fired a salvo of six torpedoes.
	13.00	Conducted a search for missing torpedoes. Two torpedoes lost.
16/10/25		Returned to Chatham.
19/10/25		Hands returned stores; wines and spirits in Customs charge.
		Normal routine recommenced.
29/10/25		Battery cells were lifted for examination.

ADM173/13238	**November 1925**

In dockyard hands for the **fitting of new Gun Trunk Glands and new Exhaust Pipes to the Auxiliary Engines.**

Normal routine. Plus Battery maintenance.

11/11/25	Landed a Party to attend the Armistice Day Memorial Service.

ADM173/13239	**December 1925**
02/12/25	Hands engaged in cleaning the ship's bottom.
21/12/25	Hands drew gas masks from the Anti-Gas School.

ADM173/13240	**January 1926**

Fitting of Gun Trunk Glands. Basin Trials of main engines.

04/01/26	Hands employed in red-leading the casings.
30/01/26	*K.26* secured alongside.

ADM173/13241	**February 1926**
12/02/26	Party from HMS *Excellent* employed on Gun Equipment Trials.
13/02/26	Dived to obtain trim.
16/02/26	Proceeded to Sheerness.

17/02/26		At sea.
	15.22	**Starboard Main Engine stopped due to hot bearing on the Vertical Drive.**

18/02/26		Weighed in company with HMS *Steadfast* and proceeded to carry out sub-calibre firing.
20/02/26		Engine Trials. 250 to 300 revs, reduced to 280. Returned to Sheerness.
22/02/26		Returned to Chatham.
23/02/26		**New Brush Springs were fitted to the main motors.**

ADM173/13242		**March 1926**
01/03/26		Main Engine and main motor Trials with Dockyard officers and workmen on board. Accompanied by HMS *Steadfast*.
03/03/26		Dived to 40 feet to test Gun Trunks.
16/03/26	13.30	HMS *Kent* was launched from No. 8 Slip.
20/03/26		Lt Commander J E Caffin joined the ship from HMS *Dryad*.
28/03/26		Sub Lieutenant C J Smith joined the ship.
29/03/26		Hands ammunitioned the ship.
30/03/26		Departed for Portsmouth.

ADM173/13243		**April 1926**
02/04/26		Departed for Gibraltar.
		Dived to 150 feet then to 190 feet.
13/04/26		Conducted Dived Turning Circle Trials.
20/04/26	11.30	Dived to commence attack on a Battle Practice Target.
	12.16	Surfaced and carried out Sub Calibre firing.
	13.18	Ditto.
22/04/26		Dived to carry out Full Calibre Shoot.
	09.52	Surfaced and opened fire.
	09.58	Ceased fire.
27/04/26		Dived to carry out Full Calibre Shoot.
	11.31	Surfaced and opened fire.
	11.37	Ceased fire.
28/04/26		Ammunition Supply Parties, Transmitting Station and Director Crews drilled.
29/04/26		Surface Full Calibre Shoot against a Battle Practice Target.
	10.55	Opened fire.
	11.02	Ceased fire.

ADM173/13244	May 1926
04/05/26	Dived to carry out Full Calibre firing.
12.56	Surfaced and opened fire.
07/05/26	Began the return voyage to Chatham.
10/05/26 07.30	Arrived at Chatham.
	Hands de-ammunitioned the ship.
13/05/26	Hands to Royal Naval Barracks during a long refit.
	Refit of the Auxiliary Engines.
31/05/26	The fore and aft pairs of 5.2in guns were hoisted out.

ADM173/13245	June 1926
	At Chatham.
	Refitting the Main and Auxiliary Engines.
	Cleaning and refitting and red-leading the Bow Buoyancy Tanks.

ADM173/13246	July 1926
	At Chatham.
	Work on the Auxiliary Engines, and the underwater service valves.
	Cleaning of the Oil Fuel and Main Ballast Tanks.

ADM173/13247	August 1926
	At Chatham.
	Work on the Auxiliary Engines, and the underwater service valves.
	Cleaning of the Oil Fuel and Main Ballast Tanks.

ADM173/13248	September 1926
13/09/26	Torpedoes were re-embarked.
14/09/26	Main Engine Basin Trials.
18/09/26	Dockyard Refit was completed.
20/09/26	Carried out Engine Trials.
21/09/26	Embarked ammunition.

22/09/26		Sailed to Campbeltown.
27/09/26		To Loch Indail, Islay. Sub Calibre Shoot using a buoy as a target. Two 2pdr cases lost overboard.

ADM173/13249		**October 1926**
01/10/26		Sailed to Portree.
04/10/26		Sailed to the Moray Firth.
05/10/26		Off Burghead carried out a Sub Calibre Exercise, using a Duffin Silhouette towing a Pattern VI Target.
06/10/26		At Moray Firth carried out a Sub Calibre Exercise, using a Duffin Silhouette towing a Pattern VI Target.
07/10/26		Ditto, from dived. Proceeded to Invergordon.
	13.00	Secured alongside *Cyclops*.
11/10/26		C-in-C Atlantic Fleet visited the ship.
14/10/26		Proceeded to Whistle Bay for a Full Calibre Shoot in 'Area F'. Proceeded to Dornoch Firth.
	17.35	Secured alongside *Cyclops*.
16/10/26		Full Calibre Shoot on a Battle Practice Target from dived.
	14.25	Dived and commenced attack.
	14.57	Surfaced and opened fire.
	15.02	Ceased fire.
	16.23	Long range surface shoot.
	16.31	Ceased fire.
		Secured alongside *Cyclops*.
19/10/26		Sailed for Portsmouth.
22/10/26		Surface torpedo firing.
25/10/26		Surface torpedo firing.
29/10/26		Surface torpedo firing.

ADM173/13250		**November 1926**
03/11/26		At sea on War Patrol Exercises.
10/11/26		C-in-C Portsmouth visited the ship.
12/11/26		Rear Admiral (S) visited the ship.
13/11/26		Sailed for Sheerness. De-ammunitioned.

16/11/26		Sailed for Chatham.
17/11/26		Officers and Ship's Company transferred to the Royal Naval Barracks for accommodation.
18/11/26		Refit commenced on Main and Auxiliary Machinery, and all underwater fittings.

ADM173/13251		**December 1926**
		In dockyard hands.
22/12/26		Torpedoes were shipped.
23/12/26		The dock was flooded.
29/12/26		The ship was undocked.

ADM173/13252		**January 1927**
		Refit of the Auxiliary Engines continued.
08/01/27		Refit completed.
10/01/27		Sailed for Sheerness.
11/01/27		Speed Trials on the Maplin Measured Mile.
12/01/27		Sea Trials.
13/01/27		Took on ammunition at Sheerness.
14/01/27		Sailed for Portsmouth.
15/01/27		Arrived at Portsmouth.
18/01/27		Carried out Sea Trials.
24/01/27		Sailed for Gibraltar. Speed around 10 knots.
27/01/27	12.30	Making 13 knots.
28/01/27	16.25	Making 14 knots.
29/01/27		Arrived at Gibraltar.

ADM173/13253		**February 1927**
		Based at Gibraltar.
02/02/27		Carried out Underwater Speed Trials. **Explosion in the Battery.**

07/02/27	Carried out Underwater Speed Trials and Depth Changing Trials.	
08/02/27	Carried out a dummy attack on *Conquest*. Fired two torpedoes during a second attack.	
09/02/27	Carried out a practice attack on *Conquest*. Carried out a second exercise with *Conquest* and S/M *L.18* and *L.26*.	
15/02/27	Carried out two practice attacks on *Conquest*.	
16/02/27	Dived and carried out a Divisional Exercise with *K.26*.	
25/02/27	Carried out a Deep Dive hunt with the 6th Destroyer Flotilla. Carried out a Divisional Attack on *Conquest* with *K.26*.	

ADM173/13254	**March 1927**	
02/03/27	At sea to meet the Mediterranean Fleet for Exercise.	
03/03/27	Deep Dive Asdic Exercise with the Mediterranean Fleet.	
04/03/27	Flotilla Manoeuvring Exercise.	
08/03/27	At sea for a combined Exercise with the Mediterranean and Atlantic Fleets.	
09/03/27	Ditto.	
10/03/27	Ditto.	
11/03/27	At Gibraltar for repairs to the Starboard Generator and the main engines.	
29/03/27	Sailed for Philippeville. *En route* carried out a practice attack on *Conquest*. Carried out specific fuel consumption trials.	
30/03/27	Used *Eagle*, *Conquest* and two destroyers of the 1st Destroyer Flotilla as targets for practice attacks.	
31/03/27	At Philippeville.	

ADM173/13255	**April 1927**	
05/04/27		Sailed for Malta.
06/04/27		Carried out submerged attacks on the Battlefleet. Targets were *Barham* and *Malaya*.
07/04/27	10.00	Arrived at Malta. Secured in Misida Creek at Buoys Nos 1 and 1A.
11/04/27		Gunnery Drills working up for an exercise.
17/04/27		Church Parties. Composed of: C of E Nil

		Presbyterians	1
		Wesleyans	2
		Baptists	3
		Congregationalists	1
		Roman Catholics	5
		Primative Methodists	1

20/04/27 Sub Calibre Shoot from submerged on Pattern VI Target.

21/04/27 Sub Calibre Shoot from submerged – same target.
Sub Calibre Shoot surfaced.

24/04/27 Church Parties.   Composed of:
C of E   20
Presbyterians   1
Wesleyans   2
Baptists   1
Congregationalists 1
Roman Catholics   5
Privative Methodists 1

26/04/27   09.36 to 09.41   Full Calibre Shoot on the surface at Battle Practice Target.

27/04/27   10.10 to 10.13   Full Calibre Shoot from submerged at Battle Practice Target.

ADM173/13256   **May 1927**

01/05/27 Church Parties.   Composed of:
C of E   Nil
Presbyterians   1
Wesleyans   1
Baptists   2
Congregationalists 1
Roman Catholics   4
Privative Methodists Nil

02/05/27 Hands embarked ammunition.

03/05/27 Full Calibre Shoot surfaced at towed Battle Practice Target.
      10.00   Opened fire.
      10.07   Ceased fire.

04/05/27   08.30   C-in-C Mediterranean Fleet came on board.
      10.01   Surfaced and carried out Full Calibre Shoot from submerged.
      10.05   Ceased fire.
      11.15   C-in-C Mediterranean Fleet left the ship.

05/05/27 Fleet Exercise with the Mediterranean Fleet. One torpedo fired at *Warspite*.

12/05/27 Sub Calibre concentrated fire with *Conquest* on the surface.

13/05/27 Full Calibre bombardment of Filfola Island. With the Vice Admiral
commanding the 1st Battle Squadron on board.
Surfaced and opened fire.

	10.54	Ceased fire.
23/05/27		To 'Area W' for concentrated Sub Calibre Exercise with *Conquest*.
	10.25	Surfaced and opened fire.
	10.32	Ceased fire.
25/05/27		To 'Area W' for concentrated Full Calibre Exercise with *Conquest*.
	11.32	Surfaced and opened fire.
	11.38	Ceased fire.
26/05/27		Hands de-ammunitioned ship at Malta into ammunition lighter and disembarked the empty cases.
27/05/27		Ditto.
30/05/27		Alongside at Somerset Wharf in French Creek. **To lift out the Rangefinder.**
31/05/27		Lt Commander Ruck-Keene joined the ship.

ADM173/13257	**June 1927**
	In dockyard hands.
01/06/27	Under tow to No 1 Dock, Dockyard Creek.
02/06/27	Refit for Main and Auxiliary Engines and underwater fittings and Batteries.
20/06/27	Hands left ship for HMS *Egmont* to man the side, on the occasion of HMS *Renown* leaving harbour with the Duke and Duchess of York on board.
24/06/27	The Gunnery Party carried out a Rapid Loading Drill.
29/06/27	The ship was undocked.
30/06/27	Hands embarked ammunition.

ADM173/13258	**July 1927**
05/07/27	Hands embarked stores. Rear Admiral Malta came on board.
06/07/27	Departed Malta for Navarino. Dived to adjust trim.
07/07/27	Arrived at Navarino.
17.00	Hands spread the awnings.
10/07/27	Divine Service held in *Cyclops*, after the Ship's Company was inspected by the C-in-C.
11/07/27	Moved alongside *Cyclops*.
12/07/27	Sailed for Port Iero, Mitylene. Took station astern of HMS *Conquest* in Cruising

Order No. 2.

En route carried out a practice attack on the Battle Squadron. No torpedoes fired.

13/07/27		*En route* to Port Iero. Carried out a Gunnery Control Exercise.
18/07/27		Exercised Fire, Collision and Gas Attack Stations.
19/07/27	09.30	Captain (S) R B Darke arrived on board to carry out an inspection.
	10.45	Captain (S) left the ship.
21/07/27		At sea. Carried out an A/S Exercise with three destroyers of the 2nd Destroyer Flotilla.
22/07/27		Inspection at sea by Captain (S).
	10.28	Dived and fired six Watershots and re-loaded.
	11.08	Surfaced. Captain (S) transferred to *K.26*.
26/07/27		To Salonika.
27/07/27	10.00	Commander C H Allen DSO joined the ship. 'Dived on account of change of commanding officer'.
28/07/27		At Salonika.
	08.00	Hauled down the pendant of Captain P E Phillips DSO. Hoisted the pendant of Commander C H Allen DSO.
	22.25	Four officers joined the ship for passage.
29/07/27		Departed Salonika for Skiathos.
	01.13	Altered course to Port to avoid a steamship who should have given way. Made a flashing signal to ascertain her nationality. She replied 'Stettin'.
30/07/27		Gunnery Party carried out a Director Test.

ADM173/13259	**August 1927**
01/08/27	At Skiathos. To sea for exercises. Leading 'L' Class into station for Captain (S) firing. Took station on HMS *Crysanthemum*. **Port Main Engine failed – bent con rod**. Proceeded on Starboard Main Engine to Skiathos and berthed alongside *Cyclops*.
02/08/27	Repairs to Port Main Engine.
03/08/27	Proceeded to sea on Starboard Main Engine for Sub Calibre Exercise (one round fired from each gun from submerged).
04/08/27	Proceeded on Exercises on Starboard Main Engine. Passed under the A/S screen and carried out a practice attack on the cruisers. HMS *Cardiff* was the target. No torpedoes fired. Proceeded to Argostoli.
06/08/27	Alongside *Cyclops* at Argostoli. Long notice for repairs to the Port Main Engine.

08/08/27		*K.26* secured alongside. Repairs completed.
10/08/27		Regatta crews away as required.
12/08/27		Gunnery Party employed in running guns in and out.
15/08/27	20.00	Lt (E) T S Lee joined the ship.
	20.10	Hoisted in boats.
16/08/27		Left Argostoli for Malta.
	02.00	Weighed.
	02.15	Submarines in line ahead on *X.1*.
	04.07	*K.26* parted company.
	04.46	*L.23* parted company.
	05.18	*L.16* parted company.
	05.50	*L.26* parted company.
		Dived.
	09.26	Sighted Red Cruisers.
		Passed through the Asdic Lines and made a submerged attack by hydrophone at 80 feet.
	11.03	Fired a smoke float.
	11.51	Fired a smoke float.
	17.45	Put the clocks back half an hour.
	18.45	Put the clocks back a further half hour.
		Proceeded on Starboard Main Engine at 9½ knots.
17/08/27		Increased speed to 13 knots. Sighted Red Cruisers. Sighted Red Battlefleet. Increased to 13½ knots to close with *Conquest*.
18/08/27		Arrived at Malta. Secured to Nos 1 and 1A Buoys, Misida Creek. HMS *K.26* secured alongside.
22/08/27		Sub Calibre Shoot from submerged.
	10.21	Surfaced and opened fire.
	10.28	Ceased fire.
	12.27	Stopped. **Helm jambed** [*sic*].
	12.28	Proceeded as required.
23/08/27		Exercises – Holding trim stopped.
	11.40	Deep dive.
		Time to dive to 80 feet from periscope depth 1 minute 30 seconds.
24/08/27		Discharged 14,570 gallons of fuel oil.
25/08/27		Attack, dummy attack and A/S Exercises with HMS *Viscount*. Target ship at high speed.
		Fired Watershots. Fired two torpedoes.
		Then took part in A/S Exercise.
31/08/27		Secured alongside Stores Wharf.

ADM173/13260	**September 1927**

01/09/27		Proceeded to Marsa Scirocco.
02/09/27		Dived for attack on Battlefleet.
		Fired six torpedoes at *Warspite* at 3,300 yards range.
	12.00	Cleaned out tanks at sea.
	12.05	Hands to bathe.
		Returned to harbour.
05/09/27		Ship in dockyard hands (in No 1 Dock).
to		
30/09/27		Bags and hammocks for transport to HMS *Egmont*.
		First Party left for Pembroke Camp.
		One Lewis Gun and six revolvers transported to HMS *Egmont*.

ADM173/13261 **October 1927**

In dockyard hands refitting machinery and gear and batteries.

ADM173/13262 **November 1927**

In dockyard hands for refit.
Hands employed in chipping the hull and painting, including the Control Room and the Hydrophone Well.

09/11/27	10.15	H M The King of Spain visited the ship.
	10.40	H M The King of Spain left the ship.

ADM173/13263 **December 1927**

In dockyard hands.
Three days spent on trials of Engines and diving equipment.

28/12/27	A/S Exercises with HMS *Winchelsea*.
29/12/27	'A' and 'Y' right guns' crews to drill.
30/12/27	'A' and 'Y' left guns' crews to drill.
31/12/27	*L.16* secured alongside.

ADM173/13264 **January 1928**

In dockyard hands.

06/01/28		To sea for Full Power Trials.
		Fault with Port Forward main motor.
09/01/28		Proceeded to the Measured Mile for Full Power Trials.
	09.33	**Starboard Main Engine Vertical Drive fractured after 3 minutes at Full Power.**

23/01/28		Range Party to Ricasoli.
24/01/28		Range Party to Ricasoli.
25/01/28		Range Party to Ricasoli.
26/01/28		Range Party to Ricasoli.

ADM173/13265	**February 1928**

In dockyard hands all month.

Hands conducted exercises all month:
Diving stations wearing gasmasks.
Raising the anchor by hand.
Diving communications.
Diving collision stations.
Gun action stations.
Fire stations.
FT exercises at Corradino.
Tubes crews to loading practice.
Route March.
Diving control parties.
Rigging the W/T masts.

21/02/28		Admiral of the Fleet Earl Beatty visited the ship.
28/02/28		2-Hour Basin Trial of Port Main Engine. Completed satisfactorily.

ADM173/13266	**March 1928**

In dockyard hands until 12 March.
Alternated Charges on Port and Starboard Auxiliary Engines.

06/03/28		Disinfecting to exterminate cockroaches.
10/03/28		Lt (E) W S Jameson left the ship, discharged to Foreign Service Leave.
12/03/28		Sub Lt Cox RNR joined the ship.
13/03/28		Sailed for Gibraltar. Exercised A/S Gear. Diving Trials at sea.
15/03/28	09.30	Increased to 230 revs Starboard Main Engine.
17/03/28	09.10	Increased to 250 revs Starboard Main Engine. Secured alongside HMS *Tourmaline* in No 2 Dock.
22/03/28		Received 22 tons of shale oil from the oiler *Prestol*.

23/03/28		At sea for exercises with the Atlantic Fleet (Blue Cruisers). Observed *Frobisher*. Observed the Blue Battlefleet.
	23.30	Two cruisers crossed the bows twice. Slowed to 8 knots ahead.
24/03/28		Returned to Gibraltar.
26/03/28		Landing Party left the ship for a rehearsal of the Review to take place on the North Front.
27/03/28		Ditto.
28/03/28		Ditto.
29/03/28		Ditto.

ADM173/13267	**April 1928**
05/04/28	Sailed for Valencia. Flotilla tactical manoeuvres at sea.
06/04/28	*K.26* was detached to fly a kite for Lewis Gun AA practice. Submarines in close order on *X.1*.
07/04/28	Arrived at Valencia.
08/04/28	Hands to Shore Leave in Valencia.
14/04/28	Departed Valencia for Malta.
17/04/28	Arrived Malta.
18/04/28	Sub Calibre Shoot. Carried out four runs.
19/04/28	5.2in Full Calibre Shoot. Dived. Fired six Watershots. Dived. Fired five torpedoes. *St Issey* recovered the torpedoes.
21/04/28	Tested the Motor Boat.
24/04/28	Full Calibre Firing. Dived to 95 feet. A/S Trials. Fired six Watershots.
26/04/28	5.2in Full Calibre Firing. A/S Trials.
29/04/28	Proceeded to sea for an attack on the Fleet.
30/04/28	Carried out a mock attack on the Fleet, cruisers and HMS *Ramillies*. No torpedoes fired.

ADM173/13268	May 1928	
		In dockyard hands. Refitting the Vertical Drive to the Port Main Engine.
01/05/28		Disembarked torpedoes and ammunition. Lost overboard by accident – one motor boat starting handle. (Previously lost overboard to date had been: one adjustable spanner; one block; one bucket and one megaphone.)
02/05/28		Proceeded to No 3 Dock. Hands engaged in scraping the ship's bottom.
03/05/28		Hands removed personal gear to HMS *Egmont* and took up accommodation there. Hands engaged in painting the ship's boats. Hands refitting the W/T Masts.
18/05/28		Undocked and moved to Somerset Wharf.
23/05/28	08.00	Landing Party left for Ghain Tuffieh to take part in Combined Operations.
24/05/28		Dressed the ship with masthead flags on the anniversary of Empire Day.
26/05/28	08.00 to 09.00	Half-masted Colours.

ADM173/13269	June 1928	
		In dockyard hands until 16 June refitting the Vertical Drive to the Port Main Engine.
		Beginning and breaking Charges.
04/06/28		Dressed ship on the Birthday of H M The King.
11/06/28		Basin Engine Trials.
12/06/28		Hands engaged in painting baggage store in *Cyclops*.
19/06/28		Proceeded on main engines out of harbour. Changed over to main motors. Carried out Diving Trials. Returned to harbour and secured alongside *K.26*.
20/06/28		Dummy dived attack on *Douglas*. Fired six Watershots. Carried out second attack on *Douglas*. Fired five torpedoes at *Douglas*. Returned to harbour and embarked a new Generator. **Armature of Midships Air Compressor defective – necessary to fit the spare.** Gunnery Party carried out a Director Test.
21/06/28		Left berth on main motors. Stopped. Proceeded out of harbour entrance on main engines. Speed 9 knots. Sub Calibre Firing. Carried out five runs. Returned to harbour. Passed entrance and stopped. Proceeded on main motors to buoys.

22/06/28		To Dockyard for examination of Air Compressors.
23/06/28		In dockyard hands until 13 July repairing the after and midships Air Compressors. Hands engaged in painting stanchions, and stowing gear in the casings.
27/06/28	08.00 to 10.00	Half-masted the Colours.
28/06/28		Exercised surface gun action stations.

ADM173/13270   **July 1928**

		In dockyard hands until 13 July repairing the Air Compressors.
01/07/28		Sunday Church Parties:

C of E   42
Roman Catholic   2
Presbyterian   2
Wesleyans   2
Baptists   3
Salvationists   1

02/07/28	11.15	Exercised surface gun action.
	11.45	Exercised gun action from submerged.
04/07/28		Fitting water polo booms. Exercised diving communications party.
07/07/28	08.30 to 09.30	Half-masted the Colours.
11/07/28	18.30	Fire Party called away to extinguish fire in T.E.O.'s locker (*Loch Long*).
	19.00	Fire Party returned on board.
13/07/28		Friday. Repairs to Air Compressors completed. Carried out trials of the Compressors. Six hands discharged sick to HMS *Egmont*.
14/07/28		Sailed for Suda Bay.
15/07/28		Maintained 240 revs on both main engines.
	17.00	Put clocks on half an hour – assumed Z-1½.
	19.00	Put clocks on half an hour – assumed Z-2.
	21.00	Increased to 260 revs (12 knots).
16/07/28		At Suda Bay. Regatta.
	20.25	Hoisted in boats.
17/07/28		A/S Exercise with *L.16*. Exercised gun action from submerged.
18/07/28		A/S Trials with *Cyclops*.
19/07/28		Proceeded from Suda Bay to Spezzia.
	20.30	Hoisted in boats.

23/07/28		Diving drills at sea. Fired five Watershots.
		Exercised gun action from submerged.
24/07/28	10.04	Stopped, and dropped Target.
	10.21	Stopped, to right capsized Target.
	10.29	At 11 knots carried out four runs of Sub Calibre Firing.
	11.13	Ceased fire.
	11.18	Stopped to pick up Target.
	11.45	Hands to bathe.
	14.00	Took on one torpedo alongside *Cyclops*.
26/07/28		Gunlayers and Transmitting Station crew to *Douglas* for drill.
29/07/28	05.40	Hands employed cleaning ship.
	06.40	Hands to breakfast.
	07.40	Hands employed cleaning ship . . .
	09.45 to 11.00	Inspecting Officer came on board, inspected Divisions, books and the ship.
	19.45	Hoisted in boats.
30/07/28	06.30	Stopped off HMS *Douglas*. Inspecting Officer embarked for sea inspection.
	06.43	Exercised Man Overboard. Dived, surfaced, exercised gun action.
	08.40	Inspecting Officer disembarked.
	10.30	Hands mustered for inoculation.
	13.30	Disembarked and embarked one torpedo.
31/07/28		Sailed from Spezzia to Skiathos.
	00.00	Submarines formed line ahead on *X.1* at 12 knots.
	00.30	Submarines formed Divisions in line ahead, columns disposed to Port. Reduced to 10 knots.
	08.30 to 19.20	Carried out a Search Exercise.

ADM173/13271		**August 1928**
01/08/28		*En route* to Skiathos. Carried out a dummy attack on *Douglas*.
		Carried out a second attack on *Douglas* and fired five torpedoes.
		Arrived at Skiathos.
02/08/28	10.11	Surfaced and carried out three runs of Sub Calibre Firing, on main motors.
	10.40	Ceased fire.
	14.00 to 18.45	Gave leave to picnic parties.
03/08/28		Saturday's Routine (Cleaning ship).
04/08/28		Surfaced Sub Calibre Firing.
06/08/28		Transmitting Station crew to *Cyclops* for drill.
	15.05 to 15.23	Carried out surface Full Calibre Firing by Gunlayers, in the presence of the Flotilla Gunnery Officer.
		Secured alongside *K.26*.
	18.00	Hands mustered for inoculation.
07/08/28	09.12	Surfaced and carried out two runs of Sub Calibre Firing.
	09.18	Ceased fire.

09/08/28	09.51	Surfaced and carried out Full Calibre Firing.
	09.57	Ceased fire.
		Carried out Fuel Consumption Test at 300 revs (13? knots).
10/08/28		Sailed for Argostoli.
	10.25 to 10.52	Inclination Exercise.
	17.10	Dummy attack on HMS *Douglas*.
	21.00 to 22.05	Night Encounter Exercise.
11/08/28		At Argostoli – Exercises.
	08.33	Red Aeroplane passed low over the ships.
	08.45	Sighted Red Cruisers.
	08.52	Stopped and dived. Proceeded on main motors. Exercise 'NV', attempting attacks on HMS *Queen Elizabeth*.
	12.00	Attempting attacks on HMS *Eagle*.
	13.30	Exercise completed. Surfaced.
13/08/28		Hands employed as required exterminating cockroaches.
15/08/28		Disembarked five Mark IV torpedoes and embarked five S.F.P. torpedoes.
16/08/28		Boats' crews away to Fleet Regatta.
17/08/28		Boats' crews away to Fleet Regatta.
		Received 5,300 galls fresh water.
		Sub Lt P J H Boutect joined the ship.
18/08/28		Secured alongside *Courageous*.
20/08/28	08.21	Vice Admiral 1st Cruiser Squadron embarked. Dived. Surfaced at gun action stations.
	09.58	Vice Admiral disembarked.
	10.14	RAF Party from HMS *Courageous* embarked. Dived and surfaced.
	12.03	RAF Party disembarked.
21/08/28	23.00	Put clocks back half an hour, assuming Z-1½.
22/08/28	02.30	Put clocks back half an hour, assuming Z-1.
	17.17	Sailed for Malta.
23/08/28		On passage. Carried out a dummy attack on HMS *Resolution*.
24/08/28		Lt Commander R S Barry RN joined the ship at sea.
		Diving exercises, surfacing and gun action exercises.
		Secured to Nos 1 and 1A Buoys at Pieta.
		Received 4,000 galls of fresh water.
26/08/28		Lt R M G Gambier left the ship.
		Lt Commander P H Ruck left the ship.
27/08/28	20.30	Landed Shore Patrol.
	24.00	Shore Patrol returned on board.

28/08/28		Fired Watershots. *L.18* and *L.23* secured alongside.
29/08/28		Lt Commander R H D Olivier left the ship.
30/08/28		To sea to act as target for *L.21*.
31/08/28		Hands employed embarking ammunition (a.m.). Hands employed striking down ammunition (p.m.).

ADM173/13272		**September 1928**
		At Malta.
05/09/28	22.45	Landed Shore Patrol.
06/09/28	03.30	Shore Patrol returned on board. Dived and carried out a dummy attack on *Douglas*. Carried out a second dummy attack on *Douglas*.
07/09/28		*En route* to Messina. Exercise 'NX'.
	12.40	Fired salvo of six S.F.P. torpedoes at *Queen Elizabeth*. Surfaced and searched for lost torpedo.
	18.05	Hands to bathe.
08/09/28		Arrived at Messina and secured alongside *Cyclops*. *L.21*, *L.23* and *L.18* secured alongside.
10/09/28		Gunlayers and Trainers to drill.
	17.00	Evening Quarters. Hands to bathe.
12/09/28		Hands employed topping up the Battery.
15/09/28	05.30 to 17.00	Taking a Charge from *Cyclops*. Diving Boat alongside. Diver employed working about the stern gland.
16/09/28		Sailed from Messina for Brindisi.
17/09/28		*En route* to Brindisi. Carried out four submerged attacks on *Cyclops* (three using Asdic).
	16.30	Started a Charge on both Auxiliary Engines.
18/09/28	09.10	Dived. Carried out an Asdic attack on *Cyclops*.
	10.05	Dived. Carried out a gun action submerged attack on *Cyclops*. Arrived at Brindisi.
19/09/28	05.30	Commenced a Charge from *Cyclops*.
	15.45	Broke the Charge.
24/09/28		Sailed for Ancona.
	09.12	Dived for an A/S attack on *Cyclops*.
	11.03	Dived for an A/S attack on *Cyclops*.
	13.13	Surface gun action attack on *Cyclops*.

25/09/28	07.20	Dived for A/S/Asdic attack on *Douglas*.
	08.20	Carried out Sub Calibre Firing.
	15.10	Arrived at Ancona. Secured alongside Clementina Quay.

ADM173/13273   **October 1928**

03/10/28	04.50	Sailed for the Brioni Isles.
	07.50	Carried out a dummy dived attack on *Cyclops*.
	16.40	Arrived at Brioni. Shifted berth twice.
12/10/28		Sailed for Fiume.
	10.45	Carried out Lewis Gun practice. (AA Target was supplied by other ships).
	16.40	Secured alongside *Cyclops* on the East side of Malo Napoli. Began a Charge from *Cyclops*.
16/10/28		Exercised the Spotting Table.
19/10/28	05.20	Sailed for Giavosa.
	12.11	Surfaced and exercised gun action.
	14.10	Carried out a dummy dived attack on *Douglas*.
20/10/28		Carried out a dummy hydrophone attack on *K.26*.
		Carried out a Sub Calibre Firing at a Target towed by *Douglas*.
	15.30	Secured alongside *Cyclops*.
26/10/28	10.00	'Blew out four torpedoes'.
	11.30	Embarked four torpedoes.
28/10/28	06.20	Sailed for Malta.
	15.45	Proceeded on main motors discharging Batteries at average speed of 6 knots, during Captain S.I. Firing, using *Douglas* as the target.
29/10/28	04.50	**Stopped Port Main Engine (defective)**. Proceeded on Starboard Main Engine at 9 knots.
	11.28	Defect on Port Main Engine made good. Proceeded on main engines.
30/10/28	09.06	Full Calibre Firing at Battle Practice Target.
	09.36	Captain S.I.'s firing by 'L' class submarine.
	1.337	Secured alongside Stores Wharf, Dockyard Creek, Malta.

ADM173/13274   **November 1928**

05/11/28		Range Party sent ashore.
06/11/28		Ditto.
07/11/28		Ditto.
08/11/28		Ditto.
09/11/28		Ditto.

12/11/28		Ditto.
13/11/28		Ditto.
14/11/28		Ditto.
15/11/28		Cast off S/M *Oxley* and *Otway*.
16/11/28		Range Party sent ashore.
17/11/28		Exercised surface gun action.
19/11/28		Exercised dummy bombardment of Filfola Island.
20/11/28		Surfaced for attack on Filfola Island.
	10.56	Opened fire with Full Calibre.
	11..02	Ceased fire.
	1215	Observed for salvo of torpedoes fired by *Douglas*.
21/11/28	09.35	Commenced Sub Calibre Firing on the surface at Part VI Target towed by 'Moy'.
	11.21	**After hydroplanes jambed** [*sic*] **and were put in hand operation.**
	12.10?	Fired a salvo of six torpedoes at *Douglas*.
23/11/28	09.26	Commenced surfacing.
	09.28	Opened Full Calibre Firing at Battle Practice Target.
	09.34	Ceased firing.
	17.03	Commenced a Charge from the shore.
30/11/28		Carried out Engine Trials on the Measured Mile.

ADM173/13275	**December 1928**
	George P Thomas took over as Captain (S) of the 1st Submarine Flotilla, Malta.
03/12/28	Annual Refit commenced. Hands disembarked personal possessions, and moved to HMS *Egmont*.
09/12/28	Ship's Company attended the 1st Submarine Flotilla Service in the Dockyard Church.
10/12/28	Docked in No. 1 Dock. Hands employed in scraping the ship's bottom.
13/12/28	Tested the Fire Mains.
14/12/28	Ditto.
22/12/28	Ditto.
24/12/28	Ditto.
25/12/28	Ditto.

26/12/28		Ditto.
27/12/28		Ditto.
28/12/28		Ditto.
29/12/28		Ditto.
30/12/28		Thirty C of E Church Party members to *Courageous*. Tested the Fire Mains.
31/12/28		Tested the Fire Mains.

ADM173/13276		**January 1929**
		In dockyard hands for Annual Refit.
14/01/29		Two ratings to Ricasoli Range.
15/01/29		Two ratings to Ricasoli Range. Discharged 44 ratings to *'Dartmouth'* for passage to the UK. 44 ratings joined the ship from *'Dartmouth'*.
29/01/29		Signalmen and Telegraphists to Ricasoli Range for Annual Musketry Course.
30/01/29		Seamen and Stokers to Ricasoli Range for Annual Musketry Course.
31/01/29		Ditto.

ADM173/13277		**February 1929**
		In dockyard hands for Annual Refit in No. 1 Dock, Malta.
01/02/29		24 ratings to Ricasoli Range for Annual Pistol Course.
14/02/29		Hands exercised in small arms drill at Conadino.
27/02/29	07.30 08.00 11.05	Commenced flooding the dock. Carried out a tilt test. Undocked the ship and moved to Stores Wharf alongside *K.26*. Remounted the Rangefinder.

ADM173/13278		**March 1929**
		In dockyard hands.
07/03/29		Hands employed embarking ammunition.
11/03/29		Hands employed embarking torpedoes.
12/03/29		The Ship's Company carried out anti-influenza treatment.
15/03/29	11.15 to 143.5	Carried out Basin Trials on both main engines.

18/03/29		At sea for Engine Trials on the Measured Mile. **On examination the Ball Races of the Camshaft Drive on both main engines were found to be broken and the Teeth were badly worn.**
23/03/29		Rifle Range party of five ratings was landed.
28/03/29		To sea to carry out 'statical' trim dived. Exercised gun action from submerged.

ADM173/13279		**April 1929**

In dockyard hands.

The Log Entry for April 1929 reads: *Owing to the main engines being out of action the ship is not considered 'ready for sea'.*

09/04/29	08.45	Cast off from tug. Left harbour on main motors. Carried out a Director Test.
10/04/29	09.26	Weighed and proceeded to sea. Exercised the Hand Steering, Planes in hand and the Sounding Machine. Exercised gun action from submerged. Tuned the Asdic gear.
17/04/29	10.15 to 11.00	Carried out a Sub Calibre Shoot at a Part VI Target.
19/04/29	11.40 to 12.10 14.20	Carried out a Sub Calibre Shoot at a Part VI Target. Dived and carried out an A/S Exercise on *Warspite*.
20/04/29		The Sub Calibre Guns were unshipped.
26/04/29		Three ratings of an advanced Camp Party marched to Ghain Tuffick Camp.
27/04/29		Three officers and the remaining 42 ratings of the Camp Party marched to Ghain Tuffick Camp.

ADM173/13280		**May 1929**

In dockyard hands.

03/05/29		37 members of the Camp Party returned. Lt R H Dewhurst left the ship and transferred to *L.23*.
04/05/29		The second Camp Party of 37 left.
06/05/29		Dressed the ship with masthead flags for Accession Day.
08/05/29		Moved the ship to No 8 Dockyard Creek to allow sounding operations to be carried out.
10/05/29		The second Camp Party returned.

16/05/29		Hands disembarked and re-embarked four torpedoes.
21/05/29	07.15	Started a Charge on the Port Generator.
	08.10	Broke the Charge due to **fracture of the Port Auxiliary Engine Crankshaft.**
	17.00	Started a Charge from the Dockyard.
23/05/29		Hands assisted Yugo Slav [*sic*] ships to moor.
24/05/29		Dressed the ship with masthead flags for Empire Day.
25/05/29		Submarine Flotilla Sports at Marsa Island.
26/05/29		Dressed the ship with masthead flags on the Birthday of H M The Queen.
27/05/29		Commander (E) L G Cowland joined the ship.
29/05/29		Lt Commander G C Harris joined the ship.
30/05/29		Hands employed transporting gear from *Cyclops* to *Lucia*.

ADM173/13281		**June 1929**
		In dockyard hands from 1 to 5 June and from 11 to 14 June.
01/06/29		Commander (E) W G Cowland joined the ship.
03/06/29		Engineer commander A Ensleigh left the ship.
04/06/29		Carried out Basin Trial on main engines.
06/06/29		At sea for Engine Trials, and Battery charging and discharging.
		Carried out a Watch Diving exercise.
07/06/29		At sea for Engine Trials, then to Pieta Creek.
14/06/29		Hands embarked torpedoes and ammunition.
	09.30 to 15.30	Basin Trial of the main engines.
17/06/29		Put to sea for Main Engine Trials, with Dockyard workmen on board.
		Carried out Sub Calibre Firing and Lewis Gun Firing.
		Anchored in St Pauls Bay.
18/06/29		Put to sea.
	09.05 to 09.40	Carried out Sub Calibre Firing.
	10.07	Fired a live torpedo.
	10.50	Dived to attack *Winchelsea*.
	12.27	Dived to attack *Winchelsea* and fired one torpedo.
	13.20	Dived for Hydrophone Exercise with *L.16*.
	14.22	Surfaced for Hydrophone Exercise with *L.16*.
	17.05	In harbour embarking two torpedoes.
20/06/29		Put to sea.
	09.47	Surfaced and carried out Full Calibre Shoot on Battle Practice Target.
	09.52	Ceased fire.
	11.25	Dived and fired one live torpedo.

	15.30	Carried out a submerged attack on *Vega*.
	16.02	Fired one torpedo.
22/06/29		Dressed the ship with masthead flags for Coronation Day.
24/06/29		Half-masted the Colours.
25/06/29		Lt H du P Richardson left the ship to join *Ramillies* for passage to the UK.
26/06/29		Proceeded with 'L' class submarines to Marsa Scirocco.
27/06/29		At sea.
28/06/29		Participated in Exercise 'OD'.
	10.25	Manoeuvres.
	10.55	Dived to carry out an A/S attack on *Douglas*.
		Carried out Equal Speed manoeuvres, Flying a Kite, gun action, firing rifle grenades, and Throw-off Sub Calibre Firing at *Douglas*.
29/06/29		Sailed for Dragamesti.

ADM173/13282		**July 1929**
04/07/29		Sub Calibre Throw-off Firing at *Douglas*.
		Carried out two dummy submerged attacks on *Douglas*.
08/07/29		Participated in Exercise 'OF'. Targets were the Battlefleet.
10/07/29		Lost overboard one Telescope No 3536.
		Participated in Exercise 'OG'. Exercise abandoned owing to bad weather.
		Returned to Navarino Bay.
11/07/29	03.30	Weighed to participate in Exercise 'OG'.
	04.20	**Explosion in No 1 Battery.**
		Returned to Navarino.
12/07/29		Sailed for Malta.
13/07/29		Arrived at Malta.
	13.30	Dockyard commenced removal of No 1 Battery.
	14.00	127 pounds of meat condemned and thrown overboard.
14/07/29 to 31/07/29		In dockyard hands.

ADM173/13283		**August 1929**
		In dockyard hands all month.
01/08/29		Lt (E) Smith joined the ship from the UK.
		Lt (E) Lee left the ship, discharged to the UK.

08/08/29		Red Watch passed the Standard Swimming Test.
10/08/29		Blue Watch passed the Standard Swimming Test.
30/08/29		Moved ship under tow.
	11.30	**Grounded off Conspicua Slips.**
	11.40	Secured alongside *L.16* at Stores Wharf.

ADM173/13284	**September 1929**
	In dockyard hands.
27/09/29	Landed 21 of the Ship's Company to act as a Funeral Party.

ADM173/13285	**October 1929**
	In dockyard hands.
31/10/29	Shifted ship to No 5 Dock.
	Hands employed scraping the ship's bottom.

ADM173/13286	**November 1929**
	In dockyard hands.
13/11/29	Lt Commander R D P Hutchinson left the ship.
	Lt K Whiting-Smith joined the ship.
28/11/29 14.30	Flooded the dock.
30/11/29	Dockyard divers working on the Bow Caps.
	Lt P J H Bartlett left the ship.

ADM173/13287	**December 1929**
	In dockyard hands for the first week.
	Thereafter 'Ready for sea at over 4 Hours notice'.
02/12/29	No 1 battery repair completed by the Dockyard.
03/12/29	**Dockyard divers performed an inspection of the Torpedo Tube Bow Caps.**
04/12/29	Dockyard divers performed an inspection of Nos 3 and 4 Bow Caps.
06/12/29	Dockyard divers worked on the Bow Caps.
07/12/29	Dockyard divers worked on the Bow Caps.
08/12/29	Carried out fumigation and opened hatches to ventilate the ship.

09/12/29		11 ratings joined from *Curlew*, 9 from *Calypso* and 3 from *Cyclops*. One rating was discharged to *L.16*.
10/12/29		Hands employed in embarking ammunition.
11/12/29		Carried out Main Engine Basin Trials.
13/12/29		Carried out Port Main Engine Trial.
16/12/29		Carried out Main Engine Trials and tested the Power Steering. Flew a Kite Aerial.
17/12/29		Half-masted the Colours.
24/12/29		Half-masted the Colours.

ADM173/13288	**January 1930**

Ready for sea for the first six days, then back in dockyard hands.

04/01/30		Proceeded to sea to discharge the bilges.
06/01/30	11.10	Carried out diving Statical Trial.
	11.22	**After Trimming Tank burst, bulging the After Bulkhead about four inches and shifting the Platform supporting the Steering and After Hydroplane Gear.** After Compartment flooding. Blew Main Ballast.
	14.00	Towed by tug to Stores Wharf. Rigged Salvage Pump for the Aft Compartment. Dockyard divers plugged the After Trim Kingston.
07/01/30	08.00	Salvage hose removed from the After Compartment.
11/01/30		In No 4 Dock.
16/01/30		Exercised Landing Parties.
17/01/30	08.00	Hands fell in for General Drill. Hands exercised Gas Stations, Collision Stations, Weighing by Hand and Tow Forward. Hands employed in replacing gear used.
21/01/30		Hands employed in scraping and red-leading the Refrigerator Compartment.

ADM173/13289	**February 1930**

In dockyard hands all month.
Hands employed in Physical Training, and on Range Parties.

05/02/30	15.00	Holy Baptism was conducted on board, for Miss Jane Mary Harris.
16/02/30	10.30	George P Thomson, Captain (S), inspected the ship.

26/02/30	09.45 to 10.25	Main Engine Trials were carried out.
27/02/30	14.10 to 14.26	Main Engine Trials.
28/02/30		Hands were employed returning empty paint drums.

ADM173/13290   **March 1930**

		In dockyard hands until 5 March. Then 'Ready for sea at over 4 Hours notice'.
06/03/30		Proceeded to sea for Trials, testing the Steering Gear and the Hand Steering, and swinging the ship.
08/03/30		Ward Room Galley Funnel recovered from overboard by divers. Proceeded to sea with *Cyclops* to Pollensa Bay.
10/03/30	09.44	Manoeuvred on main motors to be taken in tow by *Cyclops*.
	10.02	In tow.
	10.55	Stopped to slip tow.
	11.30	Tow slipped.
	16.30	Sighted two Blue Cruisers screened by a Destroyer Flotilla. Passed astern of them.
		Lost overboard by accident – two N.U.C. Lights.
11/03/30		Proceeded to Pollensa and Palma.
15/03/30	13.23	Proceeded in company with *Cyclops* to Gibraltar.
16/03/30	18.10	Parted company with *Cyclops*.
17/03/30	15.15	Secured in No 1 Dock.
24/03/30		Carried out Basin Trials.
25/03/30	11.15	Slipped for transit to Chatham.
29/03/30	09.15	Sighted the Eddystone.
	12.12	Secured to Barnpool Buoy, Plymouth.
30/03/30	09.06	Slipped for Sheerness.
	15.30	*Tetrarch* joined company.
31/03/30	09.00	Secured to No 10 Buoy, Sheerness.
		Hands employed de-ammunitioning.

ADM173/13291   **April 1930**

01/04/30	13.20	Slipped for Chatham.
	15.40	Warped into No 2 Basin. Secured alongside North Wall of No 2 Basin, Chatham.
		The Log Entry for the whole of April reads 'Ready for sea at over 4 Hours notice'.

Hands were given Foreign Service Leave.

ADM173/13292	**May 1930**
	The Log Entry for the whole of May reads 'Ready for sea at over 4 Hours notice'. Log Book signed by L M Shadwell, Lt Commander, for the Commander in Command (on leave).
01/05/30	Barometer returned to store.
05/05/30	First and Third Sea Lords and Rear Admiral (S) inspected the ship.

ADM173/13293	**June 1930**
	The Log Entry for the whole of June reads 'Ready for sea at over 4 Hours notice'. Log Book signed by L M Shadwell, Lt Commander, for the Commander in Command (on leave).
01/06/30	Lt M B Hale joined the ship.
07/06/30 09.00	Saturday. Leave granted to the First Part of Both Watches for a Wedding Party.
16/06/30	Lt (E) J H Illingworth joined the ship.
20/06/30	At Divisions: Read the Articles of War. Lt L N Brownfield left the ship.

ADM173/13294	**July 1930**
	Log Book signed by Commander Allen, returned from leave. Counter-stamped for Rear Admiral (S).
04/07/30	Worked main motors and main engines in the basin.
05/07/30 03.50	G Coleman Leading Seaman J 91594 died in RN Hospital from injuries received in a motorcycle accident.
24/07/30 09.00 09.15 11.10	Changed over to battery Lighting. Worked all auxiliary machinery and blew Main Ballast. Changed over to Dockyard Lighting.
28/07/30 11.30	Commander E M C Baraclough RN joined the ship.
29/07/30 09.00 11.30	Commander E M C Baraclough took over command from Commander Allen. Commander C H Allen left the ship.
30/07/30 1600 17.30	Model of 'Kent' secured alongside. Started the Charge on the battery of the 'Kent' Model.
31/07/30 08.30 12.00	Broke the Charge on the battery of the 'Kent' Model. Navy Week Press Representatives visited the ship.

ADM173/13295		**August 1930**
02/08/30	12.30	Saturday, Ship open to Navy Week visitors.
	19.00	Ship cleared of Navy Week visitors.
04/08/30	13.30 to 19.55	Ship open to Navy Week visitors.
05/08/30	13.30 to 19.00	Ship open to Navy Week visitors.
06/08/30	13.30 to 19.00	Ship open to Navy Week visitors.
07/08/30	13.30 to 19.30	Ship open to Navy Week visitors.
08/08/30	13.30 to 19.00	Ship open to Navy Week visitors.
09/08/30	13.30 to 19.20	Saturday. Final day of Navy Week. Ship open to Navy Week visitors.
26/08/30		Ship moved to No 9 Dock, Chatham.
	17.15	Cleared the Lower Deck. Read Warrant No 5.
27/08/30	13.15	Sale of kit of the late G Coleman Leading Seaman.
29/08/30		Lt J H Forbes left the ship for *H.31*.
30/08/30		Sub Lt J L Moreton joined the ship.

ADM173/13296		**September 1930**
02/09/30		Landed Football Party.
04/09/30		Read Warrants Nos 6 and 7.
08/09/30		Dock flooded up.
10/09/30		Ship was moved to No 2 Basin.
11/09/30		Landed Football Party.

ADM173/13297		**October 1930**
02/10/30		Conducted Basin Trials.
03/10/30		Ditto.
04/10/30		Ditto.
06/10/30		Lt J P Hunt RN joined the ship.
07/10/30		Proceeded to sea for Engine Trials.
08/10/30	14.15	**Stopped Port Main Engine – No 8 Cylinder Exhaust Valve Box Lug cracked. Starboard Main Engine – Leak developed in After Exhaust Manifold.**

		Returned to Sheerness on Starboard Main Engine only.
13/10/30		Rear Admiral (S) visited the ship.
29/10/30	14.45	Embarked one torpedo.
31/10/30		Basin Trial of main engines.

ADM173/13298		**November 1930**
03/11/30		Basin Trials of Starboard Main Engine.
04/11/30		Engine Trials.
05/11/30		Engine Trials.
	12.30	4/5 Power trial. **One cylinder of an Auxiliary Engine overheated.**
06/11/30		4/5 Power Trial. average speed 16 knots.
	15.40	**Thrust Race and Vertical Drive of Starboard Main Engine ran hot.** Returned to harbour on Port Main Engine.
07/11/30		Returned to Chatham No 2 Basin.
08/11/30	11.00	Returned Confidential Books to C-in-C's Office.
10/11/30		Lt J P Hunt left the ship.

ADM173/13299		**December 1930**
		In dockyard hands all month.
04/12/30		Disembarked one torpedo.
27/12/30		Lt M B Hale RN left the ship.

ADM173/13300		**January 1931**
		In dockyard hands all month.
01/01/31	14.05	One AB discharged from the Cells.
28/01/31		Basin Trials 50 minutes each Main Engine.
29/01/31		Basin Trials 50 minutes each Main Engine.

ADM173/13301		**February 1931**
		Log Book signed by L M Shadwell.
02/02/31		Sailed from Chatham to sea for Engine Trials, and returned to Sheerness.

03/02/31		Put to sea for Engine Trials.
	08.40	Megaphone lost overboard by accident.
	10.35	**Explosion occurred in Port Main Engine Crankcase, due to temporary seizure of No 3 Piston. Port Main Engine out of action.**
		Lost overboard by accident – 2 blankets; 2 magazine lamp cells Patt 4590.
		Proceeded on main motors for closing Tug *Robust* and embarking Medical Officer.
		Proceeded on Port main motor and Starboard Main Engine to Chatham.
06/02/31	10.00	Court of Enquiry in '*Malcolm*' held on the explosion on the 3rd inst.
09/02/31	09.00	Lt Commander L M Shadwell took over command from Commander E M Baraclough RN, who was discharged to '*Adamant*'.
	10.30	Paid men proceeding on draft.
	12.36	Draft of 47 ratings left the ship (45 ratings to HMS *Dolphin*, 1 to *Olympus* and 1 to *Oberon*).
		Lt L J Sedgwick, Sub Lt Shelford and Sub Lt J L Moreton discharged to *Dolphin*.
		The ship was reduced to 1/3 compliment [*sic*].
10/02/31	06.30	**Fire occurred in the Portside Forward Main Engine Room behind the Piston Oil Pump Starter** – Drew Main Battery Fuzes.
	06.53	Fire under control.
	07.30	Hands employed repairing damage to leads caused by the fire.
19/02/31		Lt R Edwards joined the ship.

ADM173/13302		**March 1931**
23/03/31		Repairs to Main Engine Room electrical circuits completed by the Dockyard.
25/03/31		Basin Trials of the repaired Port Main Engine.
26/03/31		Ditto.
30/03/31		Departed Chatham for Portsmouth.
31/03/31	11.30	Secured alongside *L.33* in No 3 Basin.
		Discharged 8 ratings and 1 officer to *Dolphin*.

ADM173/13303		**April 1931**
		Log Book signed by Lt Commander A L Besant in command. Countersigned by J S Morris.
09/04/31		Lt Commander A L Besant took command.
		Under Commander Besant the Log Entries begin to detail the following daily routines:
		Breakfast.
		10.30 to 10.40 'Stand easy and carry on'.
		11.00 'Up Spirits'.
		Dinner.
		Tea.
		Supper.

14/04/31		Lt Lonsdale joined the ship. Lt Edwards left the ship.

ADM173/13304	**May 1931**

11/05/31	Auxiliary engines were run.

ADM173/13305	**June 1931**

Countersigned by R B Darke, Captain (S) 5th Submarine Flotilla.

26/06/31	10.00	Ship was moved by the Dockyard from No 3 Basin.
Friday	11.00	Ship was secured in No 15 Dock.
	13.30 (approx)	**Ship assumed approx 40 degree list to Port**. All sea connections were shut off. Hands were employed bringing the ship upright.
	16.00 (approx)	**Electric fire in the Auxiliary Engine Room.**
	16.45 (approx)	Fire extinguished.
	20.35	Ship upright. Hands employed cleaning compartments. Rounds carried out every 15 minutes.
27/06/31	12.20	Ship was moved by the Dockyard to No 12 Dock.
	13.00	Ship was secured in No 12 Dock.
	19.00	Ship on the chocks.

ADM173/13306	**July 1931**

Log Book countersigned by J B Morris, Commander (S) 'Pigmy'.

Ship in Dry Dock.

01/07/31	Hands employed lifting two Main Battery Cells in No 1 Battery.
03/07/31	Hands employed lifting damaged Cells in No 2 Battery.
06/07/31	Court of Enquiry.
07/07/31	Court of Enquiry.
10/07/31	Court of Enquiry.

Meanwhile, in Dry Dock, the hands continued the work of painting and cleaning.

ADM173/13307	**August 1931**

In No 12 Dry Dock in dockyard hands.

25/08/31	Received Main Battery and Compressor Charge from *L.69*.

ADM173/13308	**September 1931**
16/09/31	Ship was undocked and moved to alongside *Regent* in No 6 Berth, No 3 Basin.
18/09/31	Ship was moved by the Dockyard to No 7 Berth, No 3 Basin.
24/09/31	Ship was moved by the Dockyard to the N W Corner of No 3 Basin (Alongside S/M *M.3*).

ADM173/13309	**October 1931**
	In Reserve.
	Main Battery charged, Basin Trial of main engines and main motors carried out.

ADM173/13310	**November 1931**
	In Reserve.
	As before.

ADM173/13311	**December 1931**
	In Reserve.
	Change of C.O. Log Book countersigned by C H Allen, Commander (S) for Reserve Half Flotilla.

ADM173/13312	**January 1932**
	In Reserve.
25/01/32	Work began on de-storing the ship.

ADM173/13313	**February 1932**
	In Reserve.
09/02/32	Ship was moved by the Dockyard to No 6 Berth No 3 Basin.
19/02/32	Ship was moved by the Dockyard to alongside *Comet* in the SW Corner of No 3 Basin.
29/02/32	Draft of 42 ratings discharged to *Dolphin*, Fort Blockhouse, and 8 ratings 'lent to *Dolphin*'.

ADM173/13314	**March 1932**
	In Reserve.

Weekly routines were established for the Machinery, and Quarterly examinations were established for the Recuperator Recoil Cylinders.

The Main Battery was charged.

23/03/32	40 per cent of the Ship's Company left on long leave.
24/03/32	The anchors and cables were disembarked.
30/03/32	Cells from No 1 Main Battery were removed.
31/03/32	Cells from No 1 Main Battery were removed.

ADM173/13315	**April 1932**
	In Reserve.
07/04/32	The remaining Cells of No 1 Main Battery were removed, followed by the Cells of No 2 and No 3 Main Batteries.
18/04/32	The ship was berthed in the pocket of No 3 Basin on *Enchantress*.
19/04/32	Victualled Stores were returned.
20/04/32	Reduced to Care & Maintenance Party with a reduced crew.

ADM173/13316		**May 1932**
		In Reserve, reduced to Care & Maintenance.
		Daily routine established:
	08.00	Each day, the ship was opened up and ventilated.
	08.15	Each day, the hands were employed on cleaning the ship and on Care & Maintenance routine.
	16.00	Each day, the ship was inspected and closed down. Then turned over to Dockyard Police Control.
26/05/32	15.30	Blew 1 to 6 to 9 and 11 to 14 Main Ballast.

❖ ❖ ❖ ❖ ❖

In November 1932 the Log Book was countersigned by George P Thomson, Captain (S), 5th Submarine Flotilla.

In June 1933 the Log Book was countersigned by M Taylor, Captain (S), 5th Submarine Flotilla.

❖ ❖ ❖ ❖ ❖

ADM173/13340	**May 1934**

The Log Book noted the ship still carried 2,445 galls of Fuel Oil remaining/Nil expended.

X.1 was shown as:

Ready for Sea	At over 4 hours notice	In Dockyard or Contractors hands
No	Yes	No

In Dockyard with Reduced Crew.

ADM173/13341	**June 1934**

Lt Commander R S Barry in command. Countersigned by M Tranter, Captain (S),
5th Submarine Flotilla on 21/06/34.

For Saturday 16 June 1934 the Log Entry reads:

12.00 Ship shut down and turned over to Police Control.
13.00 *X.1* Payed off into Dockyard Control.

Appendix B: The Plans

A selection of the official plans reduced from the original 1/48 scale showing *X.1* 'as fitted', prepared by Chatham Dockyard on 2 February 1925

Profile

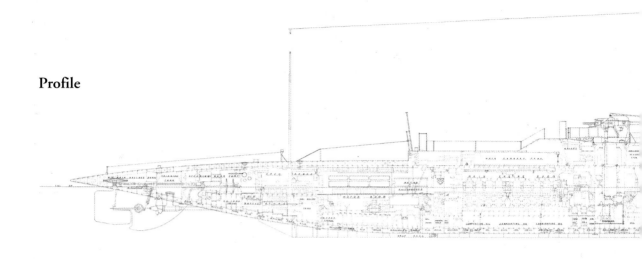

Plans of Outer & Inner hulls, Superstructure & Bridge

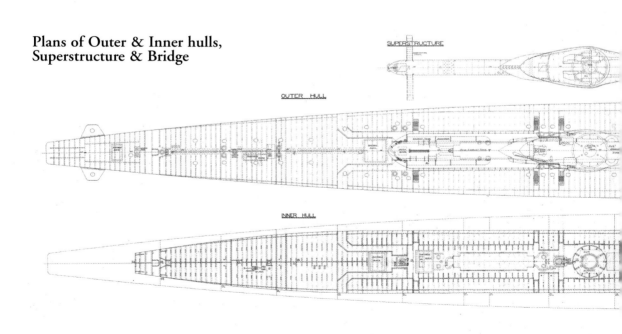

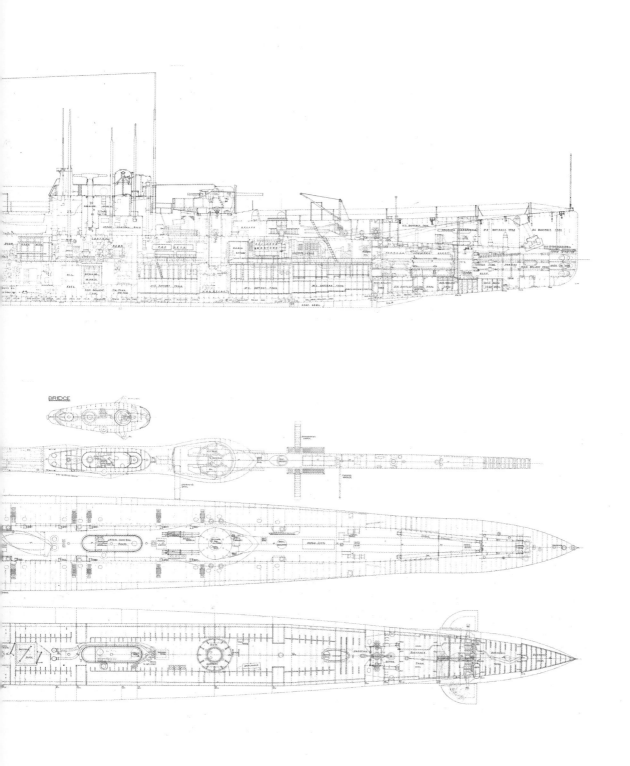

Upper Flat

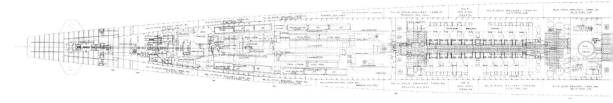

Lower Flat

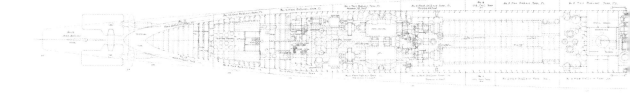

Profile

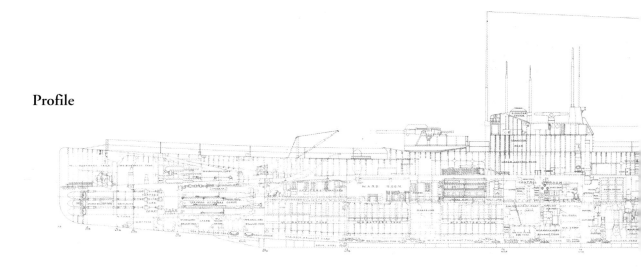

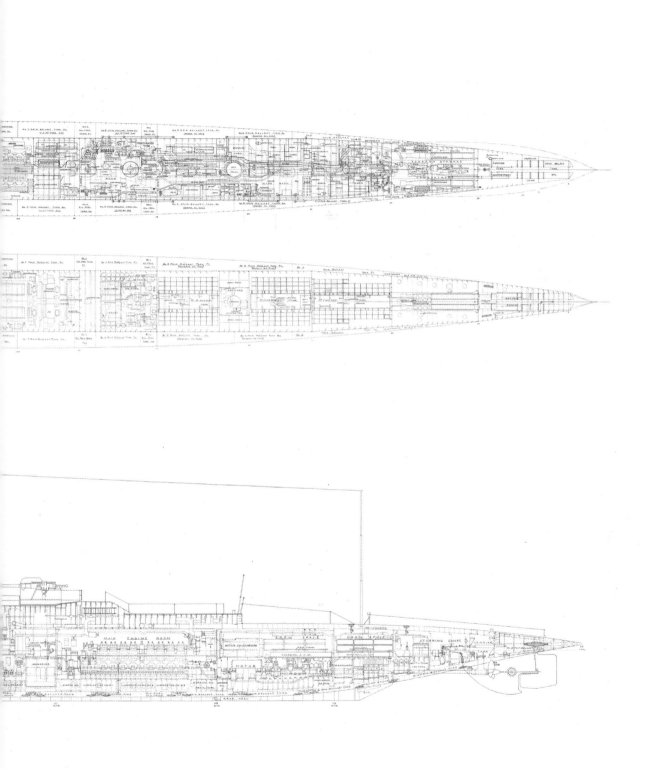

Sheer Drawing

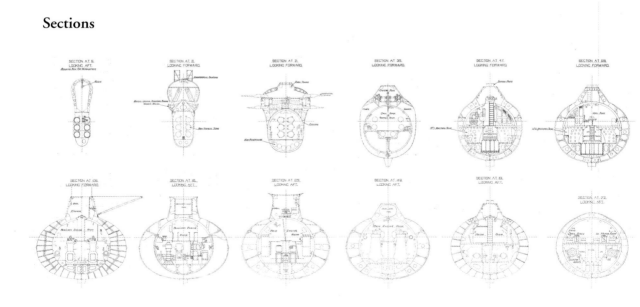

Sections

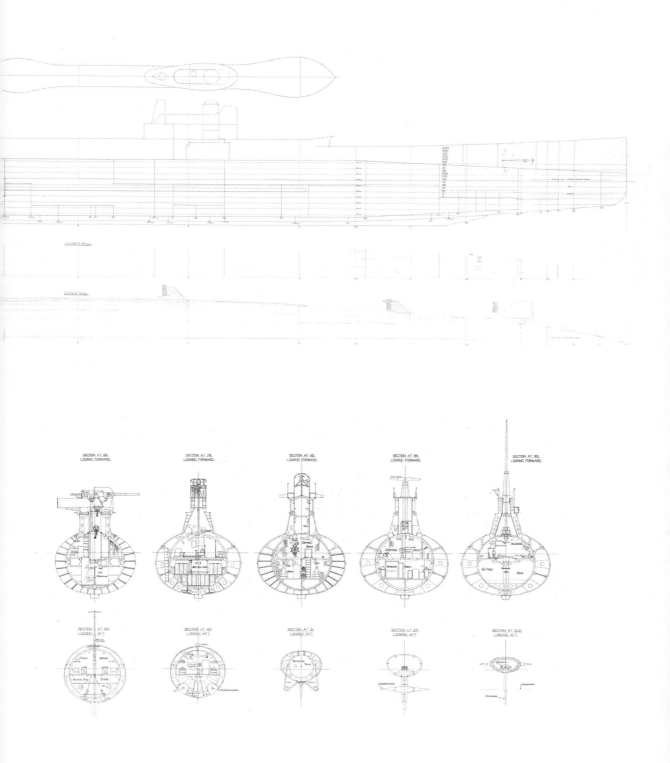

Appendix C: Comparison between the 5.2in and later 5.25in Guns

	5.2in QF Gun, Mark I	*5.25in DP Mk I*
Date in service	1924	1940
Length in calibres	42	50
Breech	Horizontal sliding wedge Manual closing/ SA opening	Horizontal sliding wedge Manual closing/ SA opening
Barrel	Tapered inner A tube, A tube, partial jacket, breech ring	Autofretted loose barrel (no liner), jacket, removable breech ring, sealing collar
Weight of twin mounting	27.15 tons	77.5 tons (*KGV*s) 96 tons (*Dido*s)
Weight of gun	3.425 tons	4.292 tons
Length of gun	230.65in	275.5in
Bore length	218.4in	262.5in
Number of grooves	N/A	36
Length of rifling	189.35in	228.5in
Chamber volume	630 cu in	894 cu in
Rate of fire per barrel	6 rounds/min normal	7–8 rounds/min (c/f 10–12 designed)
Elevation	-5/+40 degrees	-5/+70 degrees
Gun recoil	30in	24in
Maximum range @ elevation	17,288 yards @ 40 degrees	23,400 yards @ 45 degrees AA Ceiling 49,000 feet
Ammunition	Semi-fixed	Semi-fixed
Weight of shell	SAP 70lbs	SAP Mark IC – 80lbs HE – 80lbs
Propellant charge	10.78lbs MC 16 11.36lbs SC 109	18.05lbs. SC or 21.0lbs. NF/S
Cartridge case weight	17.34lbs incl SC charge	41lbs incl SC charge
Muzzle Velocity	2,300fps (701mps)	2,600fps (792mps)
Training/Elevating	Power with manual backup	Power (manual slow)

The 5.25in gun barrels are much longer than those of the 5.2in, but the major differences inside the turret are the enormous balance weights needed to achieve the high angles of elevation in this DP mounting.

Obviously, there is no hatch in the floor between the guns, as the larger size of the mounting makes for easier access. As the trunks do not have to be squeezed through water-tight glands, there are separate delivery hoists for the shells and cartridge cases of the semi-fixed ammunition. The shells emerge between the guns where *X.1*'s hoists arrived, but the cartridge cases arrive at the rear end of the loading trays.

Here the separate cartridges and shells have been placed in the loading trays, which are pivoted off to the side. The trays will swivel into line with the breech for power ramming, and then will swivel clear again to allow the breech to recoil. This arrangement is virtually identical to that on *X.1*.

Note the large cutouts in the floor plating to allow the balance weights, loading trays and breech mechanisms to achieve the high elevation needed for anti-aircraft use.

In the 5.25in turret the manual on-mounting trainer as well as the elevator sights appear to be fitted in the turret front face, between the guns, whereas on *X.1* the elevators' sights were fitted at either side.

Despite the differences in scale, it is clear that the 5.25in mounting shares a common lineage with the earlier 5.2in.

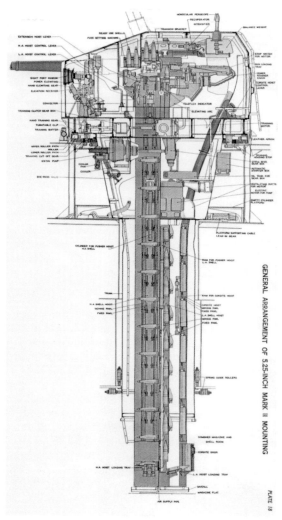

Above: A side elevation of the 5.25in twin Mark II turret, showing its gun trunk and three hoists per gun, compared with the two installed per gun in *X.1*. The propellant cases containing the cordite, and the low-angle shells, arrive vertically in pusher hoists, as in *X.1*. A third hoist (also of the pusher type with hinged pawls) has been included for the high-angle shells, which arrive in the turret in a horizontal position, ready for their nose fuses to be inserted in the fuse-setting machine in front of the top of the hoist.

Left: Interior of a 5.25in twin turret prior to fitting the sides and roof.

Notes

Chapter 1: Giant Submarines

1. *U 152* had an eventful surface gun action career during the last year of the Great War. Her victims included the armed transport USS *Ticonderoga*, which sank on 22 September 1918 after a long gun duel and a final torpedo hit, killing 213 US Navy personnel and Army soldiers. A week later *U 152* engaged in a running gun duel with the large American tanker *George G Henry*, which managed to escape although damaged and set on fire by a 15cm shell.

2. All the drawings of Project 50 and her novel 'diving boilers' disappeared after November 1918, like so many other Great War German weapons and designs, from the monster Paris Gun to the 13mm TuF, the Tank und Fleiger machine gun (although one sole example of the latter weapon can be seen in the German Army's Technical Museum in Koblenz).

3. *U 140* spawned the giant USN boats; *U 142* was copied by the Japanese as the *I-1*; experience with *U 139* persuaded the French to build *Surcouf*, although the inspiration for her armament came from *M.1*; *X.1* took up the idea of the gun-armed submarine from *U 141*, but in size and general appearance she was clearly a development of the RN 'K' class boats.

Chapter 2: Design Criteria

1. Previous Admiralty attempts at deliberate misinformation had mixed success. Their first major 'spoof' of the twentieth century succeeded in fooling the Imperial German Navy into putting 8.2in guns into their first hybrid battlecruiser *Blücher*, to match the 9.2in reportedly intended for *Invincible*, when of course the latter vessel was armed with 12in guns. The attempt to trick everyone into thinking that the second class of battlecruiser, the *Indefatigable*s, carried thicker armour than was actually the case backfired with disastrous results at Jutland. However, the designation of the 'Insect' and 'Fly' classes as 'China Gunboats' was a good cover story for their planned deployment to, respectively, the Danube and the Tigris.

2. Max Horton, who sank *T116*, later wrote 'To hit a destroyer always requires maximum luck'. Commodore Keyes commented 'To get one of those wriggling destroyers is like shooting snipe with a rifle'.

3. *T116* torpedoed in 1914 by Submarine *E.9* off the mouth of the Ems.
T188 in 1915 by *E.15* in the North Sea.
T191 in 1915 by *E.9* in the Baltic.
S33 in 1918 by *L.10* in the North Sea.

4. *TB No 10* torpedoed in 1915 by a U-boat in the North Sea.
TB No 12 in 1915 by a U-boat in the North Sea.
Recruit in 1915 in the Thames Estuary.
Attack in 1917 off Alexandria by *UC 34*.
Itchen in 1917 in the North Sea by *U 99*.
Staunch in 1917 off Gaza by *UC 38*.
Contest in 1917 in the Channel.
Comet in 1918 in the Mediterranean.
Phoenix in 1918 in the Adriatic by the Austrian *U XXVII*.
Ulleswater in 1918 off the Dutch Coast.
Scott in 1918 off the Dutch Coast by *UC 17*.

5. *X.1*'s projected sister-ship, the *X.2*, was never built. The designation 'X.2', long reserved for her, was eventually applied to the captured Italian submarine *Galileo Galilei*. *X.3* was of course the first prototype of the successful midget submarines.

6. It was this problem which would fatally handicap the Kriegsmarine during the Second World War, culminating in the humiliation of the Battle of the Barents Sea (Operation 'Regenbogen') on the last day of 1942, when the heavy cruiser *Admiral Hipper*, the panzerschiffe ('pocket battleship') *Lützow* and six large destroyers attacked Convoy JW.51B. Held at bay by a screen of destroyers and corvettes, the heavy German ships withdrew when the RN 6in cruisers *Sheffield* and *Jamaica* came on the scene. This was the action which caused Hitler to fly into a rage and order the scrapping of all large German warships. It also resulted in Grand Admiral Raeder's dismissal.

Chapter 3: Propulsion Machinery

1. The Liberty and Curtiss V-12 aero engines were small, lightweight petrol units, making extensive use of aluminium castings, and producing over 400hp – or more than half the output of the old German engines out of *U 126*. Their lightweight construction was required for use in aircraft, and of course they had an extremely short life between major rebuilds, the opposite of those qualities required for a marine engine, especially a diesel.

Chapter 5: Armament

1. Preserved in the Public Record Office, Kew, under References ADM186/268 and 269.

2. For comparison, the twin 5.25in DP mounts on the *King George V* class battleships and *Dido* class cruisers achieved only seven to eight rounds per minute per gun. The triple 6in turret on the 'Town' and 'Colony' class cruisers fired at a rate of eight rounds per minute per gun.

3. All the preserved papers deal with what was NOT considered a suitable AA armament, rather than what could be.

4 HMS *Excellent's* report of 18 February 1926 noted practical maxima of +35 degrees and -7 degrees.

5. The basic instrument was designated the Admiralty Fire Control Clock. When fitted with a plot which produced a paper record of the movements during a gun action, the instrument was known as the Admiralty Fire Control Table.

6. Notably the action off Calabria on 9 July 1940, when HMS *Warspite* landed a 15in shell on the Italian battleship *Giulio Cesare* at the unprecedented range of 26,000 yards (24,000m), while both ships were manoeuvring at high speed.

7. Examination of the wreck of *M.1* points to the likelihood that her gun mounting was dislodged in a glancing collision, leading to uncontrollable flooding into the handling spaces below. Not only was *X.1* much larger than *M.1*, but she was designed to survive an accidental flooding of her ammunition handling spaces.

8. Virtually all of the large Japanese boats would be lost to attack while submerged, including the giant aircraft carrier *I-13* during her mission to Ulithi at the very end of the Pacific War.

9. Constructor Commander Stanton had already noted this problem during *X.1*'s first cruise to Gibraltar, and in his report dated 29 April 1926 he had recommended that the gun trunk glands should be worked by a separate motor, rather than having to rely on the hydraulic pump supplying the whole turret and hoists.

10. The 2pdr pom-pom was an excellent short-range weapon providing considerable firepower. In this respect it served with distinction in Coastal Forces' motor torpedo boats and motor gun boats, and as a bow-chaser on destroyers hunting enemy S-Boats. The problems with using the pom-pom as the main medium-range anti-aircraft gun were numerous: multiple mountings were heavy and required a large crew and considerable power to operate them. In local manual control they were far too cumbersome to track a fast-moving aircraft. Combining four and also eight 2pdrs in one mounting could produce a lethal concentration of shells, but the other hand, if the gunners' aim was off, all the guns missed. Fatally, the short barrel and cartridge case gave the weapon a comparatively low muzzle velocity and therefore a shorter range than, say, the 40mm Bofors of identical calibre. Coupled to this the 40mm HE shell was designed to self-destruct at the end of its effective range, but this was severely curtailed by the length of the fuse fitted. The most disastrous example of the pom-pom's shortcomings occurred when HMS *Repulse* and *Prince of Wales* were sunk by Japanese aircraft off Malaya on 10 December 1941, when the gunners of Force 'Z', forbidden to fire on a torpedo plane after it had dropped its load, found to their dismay that the Japanese G3M2 'Nells' were dropping their two torpedoes outside the range at which the Pom-Pom's shells were self-destroying. The few Japanese planes to be lost during this disastrous engagement were almost all shot down by the gunners on *Repulse*, who disobeyed orders and fired on 'Nells' passing close overhead.

11. D J Dent, Rear Admiral (S), on 18 March 1921.

Chapter 6: The Ship, Her Hull, Fittings and Complement

1. The first all-welded warship built for the Royal Navy was the *Halcyon* class minesweeper *Seagull*, launched in the mid-1930s.

2. Published by ICT Nethercoate, Bryant, Hadley, Upper Beeding, West Sussex BN44 3TQ.

3. Against this, see the reports in Chapter 8 of swimming alongside at Malta.

4. This shade is depicted in *Warship Profile No. 16 'HM S/M Upholder'* by Captain M.L.C. Crawfurd DSC* RN (Retired).

5. The meaning of the term Asdic never appeared in any official contemporary document. It is assumed to comprise the initial letters of the Anti-Submarine Division, completed by an abbreviation of 'sonics'. The corresponding US acronym is SONAR = **SO**und **N**avigation **A**nd **R**anging.

6. At the time, it was erroneously held that the use of Asdic by RN ships would nullify the future employment of 'enemy' submarines. The primitive nature of the early sets, the initial lack of depth ranging and difficulties caused by sea layers of different density, would prove this hope to be over-exaggerated during the Second World War. The Battle of the Atlantic would be won primarily because of radar, high-frequency radio direction finding and aircraft.

7. *H.32* was also a trials submarine, like *X.1*, for closed ventilation battery cooling systems. It is likely the Admiralty wanted trials of these two innovations in both a coastal boat and an ocean-going corsair.

8. Every naval designer was only too aware of the near-tragic incident on 27 August 1862 when the huge steamer *Great Eastern* 'discovered' the uncharted pinnacle of rock in the approach to New York (which would later be named after her), when she ran into it. A historic voyage by a submarine into poorly charted waters had already resulted in tragedy. In September 1914 the Australian 'E' class boat *AE.1* had been ordered to patrol off German New Guinea to hunt the small colonial cruiser *Geier*. She had set off accompanied by the destroyer *Parramatta*, but they parted company during the voyage, and the unfortunate *AE.1* failed to return. It is suspected that she struck an uncharted reef somewhere in the Bismarck Sea, and her grave remains undiscovered at the time of writing. There is a memorial to the crew of *AE.1* at the Bitapaka War Cemetery, on Rabaul, near the site of the colonial German radio station attacked by an Allied force in the Great War.

9. Except for the high speed of 15 knots reached underwater by the special 'hunter-killer' submarines of the 'R' class.

10. *U 135* had been completed in 1918 at Danzig Dockyard, was surrendered to Great Britain at the end of the war, and in 1921 sank on her way to the breakers.

Chapter 7: Trials and Tribulations

1. The limit of 8in was set, not – as often quoted – by the RN 'Improved *Birmingham*' Class with their 7.5in guns, but because US armoured cruisers mounted 8in guns.

2. The Royal Navy alone had lost five pre-dreadnought battleships, nine cruisers, twelve armed merchant cruisers, thirteen escort ships and armed boarding vessels, one monitor, fifteen destroyers, torpedo boats and torpedo gunboats, three submarines, twelve sloops, sixteen Q-ships, two minesweepers and seven armed yachts and other auxiliaries, to direct enemy submarine torpedo attack. Dozens of other warships had been sunk or damaged by mines laid by submarines, the most notorious being the loss of HMS *Hampshire* off the Orkneys on 5 June 1916, drowning Lord Kitchener.

3. Beginning on the first day of the war when the Donaldson liner *Athenia* was torpedoed and more than 200 passengers and crew were lost.

4. The actual photograph received by the *Daily Herald* and the printing block used in the second edition have been preserved, in the file of papers on the case in the Public Records Office, Kew, under Ref: ADM1/8636/28.

5. The 'Devastator' midget submarine was conceived by Godfrey Herbert during the Great War and promoted by Max Horton as late as 1923. Displacing not more than 10 tons, and powered by multiple torpedo engines for an attack speed of 45 to 50 knots, the one- or two-man midget would carry a one-ton warhead to attack enemy vessels at sea. As per Herbert's original plans they would be launched from capital ships once the enemy fleet was sighted. Max Horton's proposals to the Admiralty in 1923 fore-shadowed the use of midget submarines in the Second World War, in that he planned to use them to attack enemy ships inside their harbours. The crew was supposed to eject from the vessel once the midget

was locked on target, in a sealed compartment which would cushion them from the warhead's blast, and hope to be picked up by a friendly vessel. It was this semi-suicidal or at least 'expendable' aspect which caused the Admiralty of the 1920s to reject the idea.

6. This use of *M.3* as a carrier for Devastators had been proposed by Horton. It would be enthusiastically taken up by the Imperial Japanese Navy, and the Type A midgets launched from mother submarines would open the attack on Pearl Harbor.

7. A British officer who according to MI5 files, spied on the US Navy for the Japanese. Frederick Rutland joined the Royal Navy as a boy and won the DSO at Jutland. A pioneer of naval air warfare, on 1 October 1917 he flew a Sopwith Pup off the roof of 'B' turret of HMS *Repulse*. Having transferred to the RAF, in 1922 he was approached by the Japanese for advice on aircraft carriers. A few months later, he resigned his commission. Watched by the British intelligence services, in 1933 his name came up in messages intercepted by codebreakers. Oka Arata, Japanese Naval Attaché in London, had recruited him as a spy. Rutland was told to go to California to set up a series of branches of an import-export business, including one in Los Angeles and one in Honolulu, from which he could spy on the American Pacific Fleet at Pearl Harbor. Codenamed Shinkawa (New River) he was given £100,000 to start up the business and £3,750 a year as salary, significant sums at the time. The British codebreakers learned that Rutland was setting up a branch of his import-export business in Regent Street as a 'post box' through which he could pass his intelligence reports to the Japanese naval attaché in London. Rutland was followed by MI6 to America where he was watched by the FBI. Over the next eight years his intelligence reports were monitored by the British. He appears to have spent much of his time living the high life in Beverly Hills. However, when in 1941 the FBI arrested a Japanese spy Rutland, fearing he would be compromised, approached the Americans offering to spy on Japan. The FBI declined the offer and put him in the hands of MI6. Rutland returned to Britain and settled down in Marlow. When war with Japan broke out, he was taken into custody. But the British were reticent to charge him because that could compromise their codebreaking operation, so in 1944 he was released.

8. The greatest irony is, of course, that if one openly behaves as if there is a threat of breakdown in relations, then such a breakdown becomes all the more likely. It is not inconceivable that the actions taken by Winston Churchill as First Sea Lord in 1914 to seize the battleships being built in Britain for the Turkish Navy, helped push the Turks into siding with the Central Powers in the Great War. The *Sultan Osman I* had been paid for partly by public subscription – the women of Anatolia had even shorn and sold their hair – to get revenge on the hated Greeks, and the heavy-handed British action outraged Turkish public opinion. This allowed the pro-German faction to gain the upper hand, and set the scene for Admiral Souchon to offer the battlecruiser *Goeben* to Turkey as a replacement. Thankfully the United States Navy never acted on one of its likely battle scenarios drawn up following the Great War, namely the possibility of armed conflict with Great Britain over world trade.

9. Advice on conversion of the *Hosho* from the oiler *Hiryu* was provided by the Semphill Technical Mission. Also, one of the eight production Parnall Peto floatplanes built for *M.2* was transferred to the Imperial Japanese Navy, which promptly produced a copy for use by their own submariners.

Chapter 9: A Litany of Failures

1. A modern misinformation parallel has emerged with disclosures about the US Air Force's 'stealth' bomber, the B-1. In the last days of Hitler's Third Reich, the Luftwaffe discovered that their 'flying wing' prototypes had a very low radar signature. When the Northrop Corporation built on Nazi research and constructed giant B-35 and B-49 Flying Wing bombers they were soon dubbed a failure. It was only in recent years, with the public revelations of the B-1 Stealth bomber that the true story has emerged. The big Flying Wings also had a surprisingly small radar signature. The Americans panicked in case the Russians discovered this feature, and constructed similar jet bombers capable of penetrating the North American radar net to launch first strike nuclear attacks. So, the Flying Wing was dropped and labelled a failure.

Chapter 10: An Unlucky Fall

1. The Royal Navy, along with several other maritime powers, was no stranger to drydock incidents. The most notorious was the capsizing of the brand-new Royal Yacht *Victoria and Albert* in 1901, when the drydock in which she was being constructed was

flooded to float her out. The cause of the disaster was uncontrolled adding of luxurious fittings high up, but the overall responsibility was Sir William White's. The affair was the cause of his fall from favour, and one of our greatest warship designers was removed from the scene prematurely.

Possibly the greatest naval shipwreck of all time was the collapse and partial sinking of the huge Admiralty Floating Dock (AFD) No. 28, on 8 August 1944 at Trincomalee. The 80,000-ton AFD was seriously damaged, and a major section sank to the seabed 160ft below. The *Queen Elizabeth* class battleship HMS *Valiant*, displacing 35,000 tons, was in the dock when it collapsed, and narrowly missed joining it on the sea bed. As it was, *Valiant* was badly holed in the stern, and her two inner shafts were bent upwards. During her voyage to Alexandria and temporary repairs, both inner shafts had to be cut off together with the propellers and the shaft bearing brackets. *Valiant* never saw action again.

Chapter 11: Only the British were Fooled

1. The large Japanese boat *I-8*'s twin 5.5in DP mounting on her foredeck was not a turret. Raeder's planned Type XI class never left the drawing board.

2. If *X.1* had been renamed *Drake* or *Grenville* then her commerce-raiding potential would have been plain for all to see.

3. From 1929 France was engaged in completing the shield of the Maginot Line in the north-east and south-east. The French Army was building up a modern armoured force of tanks, armoured cars and APCs, and re-equipping the infantry with modern machine guns, rifles and anti-tank weapons. La Royale was constructing a modern surface fleet, which would become the fourth most powerful in the world. The *Armée de l'Air* was purchasing thousands of modern French and US planes.

4. Rudder problems were apparently common to many contemporary French submarine classes, and took some time to rectify.

Chapter 12: Reflections and Epilogue

1. A friend described to the author the story of his German father-in-law, who was 'obliged' to move to the UK in 1945 to act as a consultant on factory machine tools. He had been astounded to discover that far too many UK factories still used machine tools and processes that were almost a hundred years old.

2. The workers replaced the missing cork with newspapers, dated during the period she was under construction. Hot ashes piled up against the boiler room bulkhead set the newspapers on fire and the magazine burst into flames.

3. Fatally, this rebuilding programme was begun too late to include *Hood*, *Barham* or *Repulse*.

4. The private-enterprise *R.100* was an unqualified success. The state-funded *R.101* was an overweight vessel which should have never been granted a certificate of airworthiness, let alone be allowed to depart on her fateful flight to India.

5. As with the Royal Flying Corps Great War fuselage roundels painted alongside an aircraft observer, thus turning him into a perfect target!

6. The three products of Admiral Fisher's last and wildest scheme – the Baltic Plan – were irreverently nicknamed 'Outrageous', 'Uprorious' and 'Spurious' (also known, under their correct names, as *Courageous*, *Glorious* and *Furious*).

7. The mystical sword of King Arthur, which could return to defend Britannia.

Bibliography

Primary Sources

X.1 Ship's Cover and *X.1 Ship's Plans* kept by the National Maritime Museum at the Brass Foundry, Woolwich.

X.1 and related Admiralty Files kept by the Public Record Office, Kew.

X.1 Files and Correspondence, including the notes of Ian A. Grant preserved in the Archives of the RN Submarine Museum, Gosport.

Gun Logs kept by Hampshire Records Office.

Published Sources

Bagnasco, Erminio, *Submarines of World War Two* (London: Arms & Armour Press, 1977).

Breyer, Siegfried, *Soviet Warship Development* Volume 1 (London: Conway Maritime Press, 1992).

Brown, David K, 'X.1 – Cruiser Submarine', *WARSHIP 23* (July 1982).

_____, *The Grand Fleet: Warship Design and Development 1906-1922* (London: Chatham Publishing, 1999).

Campbell, John, *Naval Weapons of World War Two* (London: Conway Maritime Press, 1985).

Chesneau, Roger (ed), *Conway's All the World's Fighting Ships 1922-1946* (London: Conway Maritime Press, 1997).

Compton-Hall, Richard, *Submarine Warfare – Monsters & Midgets* (Poole: Blandford, 1985).

Crawford, Captain M L C, *Warship Profile 16 HM S/M Upholder* (Leatherhead: Profile Publications Ltd, 1972).

Everitt, Don, *K Boats: Steam-Powered Submarines in World War I* (Shrewsbury: Airlife, 1999).

Fitzsimons, Bernard (ed), *Warships of the First World War* Purnell's History of the World Wars Special (London: BPC Publishing Ltd, 1973).

Garzke, William H Jr, and Robert O Dulin, Jr, *Battleships: Allied Battleships* (Annapolis: Naval Institute Press, 1990).

Gray, Edwin, *A Damned Un-English Weapon* (London: New English Library, 1973).

Green, William, *Warplanes of the Second World War Volume 6: Floatplanes* (London: Macdonald, 1962).

Hackmann, Willem, *Seek & Strike*: Sonar, Anti-submarine Warfare and the Royal Navy 1914-54 (London: HMSO, 1984).

Hawks, Captain Ellis, *Britain's Wonderful Fighting Forces* (London: Odhams Press, undated).

Huan, Capitaine de Vaisseau Claude, *Le croiseur sous-marin Surcouf (1926-1942)* (Nantes: Marines édition, 1996).

Jentschura, Hansgeorg, Dieter Jung and Peter Mickel, *Warships of the Imperial Japanese Navy 1869-1945* (London: Arms & Armour Press, 1986).

Institute of Naval Architects *Proceedings for the Year 1937*.

Lambert, John, 'The K Class Steam Submarines', *WARSHIP 8* (October 1978).

Le Fleming, H M *Warships of World War I, No. 3 – Destroyers, No. 4 – Miscellaneous & No. 5 – Submarines* (London: Ian Allan, 1961).

Lenton, H T, and J J Colledge, *Warships Of World War II Part Two: Destroyers and Submarines* (London: Ian Allan, 1962).

Moss, Michael, and Iain Russell, *Range and Vision: The First Hundred Years of Barr & Stroud* (Edinburgh: Mainstream, 1988).

Preston, Anthony, *Battleships of World War I* (New York: Galahad Books, 1972).

_____, and John Batchelor, *The First Submarines* Purnell's History of the World Wars Special (London: BPC Publishing Ltd, 1973).

_____, *Submarines Since 1919* Purnell's History of the World Wars Special (London: BPC Publishing Ltd, 1974)

Raven, Alan, and Roberts, John, *British Battleships of WWII* (Annapolis: Naval Institute Press, 1976).

_____, *British Cruisers of WWII* (London, Arms & Armour Press, 1980).

Rössler, Eberhard, *The U Boat – The Evolution and Technical History of German Submarines* (London: Arms & Armour Press, 2001).

Rusbridger, James, *Who Sank Surcouf? The Truth about the Disappearance of the Pride of the French Navy* (London: Century, 1991).

Whiteley, M J, *Cruisers of World War Two – An International Encyclopaedia* (London: Brockhampton Press, 1999).

Williams, Mark, *Captain Gilbert Roberts RN* (London: Cassell, 1979).

Index